# The Way to Work

## Second Edition

# The Way to Work
## How to Facilitate Work Experiences for Youth in Transition

### Second Edition

by

**Richard G. Luecking, Ed.D.**
University of Maryland
College Park

*with invited contributors*

·P A U L·H·
BROOKES
PUBLISHING Cº ®

Baltimore • London • Sydney

**Paul H. Brookes Publishing Co.**
Post Office Box 10624
Baltimore, Maryland 21285-0624
USA

www.brookespublishing.com

Typeset by Progressive Publishing Services, York, Pennsylvania.
Manufactured in the United States of America by
Sheridan Books, Inc., Chelsea, Michigan.

The individuals described in this book are composites or real people whose situations are masked and are based on the authors' experiences. In most instances, names and identifying details have been changed to protect confidentiality. Real names and identifying details are used with permission.

**Library of Congress Cataloging-in-Publication Data**

Names: Luecking, Richard G., author.
Title: The way to work: how to facilitate work experiences for youth in transition /
    by Richard G. Luecking; with invited contributors.
Description: Second edition. | Baltimore: Paul H. Brookes Publishing Co., [2019] |
    Includes bibliographical references and index.
Identifiers: LCCN 2019024634 (print) | LCCN 2019024635 (ebook) | ISBN 9781681253664
    (paperback) | ISBN 9781681253671 (epub) | ISBN 9781681253688 (pdf)
Subjects: LCSH: Youth with disabilities—Employment—United States. | School-to-work
    transition—United States.
Classification: LCC HD7256.U5 L842 2020 (print) | LCC HD7256.U5 (ebook) |
    DDC 362.4/0484—dc23
LC record available at https://lccn.loc.gov/2019024634
LC ebook record available at https://lccn.loc.gov/2019024635

British Library Cataloguing in Publication data are available from the British Library.

2023   2022   2021   2020   2019

10    9    8    7    6    5    4    3    2    1

# Contents

About the Appendices ........................................................................ vii
About the Author ............................................................................... ix
About the Contributors ...................................................................... x
Foreword    *Mary E. Morningstar* .................................................... xiii
Foreword    *Madeleine Will* ............................................................... xv
Preface ............................................................................................... xvii
Acknowledgments .............................................................................. xix
Introduction ....................................................................................... xxi

1    Recognizing Work Experiences as Indispensable
     Transition Tools ........................................................................ 1
     *Richard G. Luecking and Kelli Thuli Crane*

2    Setting the Stage for Quality Work Experiences ..................... 21

3    Planning for Work Experiences ................................................ 39
     *Richard G. Luecking, Amy Dwyre D'Agati, and
     Marie Parker Harvey*

4    Navigating Work Experience and Disability Disclosure ......... 79

5    Supporting Families to Support Work Experience ................... 95
     *Richard G. Luecking and Amy Dwyre D'Agati*

6    Finding Workplace Partners: Strategies for Recruiting
     Employers ................................................................................... 113

7    Retaining Workplace Partners: Strategies for Ensuring
     Effective Employer Participation .............................................. 135

8    Supporting Youth in the Workplace ........................................................................157

9    Facilitating Workplace Mentorship for Youth Workers....................................187
     *Richard G. Luecking and Meredith Gramlich*

10   Connecting With Professional and Agency Partners to
     Foster and Sustain Work Success.........................................................................205
     *Richard G. Luecking and Kelli Thuli Crane*

11   Pursuing Quality Work-Based Learning for All...................................................221

Index.............................................................................................................................235

# About the Appendices

The chapter appendices in this edition of *The Way to Work* offer helpful forms and worksheets to aid in the planning of work experiences for youth in transition. Purchasers of this book may photocopy the appendices from the print book for professional, educational, or personal use.

These appendices can also be downloaded by both print and e-book buyers for professional, educational, or personal use. To download these materials, follow these steps:

1. Visit the Brookes Publishing Download Hub at http://downloads.brookes publishing.com.

2. Register to create an account, or log in with your existing account.

3. Filter or search for this book's title, *The Way to Work*.

# About the Author

**Richard G. Luecking, Ed.D.,** Research Professor and Co-Director of the Center for Transition and Career Innovation, Department of Counseling, Higher Education, and Special Education, University of Maryland, 3214 Benjamin Building, College Park, Maryland 20742

Dr. Luecking is Co-Director of the Center for Transition and Career Innovation and is Research Professor in the Department of Counseling, Higher Education, and Special Education in the College of Education at the University Maryland, College Park. He previously served for 28 years as President of TransCen, Inc., a national nonprofit organization dedicated to improving the employment success of people with disabilities. During his tenures at TransCen and the University of Maryland, he has designed, implemented, and evaluated numerous model demonstration and research projects related to school-to-work transition and competitive integrated employment of individuals with disabilities. He is widely published on related topics in books, refereed professional journals, and trade publications.

Dr. Luecking's professional history includes serving as a state vocational rehabilitation counselor and the director of nonprofit competitive integrated employment service programs. He also served as a Policy Advisor to the U.S. Department of Labor, Office of Disability Employment Policy, where he helped establish its national Employment First initiative, and in the National School to Work Opportunities Office, a combined initiative of the U.S. Departments of Education and Labor. His research and professional interest is the translation of knowledge for both policy makers and practitioners.

# About the Contributors

**Kelli Thuli Crane, Ph.D.,** Center for Transition and Career Innovation, University of Maryland, College Park, Maryland

Kelli Thuli Crane is Assistant Research Professor at the Center for Transition and Career Innovation (CTCI), University of Maryland, College Park. She has extensive experience designing and implementing transition-related interventions to improve postschool outcomes for youth with disabilities, and she has served in leadership roles on several highly visible research and model demonstration projects funded by the U.S. Department of Education, the U.S. Department of Health and Human Services, and the Social Security Administration. Prior to joining CTCI, Dr. Crane worked for TranCen, Inc., as Senior Research Associate. In this capacity, she consulted with national, state, and local stakeholders to build their capacity in aligning and delivering evidence-based practices leading to improved education, employment, and financial outcomes for youth with disabilities. Dr. Crane also served as a consultant for the National School-to-Work Office (NSTWO) of the U.S. Departments of Education and Labor, where she collaborated with federal and state government entities to ensure the inclusion of youth with disabilities in high school reform and other programs and services. During her tenure at the NSTWO, Dr. Crane served in an advisory capacity on the youth subcommittee of the Presidential Task Force on the Employment of Adults with Disabilities. She has published journal articles as well as numerous products related to school-to-work transition. Dr. Crane is a Certified Rehabilitation Counselor and, early in her career, worked as a job coach and transition specialist for an urban school district.

**Amy Dwyre D'Agati, M.S.,** Center for Transition and Career Innovation, University of Maryland, College Park, Maryland

Amy Dwyre D'Agati is Technical Assistance Specialist at the Center for Transition and Career Innovation at the University of Maryland, College Park. Prior to that, she spent more than 20 years as Senior Associate at TransCen, Inc. Throughout her career, Ms. D'Agati has assisted youth with disabilities find jobs and prepare for careers and has trained transition personnel in job development, customized employment, self-advocacy, postsecondary education transition options, and marketing and business partnerships. In addition, Ms. D'Agati has led a variety of model demonstration programs and has conducted implementation on several large research projects involving employment for people with disabilities. She has also learned so much from her younger sibling Patrick, a person with a disability who lives and works in his community.

**Marie Parker Harvey, M.A.,** Center for Transition and Career Innovation, University of Maryland, College Park, Maryland

Marie Parker Harvey is Training and Development Coordinator in the Center for Transition and Career Innovation in the College of Education at the University of Maryland, College Park. This position focuses on the development of webinars and curriculum to teach workers in the education and disability fields how to create individualized work experiences for youth with disabilities. It builds upon her many years of service to youth and individuals with disabilities through direct service work, advocacy, training, and program development. This next step in her career is the result of her many years as Program Director and County Liaison for the Montgomery County Customized Employment Public Intern Project (MCPIP) for Montgomery County (MD) Government. As the County Liaison for MCPIP, Ms. Harvey identified and created more than 120 part-time positions for people with disabilities in Montgomery County government offices, based on a department's need and the candidate's specific interests, skills, and abilities. Ms. Harvey also oversaw Youth with Disabilities programs through the Workforce Investment Act (WIA) and Workforce Innovation and Opportunity Act (WIOA), assisting hundreds of in- and out-of-school youth to find employment. She developed and led her team in a successful summer youth employment program that later expanded into a year-round work-based learning program (Division of Rehabilitative Services/Summer Youth Employment/Pre-Employment Transition Services, or DORS/SYE/Pre-ETS) to place hundreds of in-school youth with disabilities in individualized work-based learning opportunities with cooperating employers. Ms. Harvey is well-known for her working relationships and collaborations with state and local government and nongovernmental agencies, local and private school systems, community service providers, nonprofits, private sector businesses, and families in need. Her experience and expertise has allowed her to serve people with a broad range of disabilities and barriers, and her work and advocacy continues to impact the field.

**Meredith Gramlich, M.A.,** Center for Transition and Career Innovation, University of Maryland, College Park, Maryland

Meredith Gramlich is Senior Faculty Specialist at the Center for Transition and Career Innovation (CTCI) in the Department of Counseling, Higher Education, and Special Education in the College of Education at the University of Maryland, College Park. She has extensive experience promoting business–education partnerships, work-based learning opportunities, customized employment solutions, and model transition services. Prior to her work with CTCI, she worked for TransCen, Inc., for 27 years as Senior Research Associate—where she provided training, technical assistance, and direct service to facilitate competitive integrated employment for youth and adults with disabilities as part of model demonstration projects, including Maryland PROMISE (a partnership of state agencies and private sector disability organizations that addressed the challenges faced by youth receiving Supplemental Security Income by promoting improved education and career outcomes), Maryland Customized Employment Partnership, Maryland Transition Initiative, and Bridges from School to Work. Ms. Gramlich is a certified special education teacher with a master's degree in transition special education with emphasis on secondary and vocational programming and business–education partnerships. She taught in Montgomery County (Maryland) Public Schools Alternative Programs, where she established its Career Program and also developed a cutting edge model education program for adjudicated youth pretrial. Ms. Gramlich is a trainer for the Employment Services Certificate endorsed by the Association for Community Rehabilitation Educators (ACRE). Ms. Gramlich's younger sister—who has disabilities and works independently in a customized, community-based, integrated job—inspired her to dedicate her career to finding creative solutions for independence.

# Foreword

I was so thrilled when Rich asked me to write a forward for the new edition to his book, *The Way to Work*. It was not just the honor of being asked, which of course, coming from Rich Luecking, is quite the honor. More important, as a long-time transition educator who has taught probably hundreds of secondary and transition practitioners, I have used the first edition of *The Way to Work* for years, hoping that sooner or later Rich would get around to updating the content. For the many students who have enrolled over the years in the Employment and Career Development classes I have developed and taught, *The Way to Work* was a cornerstone.

The second edition continues to maintain the strong emphasis on ensuring that youth with disabilities make positive transitions from school to competitive integrated employment by continuing to engage transition practitioners in supporting youth to learn how to work. As is now well established in our field, students with disabilities must obtain high-quality work-related experiences in order to exit school with successful work experiences leading to employment (Test et al., 2009). The critical impact of *The Way to Work, Second Edition,* is the emphasis on supporting transition stakeholders to understand the importance of career development and work-based learning, given the emergent research associated with programs and experiences that predict future job success. Since the first edition was published, the research associated with what we know as a field about how best to support youth with disabilities to transition successfully from school to integrated employment has continued to grow. Especially important is emergent research indicating that vocational education and work-based learning while in school is one of the strongest factors impacting postschool employment for a wide range of youth with disabilities (Carter, Austin, & Trainor, 2011; Luecking, Fabian, Contreary, Honeycutt, & Luecking, 2018; Mazzotti et al., 2016).

In addition to emerging research, recent work-related policy developments associated with employment for individuals with disabilities demonstrate the critical need for a current perspective on work, such as is found in *The Way to Work*. It is essential for transition practitioners to understand and collaborate with the outside agencies responsible for supporting work-related transition services, in particular preemployment transition services, as described in the Workforce Innovation and Opportunities Act (WIOA) of 2014 (PL 113-128). Given the now substantially increased role of vocational rehabilitation to support and implement Pre-Employment Transition Services requirements, it is vital that secondary schools refocus their school- and work-based learning to incorporate high levels of collaboration for the benefit of students. This book lays out these critical changes and how transition practitioners can engage with the wide array of outside agencies and services. In addition, Rich has updated and enhanced the core information pertaining directly to building strong and essential school–business partnerships that is found in Chapters 6 and 7.

Given the emphasis on college and career readiness models for youth with disabilities (Morningstar, Lombardi, Fowler, & Test, 2015), it is not surprising that *The Way to Work* focuses on strategies that create necessary opportunities for successful work experience tied to a relevant, rigorous curriculum and to instruction that increases the likelihood of career pathways leading to productive postschool employment. I appreciate the book's clear and compelling organization because it carefully scaffolds each topic in a logical approach, with information and strategies building upon one another for the reader. The heart of the book offers specific and applicable approaches for planning, implementing, and sustaining successful career and work experiences. A new and exciting element of this edition is the inclusion of Learning Labs that are designed to guide the reader toward implementation of work-related strategies. To hook the reader and illustrate strategies in a real-world context, case studies are used throughout each chapter. As a long-time user of the original book, I'm happy to see that updated forms are available for use. I have always used the forms as a starting point for practitioners to practice newly acquired content and then, as they gain confidence and experience, to adapt and modify to meet their unique contextual needs. From my perspective as a transition researcher and teacher educator, the second edition of *The Way to Work* was long overdue. For those concerned about ensuring that every student leaves school prepared for a career-focused employment outcome—from higher education faculty, secondary school administrators, and transition stakeholders (including school and community providers)—the book serves as a complete package that combines the most current research, evidence-based practices, and critical school and community strategies for positive outcomes.

*Mary E. Morningstar, Ph.D.*
*Department of Special Education*
*College of Education*
*Portland State University*

## REFERENCES

Carter, E. W., Austin, D, & Trainor, A. A. (2011). Predictors of postschool employment outcomes for young adults with severe disabilities. *Journal of Disability Policy Studies*, *20*, 1–14.

Luecking, R., Fabian, E., Contreary, K., Honeycutt, T., & Luecking, D. (2018). Vocational rehabilitation outcomes for students participating in a model transition program. *Rehabilitation Counseling Bulletin*, *61*, 154–163.

Mazzotti, V. L., Rowe, D. A., Sinclair, J., Poppen, M., Woods, W. E., & Shearer, M. L. (2016). Predictors of post-school success: A systematic review of NLTS2 secondary analyses. *Career Development and Transition for Exceptional Individuals*, *39*(4), 196–215.

Morningstar, M. E., Lombardi, A., Flower, C. H., & Test, D. W. (2015). A college and career readiness framework for secondary students with disabilities. *Career Development and Transition for Exceptional Individuals*. Retrieved from https://doi.org/10.1177/2165143415589926

Test, D. W., Mazzotti, V. L., Mustian, A. L., Fowler, C. H., Kortering, L., & Kohler, P. (2009). Evidence-based transition predictors for improving post school outcomes for students with disabilities. *Career Development for Exceptional Individuals*, *32*, 180–181.

Workforce Innovation and Opportunity Act of 2014, PL 113-128, 29 U.S.C. §§ *et seq.*

# Foreword

If you listen carefully you can hear the rumbling of a strengthening current in American society: the insistence on the part of more and more youth and adults with disabilities and their families for more and better employment opportunities. Since the mid-1980s, this current has led slowly to a larger body of knowledge about how to prepare people with disabilities for employment and a subsequent solidifying commitment on the part of policy makers to encourage and expand employment and career opportunities for individuals with disabilities choosing the path to employment.

In fact, when the concept began to emerge that people with disabilities could become employed and should have the supports and services required to make employment possible, the federal government placed increasing emphasis on improving the practice of supported employment and the processes it entails to increase employment outcomes for transitioning youth. But this has not been an easy matter given the necessity for painstaking effort 1) to raise expectations regarding the competencies of people with disabilities in the workforce, 2) to discern the factors that contribute to better outcomes for these individuals, and 3) to design and implement the ideas, processes, and strategies necessary to deliver improved outcomes.

As new knowledge and practice emerged, the necessity of communicating this information clearly to transition professionals, vocational rehabilitation counselors, job specialists, job developers, and individuals with disabilities and their families became compelling and continues to be so. Few who have accepted this challenge have contributed as much to the endeavor as the author of this book.

For his entire career, Rich Luecking has been immersed in the change of culture from sheltered work and nonwork to competitive integrated employment. An esteemed researcher, practitioner, author, and teacher, he has played an enormous role in maturing our thinking about what constitutes effective transition from school to work and adult life. This book follows up on the 2009 publication of *The Way to Work: How to Facilitate Work Experiences for Youth in Transition,* and it must be underscored that the timing of this new edition is fortuitous.

In the decade since the first book was released, a more robust and nuanced understanding of the processes of preparing and successfully placing individuals with disability in work-based experiences—which is a significant correlate to successful employment—has evolved and, more recently, has been embedded in legislation. In 2014, Congress successfully reauthorized the Workforce Innovation and Opportunity Act, which requires greater alignment of programs, collaboration across agencies, movement away from the use of subminimum wage certificates, and more efficient use of funds to achieve competitive integrated employment for people with disabilities. In that same year, Congress also enacted a law (the Achieving a Better Life Experience [ABLE] Act, PL 113-295) creating a tax-advantaged savings account for people with disabilities and their families to encourage work, earnings, and savings. In addition, initiatives, such as paid internships and apprenticeships and postsecondary education programs for students with disabilities—including those with intellectual disability—have begun to multiply. Perhaps most important, a new model of supported employment for those in transition—customized employment—is being utilized to a greater extent to support individuals who have significant disabilities.

From my perspective, the system of adult services and supports that has been in place for longer than the last half-century is in the early stages of great transformation, but transformation is impeded—it cannot successfully occur without transmitting the knowledge of practice necessary to implement new ideas and execute new processes and strategies. In a sense, this book has anticipated the coming transformation; it is expressly designed to facilitate it.

*Madeleine Will*
*President*
*Collaboration to Promote Self-Determination*

## REFERENCES

Achieving a Better Life Experience (ABLE) Act of 2014, PL 113-295.
Workforce Innovation and Opportunity Act of 2014, PL 113-128, 29 U.S.C. §§ *et seq*

# Preface

Two noteworthy developments have occurred since the first edition of this book. First, federal policy continues to move in the direction of presuming that anyone with any disability who wants to work can work. The presumption of employability is the underpinning of current special education transition planning requirements, vocational rehabilitation eligibility guidelines, and other federally supported programs that include employment as a service for people with disabilities. Second, more is known about how to make employment happen. Yet, policy is still not where disability employment advocates would like it to be, and advocates are still learning how to take effective services and strategies to scale so everyone can benefit no matter what their support needs might be and no matter where they live. But things are moving in the right direction.

To keep things moving forward, this edition of *The Way to Work* incorporates new strategies, along with long-standing proven approaches to helping youth experience work. All the techniques covered in this book have come from over 3 decades of developing, implementing and evaluating transition models that feature work experiences as a centerpiece of transition service to youth with disabilities. They come from everyday application by schools and their partners in communities throughout the country. They also come from large-scale national programs and initiatives, which have lent themselves to thorough evaluation. From all of them, the evidence continues to build supporting the idea of work as both an essential transition service component and as the desired outcome of transition service. In other words, to get work and have a career, one has to learn how to work. When this happens, the ideal culmination of education service for students with disabilities will be productive and meaningful employment and careers as adults. Our success as transition professionals should be judged against this standard.

To that end, this edition of *The Way to Work* intends to elevate the effectiveness of transition specialists. It uses numerous real-life examples to illustrate strategies and techniques that my contributors and I have found successful. These examples come from our work on national scale projects such as the Marriott Foundation's Bridges program, the National Youth Transition Demonstration, and Promoting Readiness for Minors in SSI (PROMISE). They come from statewide initiatives such as the Maryland Seamless Transition Collaborative. And they come from working with individual school systems in communities around the country. The approaches detailed in this book, then, come from actual practice in the field where dedicated transition professionals use them. Furthermore, they are supported by rigorous research that has evaluated their application. In short, the strategies in this book have been field tested, and we know they work.

The challenge is now to take to scale what is known to work. To say work experience should be central to good transition service is one thing. To make sure that all youth have the opportunity to be exposed to work experience is another thing. Schools and communities, of course, will have to commit to making work experience available to all youth with disabilities. But even when that commitment is made, youth with disabilities still struggle with employment preparation in the absence of transition professionals who know how to help them experience work. It will always be necessary to build the capacity of those professionals who have been tasked with facilitating work experience for youth in transition. That is, those who are new to this work need to be trained how to do it, and experienced professionals need ongoing training to continually improve their work experience facilitation skills. The intention of this book is to do both of these things. *The Way to Work* is meant to be a resource for both the aspiring and the experienced transition professional.

My previous work at TransCen, Inc., and my current work at the Center for Transition and Career Innovation at the University of Maryland has been driven by the potential of all youth to achieve employment success. In various ways, activity continues at both places to illustrate "the way to work." In particular, the Center's mission is threefold: 1) to study how, when, and under what circumstances youth achieve employment success; 2) to translate knowledge gleaned from that study so as to influence both policy and practice, which will impact transition and employment success for youth with disabilities; and 3) to help professionals learn and put into practice those techniques known to be successful. I invite readers to follow our work at https://education.umd.edu/CTCI.

# Acknowledgments

As with the first edition, this second edition of *The Way to Work* owes much to the many dedicated and effective professionals who work every day to help youth learn the way to work. At the top of that list are my long-time colleagues and friends Kelli Thuli Crane, Amy Dwrye D'Agati, Meredith Gramlich, and Marie Parker Harvey. They are incredible people and professionals who have directly assisted youth in finding the way to work, taught others how to do the same, and been key contributors to implementing the many transition models we have established and studied. In other words, they know how to do it, they know how to show others how to do it, and they have helped provide evidence of how it works. I am grateful to them for all of that, for their contributions to selected chapters in this book, and for their diligence in collecting the numerous examples of youth work experiences included throughout this book.

Ellen Fabian is another longtime "partner in crime" who deserves acknowledgement. From the very first transition supported employment model we tested together in the late 1980s to our current work on the rigorous evaluation of large-scale transition models that feature work experience, her contributions have been enormous and invaluable. She has led the way in documenting the value of work experiences.

I give special thanks to Mary Morningstar, who graciously agreed to provide a foreword for this book. The source of my gratitude is twofold. First, she is one of the preeminent teacher educators and transition researchers in the county. Second, she was a public school teacher and collaborator when we first tested a seamless transition model in Montgomery County, Maryland, in the late 1980s. She is a true pioneer and remains a key leader in the school-to-work transition field. It is an honor to have her weigh in here on the importance of work experience to the career development of youth.

Speaking of honors, it is hard to think of a higher one than to have Madeleine Will also provide a foreword. To say that she has been one of the most tireless advocates on behalf of individuals with disabilities would be an understatement. Among a host of other important contributions, she is the "Godmother" of the national focus on transition as a policy and as a practice. The field owes much to her work as a high-level federal official, to her ongoing national leadership in this movement, and to her voice as a parent who knows whereof she speaks.

A big thank you goes to my colleague, friend, and wife, Debra Martin Luecking, who has been a partner in many of the seamless transition models we have implemented and whose ideas and encouragement were invaluable during the production of both editions of this book.

Most important, I want to thank the many youth and families who kindly agreed to let their stories be told about the value of work experience in the pursuit of employment and careers. It is they who have inspired this work.

# Introduction

The research on effective transition service can be summed up in three words: Work is good! The evidence continues to grow that work experience in high school is one of the strongest predictors of adult employment for youth with disabilities (Luecking, Fabian, Contreary, Honeycutt, & Luecking, 2018; Wehman et al., 2014). Effective transition professionals already know this. In fact, anyone who has watched youth blossom in self-confidence and skill as they perform in an authentic workplace can attest to this phenomenon.

The implications of the value of work are wide reaching, especially for youth with disabilities currently in the nation's secondary schools—almost 400,000 of whom exit school each year (National Center for Educational Statistics, 2016). Ever since school-to-work transition became a federal policy priority (Will, 1984) and transition planning became a legal requirement (Individuals with Disabilities Education Act [IDEA] of 1990, PL 101-476; Individuals with Disabilities Education Improvement Act [IDEIA] of 2004, PL 108-446), the value of work experience for youth with disabilities as they prepare to exit publicly mandated education has become increasingly obvious. It has long been known that it is critically important for youth with disabilities to experience learning in work-based environments— that is, situations in which they spend concentrated and structured time in actual work settings provided by cooperating companies and employers.

Notably, two national developments illustrate increasing recognition of the importance of work experience for youth in transition from school to adult life. The first is legislative. The Workforce Innovation and Opportunity Act (WIOA) of 2014 (PL 113-128) requires that state vocational rehabilitation (VR) agencies allocate 15% of their service funds to transitioning students and youth for what are called Pre-Employment Transition Services, or Pre-ETS. Pre-ETS include five categories of service to students with disabilities for which VR can pay: job exploration counseling, counseling on opportunities for enrollment in postsecondary education and training, workplace readiness training, instruction in self-advocacy, and work-based learning experiences. This means that VR can now pay for the development and support of work experiences for students with disabilities while they are in secondary school. This has the potential to significantly boost the ability of students with disabilities to exit school better prepared for successful adult employment.

The second development is the increasing advocacy for adult employment for all individuals with disabilities. This advocacy is embodied in the Employment First movement. Per ODEP (2018), this initiative urges publicly financed systems "to align policies, service delivery practices, and reimbursement structures to commit to integrated employment as the priority option with respect to the use of publicly-financed day and employment services for youth and adults with significant disabilities." In other words, government should fund those services that promote employment and minimize funding to those services that do not. In many states and federal initiatives, Employment First activities have prioritized work and work experiences for youth with disabilities who are still in high school (ODEP, 2018). This movement has provided strong impetus to the notion that employment is presumed desirable and possible for *all* people with disabilities, including those who might need unusual or significant support to make that happen.

## JOB SUCCESS

Although the case is strong that work experience is best predictor of postschool job success, it is not the only one. There are, of course, other circumstances that contribute to successful transition to work and adult life. Near the top of that list is the involvement and support of families. Simply put, when families expect that their family members with disabilities will become employed, these youth are highly likely to do so (Carter, Austin, & Trainor, 2011; Wehman et al., 2014). Furthermore, when family members actively support work experience, including by providing important perspective about interests and preferences, young people with disabilities tend to succeed in work experiences and in adult employment (Test et al., 2009).

Another contributor to successful employment is self-determination, or self-advocacy. That is, youth with disabilities succeed in the workplace when they have the ability and opportunity to express themselves regarding what they prefer, what they can do, and what kind of help they need to perform effectively in the workplace (Shogren, Wehmeyer, Palmer, Rifenbark, & Little, 2015). There has been a long-standing movement within the disability community that says "nothing about us without us." This means that individuals with disabilities do not want things done to them or for them without their input and consent. It also means that no one should assume what type of work experience or ultimate employment goal should be pursued without express input from students preparing to work. Furthermore, it means that a disability label should not determine whether someone can work or what kind of job someone should aspire to. Indeed, disability advocacy and current federal policy direction presume that not only do all people with disabilities have the potential to work but also that what type of work they pursue should be determined only with the informed input and consent of the job seeker (Martinez, 2013).

Interagency collaboration, under the right conditions, also contributes to the achievement of work experience and employment goals of young people with disabilities. Many students and youth with disabilities are served by multiple systems and professionals. However, it has often been the practice among schools and collaborating agencies to merely make a hand-off to another responsible organization for an employment or transition-related service. Yet, to achieve the best outcomes, the context of the collaboration is important. When collaboration is jointly and directly focused on outcomes for youth, such as work experience or integrated paid employment, higher rates of employment are more likely (Fabian, Simonsen, Deschamps, Dong, & Luecking, 2016; Luecking et al., 2018).

The evidence about what works when helping youth with disabilities make the transition from school to work and adult life continues to grow. It builds on past attempts to synthesize what research, experts, and advocates point to as essential components of effective transition service. The Guideposts for Success (NCWD/Y, 2005, 2019), for example, is a widely used framework to conceptualize optimum service delivery for youth in transition. It is based on extensive review of research, demonstration projects, and acknowledged effective practices. The Guideposts identify five general areas of intervention:

1. *School based preparatory experiences*—that is, academic instruction and targeted curriculum

2. *Career preparation and work-based experiences*, including vocational training and work experiences

3. *Youth development and youth leadership*, especially as they relate to self-determined transition planning

4. *Family involvement and support*

5. *Connecting activities*—that is, those activities that enable youth to be linked with organizations and services that complement their transition services and/or enable necessary postsecondary supports

Although this edition will touch on all of these factors, work is the obvious thrust of this book. Work is the strongest forecaster of postschool employment success. The other features of the Guideposts, and thus other relevant evidence, will be discussed intermittently as they are often critical to making work experiences and work successful. Many publications are available that highlight aspects of each and all of these factors, but even in the ensuing time since the first edition of *The Way to Work* (Luecking, 2009), still too few exist that exclusively address how to help youth learn how to work and how to build their employment portfolio so that they begin their adult careers *before* they exit school. This book builds on the first edition to continue to fill that void.

## THE NEED FOR A CONTINUED EMPHASIS ON WORK

Given the growing evidence about effective transition interventions and services, there is every reason to look forward to the day when young people with disabilities enter the workforce for what ideally will be the start of a long career. The statistics, however, suggest that these expectations are still not the norm and that employment is still an elusive postschool outcome for many youth with disabilities. Since the late 1990s, there have been modest improvements in postschool employment for youth with disabilities (Wagner, Newman, Cameto, & Levine, 2005; Wehman, 2013). However, there continue to be lags in youth participation in paid jobs outside of school (Lipscomb, Lacoe, Liu, & Haimson, 2018). Significant disparities, including the following, continue between youth with disabilities and their same-age peers without disabilities:

- Youth with disabilities are less likely than their peers without disabilities to finish high school (Stark & Noel, 2015).

- Youth with disabilities are less likely to pursue postsecondary education that will prepare them for good jobs and careers (National Center for Education Statistics, 2016).

- Some groups of special education students need connections to ongoing support to sustain the benefit of public education, and these supports are not always available (Wehman, 2013; Windsor et al., 2018).

- Subminimum wage and sheltered employment remains the fate of thousands of people with intellectual and other significant disabilities (Hiersteiner, Butterworth, Bershadsky, & Bonardi, 2018).

- Unemployment, poverty, and dependence on public assistance programs await many transitioning youth as they exit school (Davies, Rupp, & Wittenberg, 2009; DeNavas-Walt & Proctor, 2015).

In effect, less-than-optimal postschool employment outcomes could be cited for all categories of youth with disabilities. That is, whether youth have the label of intellectual disability, behavioral disabilities, mobility disabilities, sensory disabilities, learning disabilities, or multiple disabilities, the field can do better in helping them achieve adult employment. It remains clear that special education transition services must improve the way in which they create and offer to students important work experience opportunities, how they complement curricula requirements, and how these experiences and the rest of public education lead to productive postschool employment. The field may be moving in the right direction, but it is not there yet. The good news? So much more is now known about how to make work happen for all categories of youth with disabilities. That is what this book hopes to impart.

## EMPLOYMENT FOR ALL

Youth and their families no longer have to settle for historically disappointing postschool outcomes. Work-based experiences, such as job shadowing, internships, cooperative work placements, service learning, and volunteer work experiences, are effective and important prerequisites to successful postschool employment success. Moreover, when *paid work*, the gold standard of youth in the workplace, is paired with education, either as an ancillary activity or as an integral aspect of curriculum, youth are considerably more likely to obtain and retain employment as adults (Wehman et al., 2014).

In essence, focused work experiences throughout secondary education can be the antidote to obstacles to adult employment. Carefully organized and supervised work experiences, where there are opportunities to receive guidance and feedback on work performance, would go a long way to improve postschool employment outcomes. Furthermore, these experiences serve as career building blocks as adolescents exit school, especially when upon exit they require connections to supports that will help them to continue pursuing work and career opportunities to which they were exposed during secondary education. Thus, this book's purpose is to offer strategies essential for creating opportunities for successful work experiences, for pairing them with curricula requirements, and for bolstering the likelihood that publicly supported education leads to productive postschool employment. Indeed, a case could be made that the nation's education system can only be deemed to have achieved its aims when the climax of each student's educational experience is the beginning of a productive adult life. For most people this means a job—or, even better, a career.

This book is framed by the belief that the culmination of publicly supported education for youth with disabilities can and should be real adult employment. The book guides the reader in helping youth choose and pursue work experiences. It provides approaches for identifying, developing, organizing, and monitoring work experience opportunities in the workplaces of a community's employers.

My experience and that of committed colleagues around the country have led to the driving philosophy of this book: *All youth who want to can achieve an adult life of productive and successful employment, regardless of disability label, the need for support and accommodation, the intensity of special education services, or even the economic vitality of their communities.* The approaches described in this book can be applied to help all of these youth achieve this goal. This book shows how work experiences become opportunities for learning how to work so that postschool employment becomes the rule rather than the exception for youth with disabilities.

## HOW THIS BOOK IS ORGANIZED

The chapters in this book are arranged so that ideas and strategies presented in each chapter are logical precursors to the ideas and strategies presented in the subsequent chapter. They are ordered to build a continually reinforcing knowledge base. However, although the chapters are organized to follow a logical sequence, the reader may extract ideas and strategies directly from any one of them at any time. Each chapter has stand-alone strategies that can be applied in direct practice related to the chapter topic.

The first two chapters set the stage for the practical strategies that will be presented later throughout the book. Chapter 1 illustrates the need for work experiences and how they foster the development of a career pathway for youth. Chapter 2 goes into some detail about the types of work experiences and their respective uses and importance in job and career pursuits. It also provides the framework for making sure that quality is built into youth work experiences and that the roles of youth, educators, families, employers, co-workers and other interested parties are carefully considered and well defined. These chapters are intended to provide a basis for proceeding with the strategies found in subsequent chapters.

The process of and strategies for organizing and supporting quality work experiences begin in Chapter 3 and continue through Chapter 10. It is in these chapters that the practitioner will be able to take away specific and directly applicable strategies for planning, developing, and supporting successful work experiences. Again, although these chapters are ordered in a sequence that suggests a practical progression, readers can access them out of order if their experience and learning needs are more in one area or another. Since these chapters represent the heart of work experience practice, they include specific Learning Labs, designed to help the reader practice and implement the strategies the chapters present.

Every chapter contains specific case examples of youth and/or case examples of how strategies have been applied to good effect. These are meant to illustrate real-world application of these ideas and strategies. They are all derived from actual examples taken from field experiences, using pseudonyms to protect confidentiality. Many chapters also contain sample forms that the reader is free to reproduce or adapt for direct use in transition practice. They are samples of forms transition professionals have found useful for advancing transition, but they are by no means the only or necessarily the best way to do it. Readers are encouraged to adopt and adapt them as they find helpful.

Finally, Chapter 11 presents issues and trends that may affect the future of work experience and employment for youth with disabilities. It presents a context for thinking about how transition practice might be affected by these trends and how transition professionals and advocates might work to ensure that the way to work might be constantly improved, rather than hindered, by these developments.

## AN IMPORTANT NOTE ON CHARACTERIZING YOUTH, EMPLOYERS, AND THOSE WHO LINK THEM TOGETHER

When a disability label serves as a major descriptor of a student, too often assumptions are made about youth circumstances that are either stereotypical or limiting. Therefore, throughout the book, specific disability labels are used sparingly when referring to youth in the case studies. Such references are used only if there is a compelling reason to identify a disability for case study clarity. It is important, of course, to factor in accommodations that individual youth may need in order to succeed in the workplace. However, it is also essential to know that even within particular disability categories, the range and type of accommodations are broad. They depend entirely on each individual's circumstances. Thus, in general discussion, the book almost always refers to young people with disabilities simply as students or youth. The reader, with noted exceptions, will be able to apply the concepts discussed to any youth seeking or participating in a work-based experience, regardless of disability label, nature of disability, or need for support.

It should also be noted that employers are absolutely essential partners in creating work experiences for youth. Chapters 6 and 7 discuss the importance of employer cooperation and of viewing employers as another ultimate customer of transition programs that promote work experiences and jobs for youth. Employers are as heterogeneous as the youth with whom they may come in contact. They come in all sizes and descriptions: private sector; for-profit entities; local, state, and federal government entities; and nonprofit and civic entities. Some have a handful of employees; others hire thousands. In addition, a host of industry sectors exist under which various employer entities could be classified. To simplify matters, the book uses in general discussion the terms *employer, business,* and *company* interchangeably to refer to any entity—public or private, large or small—that could potentially offer work experiences and jobs to youth. Again, the issues and strategies that successfully link employers on behalf of and with youth ultimately frame the success of this work, no matter what labels are used to describe it.

Finally, many types of professionals come in contact with youth with disabilities. There are, of course teachers and educational staff. There are vocational rehabilitation counselors. And there are job developers and job coaches who may work for schools or for community employment service agencies. Any of these people may have the responsibility of connecting youth to workplaces for work experiences and for supporting them during these experiences. In this book, all those who have the responsibility for facilitating work experiences—regardless of job title or affiliation—are referred to universally as transition specialists. The strategies presented throughout are meant to useful to anyone who does this important work.

As readers consider the ideas and strategies that the book offers, I sincerely hope that more and more people will adopt the belief that work is good! It is good for youth to learn in real work environments, to learn how to work, to learn where to work, to find the best ways to be supported and accommodated at work, and to produce at work to the satisfaction of current and future employers. The intent is that through these activities the ultimate good is that youth can find life satisfaction as contributing citizens and self-supporting adults.

## REFERENCES

Carter, E. W., Austin, D, & Trainor, A. A. (2011). Predictors of postschool employment outcomes for young adults with severe disabilities. *Journal of Disability Policy Studies, 20*, 1–14.

Davies, P. S., Rupp, K., & Wittenburg, D. (2009). A life-cycle perspective on the transition to adulthood among children receiving Supplemental Security Income payments. *Journal of Vocational Rehabilitation, 30*(3), 133–151.

DeNavas-Walt, C., & Proctor, B. (2015). *Income and poverty in the United States: 2014* [U.S. Census Bureau, Current Population Reports P60-252]. Washington, DC: U.S. Government Printing Office.

Fabian, E., Simonsen, M., Deschamps, A., Dong, S., & Luecking, D. (2016). Service system collaboration in transition: An empirical exploration of its effects on rehabilitation outcomes for students with disabilities. *Journal of Rehabilitation, 82*, 3–10.

Hiersteiner, D., Butterworth, J., Bershadsky, J., & Bonardi, A. (2018). *Working in the community: The status and outcomes of people with intellectual and developmental disabilities in integrated employment—Update 3* [NCI Data Brief, April 2016]. Cambridge, MA: Human Services Research Institute.

Individuals with Disabilities Education Act of 1990, PL 101-476, 20 U.S.C., 1400 *et seq.*

Individuals with Disabilities Education Improvement Act of 2004, PL 108-446, 20 U.S.C., 1400 *et seq.*

Lipscomb, S., Lacoe, J., Liu, A., & Haimson, J. (2018). *Preparing for life after high school: The characteristics and experiences of youth in special education: A summary of key findings from the National Longitudinal Transition Study 2012* [NCEE Evaluation Brief]. Washington, DC: Institute of Educational Sciences.

Luecking, R. (2009). *The way to work: How to facilitate work experiences for youth in transition.* Baltimore, MD: Paul H. Brookes Publishing Co.

Luecking, R., Fabian, E., Contreary, K., Honeycutt, T., & Luecking, D. (2018). Vocational rehabilitation outcomes for students participating in a model transition program. *Rehabilitation Counseling Bulletin, 61*, 154–163.

Martinez, K. (2013). Integrated employment, Employment First, and U.S. federal policy. *Journal of Vocational Rehabilitation, 3*, 165–168.

National Center for Educational Statistics. (2016). *Digest of education statistics: 2015.* Retrieved from https://nces.ed.gov/programs/digest/d15/index.asp

National Collaborative on Workforce and Disability for Youth (NCWD/Y). (2005, 2019). *Guideposts for success.* Washington, DC: Institute on Educational Leadership.

Office of Disability Employment Policy (ODEP). (2018). *Employment First*. Retrieved from https://www.dol.gov/odep/topics/EmploymentFirst.htm

Shogren, K., Wehmeyer, M., Palmer, S., Rifenbark, G., & Little. T. (2015). Relationships between self-determination and postschool outcomes for youth with disabilities *Journal of Special Education, 48*, 256–267.

Stark, P., & Noel, A. (2015). *Trends in high school dropout and completion rates in the United States: 1972–2009*. Washington, DC: U.S. Department of Education. Retrieved from http://nces.ed.gov/pubsearch/pubsinfo.asp?pubid=2015015

Test, D. W., Mazzotti, V. L., Mustian, A. L., Fowler, C. H., Kortering, L., & Kohler, P. (2009). Evidence-based transition predictors for improving post school outcomes for students with disabilities. *Career Development for Exceptional Individuals, 32*,180–181.

Wagner, M., Newman L., Cameto, R., & Levine P. (2005). *Changes over time in the early postschool outcomes of youth with disabilities*. Menlo Park, CA: SRI International.

Wehman, P. (2013). *Life beyond the classroom: Transition strategies for young people with disabilities* (5th ed.). Baltimore, MD: Paul H. Brookes Publishing Co.

Wehman, P., Sima, A., Ketchum, J., West, M., Chan, F., & Luecking, R. (2014). Predictors of successful transition from school to employment for youth with disabilities. *Journal of Occupational Rehabilitation, 25*, 223–234.

Will, M. (1984). *OSERS programming for the transition of youth with disabilities: Bridges from school to working life*. Washington, DC:, U.S. Department of Education, Office of Special Education and Rehabilitative Services.

Winsor, J., Timmons, J., Butterworth, J., Migliore, A., Domin, D., Zalewska, A., & Shepard, J. (2018). *StateData: The national report on employment services and outcomes*. Boston: University of Massachusetts Boston, Institute for Community Inclusion.

Workforce Innovation and Opportunity Act of 2014, PL 113-128, 29 U.S.C. §§ *et seq.*

*To Nick Certo (1949–2017), who was a friend and colleague and whose belief in the employability of all youth was the cornerstone of his pioneering work on seamless transition programs for youth with disabilities*

# Recognizing Work Experiences as Indispensable Transition Tools

Richard G. Luecking and Kelli Thuli Crane

---

**By completing this chapter, the reader will**

- Discover the primary benefits to youth who participate in work experiences
- Understand the types and purposes of work experiences
- Learn the types and purposes of work experiences
- Consider what constitutes a quality work experience
- Engage with examples of transition models that feature work experience and that provide evidence of their value

---

Marquita has two strong interests. She wants to be a lawyer and she wants to "make a difference." She is a hard-working, meticulous student. Her accommodations at school include voice recognition software on her computer. Her teacher helped her find a job shadowing experience at a small law firm where she observed the processes for legal research. She had a subsequent internship at a large law firm where she performed a range of administrative tasks and where she learned how her need to use voice recognition software could be accommodated. These experiences helped solidify her interest in law. She is now enrolled in a local university majoring in political science. Next stop: law school.

Erika always wanted to have a job and make money. Until her last year in school she had almost no exposure to work other than knowing her family members had jobs. Even her teachers had doubts about her ability to ever work in a "real" job due to her blindness and need for close supervision to perform many basic tasks. She participated in a work experience program in her last year of school, where she learned—with specific accommodations—to perform clerical tasks such as preparing mailings. She did so well that she was offered a job at that company at the end of her work experience. Many years later, she still works there.

Roberto had no notion of what kind of job or career he wanted. But he liked to be busy and active. As part of his high school transition program, he had work experiences as a grocery store shopping cart attendant and as a janitor at a shopping mall food court. He didn't do well in either work experience. As he is nonverbal, he could never say what he liked or did not like about the experiences. Then, he sampled tasks at a recreation center's ropes course. He was always busy at the center, filling water jugs, sorting equipment, and packaging marketing materials. His smile and his proficient work made it clear this was a good match. Now that he is out of school he works as a fitness center attendant with support from an adult employment agency.

Declan struggled in the early years of high school. He faced many behavioral challenges, and bounced back and forth between his neighborhood school and an alternative high school. Things turned around for him when he began an internship as an information technology (IT) assistant with a large research company. It challenged him and engaged his interest. He found his niche and purpose. He finished high school, completed an associate degree in IT, and is now employed as an IT technician at a small nonprofit organization.

Marquita's, Erika's, Roberto's, and Declan's stories are examples of the employment and career success that students and youth with disabilities can achieve, especially when we assume that all youth with disabilities can work and when we apply effective, evidence-based practices to make that happen. Over the past few decades, the postschool employment rates for students with disabilities are slowly but steadily inching upward. Youth in all categories of disabilities are faring slightly better in terms of postschool employment rates, with an overall employment rate now above 50% (Liu et al., 2018). This compares with overall postschool employment rates for all categories of youth with disabilities of well below 50% in the late 1980s (Blackorby & Wagner, 1996). Although these rates are not as high as they should be, they are improving, thanks in large part to newly focused policy and improved practices to plan for and facilitate work experiences. As the field continues to identify evidence-based practices that promote work, it is logical that youth with disabilities become better prepared for the world of work.

This is good news for youth, their families, disability advocates, professionals, and policy makers. It means that school-to-work transition outcomes are starting to catch up to the original legislative intent reflected in the Individuals with Disabilities Act (IDEA) of 1990 (PL 101-496), which mandated transition planning, and, more recently, the Workforce Innovation and Opportunities Act (WIOA) of 2014 (PL 113-128), which mandates state vocational rehabilitation (VR) agencies provide services, including work experiences, for students with disabilities before they exit high school. The underpinning of each of these laws is the notion that anyone eligible for services provided through the agencies supported by these legislations has the potential to benefit from them. That is, employability is presumed.

Increased employment rates and legislation that presumes employability for youth with disabilities are the result of learning better ways to educate and prepare students and youth for transition to employment and adult life. The transition field has learned improved ways to structure resources and services to ensure that better connections are made to support youth. Most important, it has become clear that connecting youth to workplaces early and often throughout the secondary school years is a valuable way to help youth get started on productive postschool careers.

Unfortunately, many students with disabilities continue to struggle to successfully make the transition from school to adult employment. For every Roberto, Erika, Marquita, and Declan, there are other youth with disabilities who will not be so fortunate as to have their education lead directly to a job and career path. This does not have to be the case. The field of transition from school to work is ever evolving and its methodology improving. Carefully organized and monitored work experiences are part of this evolution. This chapter elaborates on why work experiences are so important, illustrates the potential they have for benefiting youth, introduces components of quality work experiences, and briefly discusses transition models that feature work experience as a centerpiece intervention.

## WHY WORK EXPERIENCE IS IMPORTANT

A work-based learning experience includes essentially any activity that puts youth in the workplaces of employers and that offers an opportunity to learn about careers, career preferences, work behaviors, and specific work and occupational skills. For youth with disabilities, work-based learning has the additional benefit of helping to identify any necessary supports and accommodations that might be essential to perform tasks and engage in behaviors that are necessary for workplace success. This book refers to this type of purposeful educational and transition activity as *work experience*. Work experiences can include such sporadic and brief activities as job shadowing, informational interviews, and workplace tours; more intensive activities of various durations such as workplace mentoring; and other more-protracted experiences, including work sampling, service learning, on-the-job training, internships, apprenticeships, and paid employment. Each of these activities contributes to the career development, career choice, and career success of individuals with disabilities.

### Benefits to Students and Youth

The textbox titled Benefits of Work Experiences summarizes research-supported benefits associated with work experiences as transition tools. For all youth, with and without disabilities, work experiences have long been shown to improve self-esteem, teach and reinforce basic academic and technical skills, promote an understanding of workplace culture and expectations, and help youth develop a network for future job searches (Haimson & Bellotti, 2001; Hoerner & Wehrley, 1995; Wehman, 2013). For youth with disabilities, these experiences further serve as opportunities to identify the particular workplace supports they may require as they pursue later employment and career prospects (Wehman, 2013).

Such experiences also serve to expose students to work and career options that would otherwise be unknown to them. This is especially critical to youth with disabilities for whom exposure to the range of career options is often very limited. For anyone, it can be said that exposure precedes interest. That is, how can anyone know if he or she likes or is interested in something without first knowing about it? One of the key values of work experiences for youth with disabilities is that they often function to introduce youth to tasks, jobs, and careers they would not know about otherwise.

**Benefits of Work Experiences**

Students and youth who participate in work experiences benefit by having the opportunity to

- Gain exposure to new experiences that will inform career interests

- Explore career goals

- Identify on-the-job support needs

- Develop employability skills and good work habits

- Gain an understanding of employer expectations

- Link specific classroom instruction with related work expectations and knowledge requirements

- Develop an understanding of the workplace and the connection between learning and earning

- Gain general work experience as well as experience connected to a specific job function that can be added to a work portfolio or résumé

## Legal Special Education Requirements

Although not specifically cited in current special education law, work experiences can be valuable tools for education systems to meet requirements for monitoring the transition components of the law. For example, states are required by special education legislation, such as the Individuals with Disabilities Education Improvement Act (IDEIA) of 2004 (PL 108-446), to measure the "percent of youth aged 16 and above with transition planning that includes coordinated annual goals and transition services that will reasonably enable the student to meet his/her postsecondary goals in the identified areas" (Indicator 13, IDEIA 2004). Obviously, if those goals include employment and/or postsecondary education, then work experiences are critical to help students meet postsecondary goals.

States also are required to monitor the "percent of youth who had IEPs [individualized education programs], are no longer in secondary school, and who have been competitively employed, enrolled in some type of postsecondary school, or both, within one year of leaving high school" (Indicator 14, IDEIA 2004). If this percentage is high, then it can be inferred that youth were adequately prepared for postschool life, including employment. Of course, previously cited research indicates that work experiences are important to adequate preparation for positive postschool employment outcomes (e.g., Carter et al., 2012; Wehman et al., 2014). The incentive exists, therefore, for state school systems to monitor their local systems so that they adopt curriculum and teaching methodology that helps address these indicators. The clear intent is for local school districts to receive the help they need to deliver the best possible transition services for their students. Transition planning, as required by law, is important to meeting the intent of IDEIA and, more important, help facilitate an effective transition from school to work and adult life for students with disabilities. The fact that students in special education are showing gains in postschool employment rates, however modest, illustrates the value of these requirements.

Local education agencies are also required to report the percentage of students with IEPs who have dropped out of school compared with the percent of all students in the state who have dropped out (Indicator 2, IDEIA 2004). There are thousands of students who, like Roberto introduced at the beginning of this chapter, likely would drop out of school without appropriate incentives and relevant curriculum to engage them in career development activities. Although it would be naïve to suggest that work experience alone will mitigate this problem, it certainly is an important action to consider. In any case, special education law recognizes that it is crucial for schools to find ways to address an alarmingly high drop-out rate among students receiving special education services.

Compliance with special education law is important to schools, as both federal and state funding support depend on it. However, the law exists to ensure that students benefit from the education they receive from the schools—it is students who ultimately realize the benefits of transition planning, especially when that planning includes work experiences. These experiences have direct, tangible benefit for youth, as illustrated by the brief examples at the beginning of this chapter. Each of the youth in these examples had opportunities to identify career interests, explore the need for on-the-job support needs, learn work skills, become aware of employer expectations, and connect learning in the school with its relevance to the world of work. Most important, these experiences resulted in either direct adult employment success or the path to obtain it.

## Systemic and Program Benefits

Although youth are the obvious beneficiaries of work experiences, it is instructive to point out that advantages accrue to those entities that provide and fund education, transition, and employment services. For example, when work experiences are included in educational curricula, or as adjunctive experiences to education, or as integral features of the IEP, school systems stand to have better results related to Indicators 2, 13, 14 of the special education law described earlier. For example, a recent initiative in Maryland is specifically requiring local school systems to track the work experiences of all students as part of the State Department of Education's objective to increase the number of students participating in work experiences before exiting high school. As stated by the Assistant State Superintendent of Education Marcela Franczkowski, "What gets measured gets done" (personal communication, November 18, 2018).

Similarly, state VR agencies that provide services to eligible youth can benefit. In particular, when youth with disabilities engage in work experiences as part of their services, VR agencies can expect better returns on the service dollars (Luecking et al., 2018). In effect, when students achieve employment, state VR agencies can report more successful case closures for the students and youth they serve. Moreover, WIOA also now requires VR agencies and schools to increase collaboration on behalf of students with disabilities. One study illustrated a significant difference both in money spent and in the number of successful case closures for VR service recipients who participated in work experience as part of their

**Table 1.1.** System and program benefits of collaborating on work experiences

| Schools/ school districts | Vocational rehabilitation | State I/DD, mental health, and other service agencies | Community employment service programs |
|---|---|---|---|
| More meaningful IEPs and transition plans required by special education law | Clear opportunities to meet WIOA requirements to collaborate with schools | More efficient application of resources | Improved capacity to serve youth |
| Additional positive outcomes for Indicators 2, 13, and 14 of IDEIA | More efficient application of resources | Improved employment outcomes | More efficient application of resources |
| | More successful case closures | | Improved employment outcomes |

*Key:* I/DD, intellectual/developmental disabilities; IEPs, individualized education programs; IDEIA, Individuals with Disabilities Education Improvement Act of 2004; WIOA, Workforce Innovation and Opportunity Act of 2014.

transition service when compared to VR service recipients who did not (Luecking et al., 2018).

State agencies for intellectual and developmental disabilities, and state mental health agencies, are often in a position to provide employment-related postschool services to transitioning youth. These programs have much to gain when individuals entering their service system have experienced work before exiting school or, even better, already have jobs at the point of exit. In such cases, there will be less need for work assessment and job development services from these agencies. Not only will it maximize resources, but the outcomes of service provision will improve (Certo & Luecking, 2006). Agencies can spend less money for better outcomes.

Finally, there are advantages to community employment service programs that might directly collaborate with schools in the facilitation of work experiences. They can essentially bring young people into their programs who are either already working or who have had the benefit of work experiences. This makes the application of job development and job support resources all that much easier and more efficient. It also improves service capacity and effectiveness. Of course, the sharing of resources and collaboration between schools, VR agencies, and other community partners to facilitate transition is often easier to say than to do. Where collaboration includes work experience, however, all partners benefit and outcomes improve (Fabian, Deschamps, Simonsen, & Luecking, 2016). Table 1.1 summarizes these benefits.

## TYPES AND USES OF WORK EXPERIENCES

Work experiences may include any combination of the following: career explorations, job shadowing, volunteer experience, service learning, paid and unpaid internships, apprenticeships, and paid employment. These experiences offer opportunities for youth to learn specific work and occupational skills, as well as appropriate work behaviors—often referred to as "soft skills" (e.g., following instructions, getting along with coworkers)—needed to succeed in the workplace. In addition, work experiences can help identify the youth's employment and career preferences, and the supports and accommodations that might be essential to long-term workplace success. A range of work experience is presented and defined in Table 1.2.

**Table 1.2.** Types of work experiences

| | |
|---|---|
| Career exploration | Career exploration involves visits by youth to workplaces to learn about jobs and the skills required to perform them. Visits and meetings with employers and people in identified occupations outside of the workplace are also types of career exploration activities from which youth can learn about jobs and careers. Typically, such visits are accompanied by discussions with youth about what they saw, heard, and learned. |
| Job shadowing | Job shadowing is extended time, often a full workday or several workdays, spent by a youth in a workplace accompanying an employee in the performance of his or her daily duties. For example, many companies have take your son or daughter to work days and some companies organize annual official job shadow days when they invite youth to spend time at the company. |
| Work sampling | Work sampling is work by a youth that does not materially benefit the employer but allows the youth to spend meaningful time in a work environment to learn aspects of potential job tasks and to learn soft skills required in the workplace. It is important for transition specialists to be familiar with the Fair Labor Standards Act requirements for volunteer activity. |
| Service learning | Service learning is hands-on volunteer service to the community that is integrated with course objectives. It is a structured process that provides time for reflection on the service experience and demonstration of the skills and knowledge acquired. Many school districts require service learning time as a condition for graduation, which offers opportunity to structure them as meaningful work experience. |
| Internships | Internships are formal arrangements whereby a youth is assigned specific tasks in a workplace over a predetermined period of time. Internships may be paid or unpaid, depending on the nature of the agreement with the company and the nature of the tasks. Many postsecondary institutions help organize these experiences with local companies as adjuncts to specific degree programs and are alternatively called cooperative education experience, cooperative work, or simply co-ops. |
| Apprenticeships | Apprenticeships are formal, sanctioned work experiences of extended duration in which an apprentice learns specific occupational skills related to a standardized trade, such as carpentry, plumbing, and drafting. Many apprenticeships also include paid work components. |
| Stipend jobs | Stipend jobs include those in which wages are paid through an external source, such as a youth employment program, rather than directly by the employer. These jobs are typically customized or created to match student and employer circumstances, rather than match a specific existing job description. Some youth employment programs feature stipend jobs. |
| Paid employment | Paid employment may include existing standard jobs in a company or customized work assignments that are negotiated with an employer, but they always feature a wage paid directly to the youth by the employer. Such work may be scheduled during or after the school day. It may be integral to a course of study or simply a separate adjunctive experience. |

Work experiences during secondary school can be organized in many different ways. They can be

- Structured as essential elements of educational instruction, such as when they are a primary element of the transition plan and most of the educational instruction happens in relation to the work experience

- Complements to classroom instruction, such as when a youth has a work experience related to the course content

- Adjuncts to classroom instruction, such as when a youth has a full complement of mandated coursework related to achieving a diploma, but has a work experience assignment that counts as class credit

- Unrelated to any specific classroom or educational instruction, such as a part-time job after school, but nevertheless useful and important to career development

The key aspect of any work experience is the contribution it makes to the youth's path to adult employment. Regardless of how they are structured, how long they last, or when they occur, all work experiences during secondary school help students find the way to work. The sections that follow further explain and explore the types of work experiences.

## Career Explorations

Career exploration generally involves the youth visiting a workplace for brief exposure to a specific kind of work environment or job type. One middle school teacher organized half-day trips to three different local companies every semester for her students to learn about different jobs in those companies and the skills required for performing them. After each visit the class discussed what they saw, what jobs existed in the companies, what skills were necessary, and whether these would be jobs of interest to them.

Similarly, employment specialists with community rehabilitation agencies often arrange company visits and informational interviews for young job seekers on their caseloads. This allows youth to ask key employees what the company is most known for, what skills and traits they look for in new employees, and what they see as future workforce needs. After these visits, the employment specialist might lead a discussion for youth to consider how these job requirements might relate to jobs and careers they might want to pursue.

## Job Shadowing

One way to understand the requirements of a job or job type is to spend a whole day with someone who is performing that job. Many high schools participate in "Groundhog Job Shadow Day" which happens annually in February. On that day, both general and special education students shadow an employee at a company to learn about their daily job duties. In some instances, schools require students to prepare a report and/or participate in a discussion on what they learned about the job and the company during a shadowing experience, whether it occurs on a designated job shadow day or any time during the school year. Job shadowing experiences are unique ways young people can be introduced to jobs, job requirements, and potential career options. This introduction to the workplace often provides a foundation upon which youth can begin identifying other work experience options for the rest of their high school years as well as the beginning considerations for career options after high school.

Other job shadow experiences can be less formal but no less valuable, such as when youth participate in "take your child to work days" sponsored by many schools and communities. In short, these types of episodic experiences are ways to introduce youth to workplace circumstances and to provide them with initial knowledge about work and careers.

## Work Sampling

Youth can also be exposed to work by spending time in a workplace as an unpaid worker. For example, many schools and community employment services will provide rotations through several workplaces so that youth can "sample" different types of job tasks and different work environments. These experiences also help youth to learn "soft skills" required in the workplace. Volunteer work experiences take many forms and can be conducted in the workplaces of almost any employer. They are especially useful for youth for whom learning in simulated environments is difficult to generalize to authentic work environments. Sampling work experiences is another way for students to be exposed to a variety of workplace environments, discover work preferences and interests, and identify accommodation needs.

Although these are common and valuable work experience options for many youth, transition specialists need to be aware of Fair Labor Standards Act (FLSA) requirements. FLSA is in place so that employers do not take advantage of workers or benefit from free labor. Essentially, as long as the youth in the work sampling experience does not perform work that materially benefits the employer's operation, there is no violation of FLSA. More is said about these requirements in Chapter 2.

## Service Learning

Another common type of volunteer work experience is when youth provide purposeful volunteer service, such as assisting with delivering Meals on Wheels or helping at a public library. When these types of volunteer experiences are formalized into a structured and purposeful process that contributes to community improvement or addresses a community need in some way, as well as integrates with course objectives, they are often considered for service learning hours by schools.

For example, some school districts require a certain number of service learning hours for students to graduate. One teacher helped students participate in an oral history project where they recorded the stories of military veterans for consideration for inclusion in a Library of Congress archive on veteran history. For the community, this activity helped maintain and capture the contributions veterans provided their country. For the students, this activity helped them learn valuable lessons on planning, organizing, and carrying out purposeful tasks. And, of course, they earned service hours that counted toward their graduation requirements. For some, it also can suggest a career path. For example, one student decided to pursue a postsecondary education program in media communications as a result of learning about audio and video recording during this service learning project.

Regardless if service learning is for school credit or not, by participating in this type of activity, youth learn valuable work behaviors such as being on time, completing assigned tasks, working as a team, and dealing with distractions—all the while serving the community.

## Internships

Internships are extremely valuable experiences as they provide opportunities to learn while completing specific tasks under a formal agreement with employers. They can be either stand-alone experiences or paired with a particular curriculum requirement, such as when a vocational preparation program requires cooperative work, or co-ops. They may be paid or unpaid, depending on the arrangement with the employer and the nature of the internship. One example of stand-alone internship experiences that are adjunctive to the high school experience is the Bridges program of the Marriott Foundation for People with Disabilities described later in this chapter (MFPD, 2018). Students referred to this program participate in a semester-long experience in a local company where the youth is paid directly by the employer. The youth learns real job skills in a real workplace, but neither he or she nor the employer are under any obligation to continue the relationship at the conclusion of the internship. For the participating youth, it serves a number of purposes, including learning both specific and soft work skills, learning employer expectations for performance, building a résumé, and earning extra spending money.

## Apprenticeships

Apprenticeships are primarily associated with a particular trade and are available in a wide range of occupations, including traditional fields (e.g., construction), and high-growth fields (e.g., health care, information technology). Apprenticeship programs are highly structured and typically include supervised on-the-job training by a qualified journey-level worker, as well as outside related instruction, which is generally classroom based. Apprenticeships offer not only skill development under a set of predetermined requirements, but also a direct path to postschool employment. Many apprenticeships feature a paid work experience along with classroom work that leads to both a diploma and an apprentice certificate. Participation by youth with disabilities in apprenticeships has been sporadic, but interest is growing due to an initiative from the U.S. Department of Labor, Office of Disability Employment Policy (ODEP), which is supporting projects focused on preapprenticeship and apprenticeship opportunities for youth and adults with disabilities in high-growth industries (ODEP, 2018).

## Stipend Jobs

The primary goal of any work experience is to teach the skills, knowledge, and competencies needed to perform specific tasks in the workplace. Work experiences can be paid or unpaid, but sometimes youth may be part of a program that offers stipends during work training. That is, the payment comes from an agency or program rather than directly from the employer. Employment agencies or youth service programs that sponsor vocational preparation programs, such as summer youth employment programs or some VR programs, will occasionally provide stipends to participants. These stipends can be an incentive to participate in work experiences and a demonstration of another benefit of working—that is, earning money.

## Paid Employment

These experiences can be full or part time, regular or customized jobs, and during or after school. However, the common denominator is that youth are paid a wage directly by the employer. Paid employment may occur because a student's IEP specifies a work objective; other times, it is simply an after-school job. For reasons already stated and that will become more obvious by the end of this book, paid work in authentic community settings is what contributes most strongly to postschool employment success for youth. It is therefore the gold standard of work experiences. Paid employment is a key intervention associated with effective transition preparation and it represents the desired outcome against which transition success can be measured.

Chapter 2 discusses when and how to incorporate each of these types of work experiences. Subsequent chapters share how to use various strategies for planning, developing, organizing, and monitoring work experiences regardless of the type of experience. So, how can we ensure that youth get the maximum benefit from their work experiences?

## QUALITY WORK EXPERIENCES

Work experiences can be created through school-sponsored work study programs, through established school curricula, through resources such as VR pre-employment transition services (Pre-ETS), as adjuncts to transition planning, or combinations of these approaches that may be available to students with disabilities. Irrespective of the particular route students may take to gain these experiences, there are several factors that require consideration when organizing work experiences. Among these are connections between workplace and school-based

---

### Quality Work Experience Characteristics

- Clear program goals

- Clear expectations and feedback to assess progress toward achieving goals

- Clear roles and responsibilities for worksite supervisors, mentors, teachers, support personnel, and other partners

- Convenient links between students, schools, and employers

- On-the-job learning

- Range of opportunities, especially those outside traditional (e.g., hospitality, retail) youth-employing industries

- Mentor(s) at the worksite

- Youth and employer feedback on the experience

learning, clear expectations of student activity at the workplace, clearly defined roles of transition specialists and worksite supervisors, and well-structured feedback on student performance. In addition, it is important for youth with disabilities to have appropriate supports and accommodations in place. Training and guidance for workplace personnel also is an important feature of creating a welcoming and supportive environment in which students can thrive. The textbox titled Quality Work Experience Characteristics summarizes the characteristics of quality work-based programs that are supported by research (e.g., Cease-Cook, Fowler, & Test, 2015). These characteristics and how to achieve them are discussed in detail in subsequent chapters.

Quality work experiences are especially dependent on everyone knowing and fulfilling their roles in the arrangement. Students must know what is expected of

---

**Shared Responsibility for Work Experience Success**

**Student/youth responsibility in work experiences**

- Perform job responsibilities

- Communicate needs and suggest support strategies

- Adhere to workplace guidelines and procedures

- Comply with expectations for job performance, behavior, and social interactions

- Show respect, be responsible, and follow through on commitments

- Learn as much as possible about the work environment and the job

**Transition specialist responsibility in work experiences**

- Orient youth to the workplace

- Orient youth to their roles and responsibilities

- Communicate expectations for job performance, behavior, and social interactions

- Explain consequences for inappropriate behavior

- Orient employers to their roles as mentors and supervisors

- Help students communicate their support needs and strategies

- Help employers capitalize on youths' learning styles and identify support strategies

- Communicate with youth and employers on a regular basis

- Link work experiences to classroom learning and academic curriculum

**Employer responsibility in work experiences**

- Model expectations

- Give clear, detailed, and repeated directions

- Communicate expectations for job performance, behavior, and social interactions

- Explain consequences for inappropriate behavior

- Identify the best methods of communication for each student

- Capitalize on each youth's learning style and identify support strategies

- Teach skills needed for successful job performance

- Provide feedback on youth performance

- Communicate with youth and transition specialists on a regular basis

them, how they are expected to behave on the job, and general and specific workplace guidelines. Transition specialists must carefully and thoroughly orient the student to the workplace, communicate and coordinate procedures with the hosting employer, ensure that everyone is clear about their respective responsibilities, and link the work experience to the student's course of instruction, if applicable.

For their part, employers are often viewed as "donating" their places of work as the learning environment. More will be said in Chapters 6 and 7 about minimizing this perception and about making sure cooperating employers receive reciprocal benefit from work experiences. For now, it is important to know that employers will have critical basic responsibilities to fulfill if the work experience is to be productive for both them and the youth. These responsibilities include, among a host of other possible roles, communicating behavior and performance expectations, informing the youth and transition specialist about workplace requirements, and training youth on necessary job skills. The textbox titled Shared Responsibility for Work Experience Success lists the basic responsibilities of students, transition specialists, and employers that contribute to the effectiveness of work experiences. These respective responsibilities also are discussed in considerable detail in subsequent chapters.

## MODELS THAT WORK

A host of models throughout the country feature successful implementation of work experience. Most transition specialists organize work experiences with students through a locally designed, and usually school-specific, approach where students regularly access community workplaces for various types of work experiences. Some are able to help youth access specially designed and well-known programs. In either case, these programs offer further useful insight into the importance of work experiences and their potential to launch youth with disabilities into adult careers. A few are summarized in this chapter to show what is possible. These examples also provide empirical evidence of the impact of work experience. However, schools and communities do not need to have formal and highly visible models like the examples described here to successfully incorporate work experiences into the individual student's educational program or transition plans. In fact, most often, it is individual professionals working in individual school systems or with workforce agencies that make work experiences successful for individual youth.

## Bridges From School to Work

Bridges From School to Work, or simply Bridges, developed by the Marriott Foundation for People with Disabilities, continues to illustrate the power of paid work experiences for youth with disabilities. Since its inception in 1989, Bridges has served more than 21,000 youth (MFPD, 2017). It operates in 11 major metropolitan areas: Atlanta, Baltimore, Boston, Chicago, Dallas, Los Angeles, New York City, Oakland, Philadelphia, San Francisco, and Washington, D.C. Bridges was originally designed to create paid internships in local companies for youth with disabilities who are in their last year of high school (Luecking & Fabian, 2000). It has since made several adaptations to serve more youth and to ensure postschool follow up to some participating youth. Today, Bridges is delivered during a 15- to 24-month period. Its component parts include skills assessment, career planning, job development, placement, evaluation, action planning, and follow-up. Bridges partners with school systems, VR agencies, and workforce agencies in local communities to identify young people with disabilities for program participation who are in their last year of high school or have just exited. Bridges also serves out-of-school youth who are 17–22 years old.

Bridges produces universally high employment placement rates, up to 90%, across socioeconomic and disability characteristics, and across diverse urban areas throughout the United States (Gold, Fabian, & Luecking, 2013). Bridges also produces universally high employment placement rates regardless of school characteristics (Dong, Fabian, & Luecking, 2015). That is, the job placement services represented by Bridges can benefit youth with disabilities regardless of the quality, structure, or available resources of the schools in which they are enrolled.

These results did not happen by accident. Bridges pays particular attention to building staff competence to facilitate these work experiences. One study showed that Bridges staff who have highly successful track records in job placement and retention exhibit four distinct personal attributes: 1) principled optimism, meaning a belief that all youth regardless of disability have the ability to work; 2) cultural competence, meaning they are aware of and sensitive to the context in which youth live; 3) business-oriented professionalism, indicating they have a work ethic that also helps them see their work through a "business lens"; and 4) networking savvy—that is, they are good at connecting with people and resources (Tilson & Simonsen, 2013).

For their part, employers see successful engagement with Bridges as related to their confidence in the Bridges staff (Simonsen, Fabian, & Luecking, 2015). Employers say that matching particular skills of the Bridges job candidate to the specific demands of the business operation is more important than filling vacant positions.

That is, they will hire individuals who can show they will help the operation even if there are no specific job openings. Furthermore, they indicate that hiring youth with disabilities as a way of giving back to the community is a less important factor in hiring decisions than performance capacity of youth and meeting specific business needs.

The success of Bridges suggests two things about the practice of pairing paid work experiences with other educational activities. First, the youth obviously benefit since as an aggregate group they are achieving employment at a rate that notably exceeds typical employment rates of transitioning youth with disabilities. Second, employers are benefiting as well. It is apparent that exposure to youth with disabilities—along with the competent support of Bridges professionals—enables employers to access workers who can contribute to employers' operations. Chapters 6 and 7 explore this latter point in some detail, as it has implications for how transition professionals interact with employer partners who are so essential to making work experiences happen.

## Project SEARCH

The Project SEARCH Transition-to-Work Program is a branded, business-led, 1-year employment preparation program for students with significant disabilities that takes place entirely at the workplace of employer partners (Rutkowski, Daston, Van Kuiken, & Riehle, 2006). Since its establishment in 1996 at Cincinnati Children's Hospital Medical Center, Project SEARCH models have literally expanded to locations around the world. More than 3,000 students participate in Project SEARCH around the United States each year (Project SEARCH, 2019).

Project SEARCH features total immersion in the workplaces of participating companies from medical, banking, and other industries that might have large enough locations to offer multiple integrated job task learning opportunities. It includes a combination of classroom instruction, career exploration, and hands-on training through worksite rotations within the company (Persch et al., 2015). Each site is staffed by a special education teacher and one to three skills trainers to meet the educational and training needs of the interns. The Project SEARCH instructor, host business liaison, state vocational rehabilitation counselor, and community rehabilitation provider staff work together for intern referral and program oversight.

Project SEARCH interns attend the program for a full school year in the host business. The host business provides access to an on-site training room that can accommodate up to 12 interns. The program culminates in individualized job development. The program regularly achieves a 75% postproject placement rate in competitive integrated employment, defined as year round and nonseasonal, at least 16 hours per week, at the prevailing wage, and working among coworkers with and without disabilities (Project SEARCH, 2019).

Project SEARCH illustrates several key points related to the value of work experiences. First, it is not only heavily invested in the participation of businesses, but these businesses play a leadership role. Like Bridges, this suggests perspectives about employers that are important in all work experience development. Second, it involves a collaboration between several partners whose programs and services might otherwise overlap but not necessarily intersect. Here schools, VR agencies, and community rehabilitation service providers are working together at the same time with the same students. The example of seamless transition in the next section shows how this might work in typical transition efforts where there are no programs like Bridges or Project SEARCH available. Finally, the outcomes speak for themselves. When the norm for employment in community integrated employment for individuals with significant disabilities is less than 20% (Winsor et al., 2017), Project SEARCH is achieving outcomes that are more than three times higher.

## Seamless Transition Models

One common approach to transition service includes components that lead to students exiting school already employed or enrolled in postsecondary education that will lead to employment. Moreover, they have been linked to the necessary supports to maintain job and career achievement into adulthood. That is, they move seamlessly from being a student to an employed adult. Certo et al. (2009) first promoted what was called the Transition Service Integration Model (TSIM), whereby the first day after school exit looks the same to the youth as the day before—that is, the same job, same supports. During participating students' last year in school, their school system enters into a formal service contract with a local private nonprofit community rehabilitation program that serves adults with significant support needs and that agrees to work with pending graduates *before* and *after* school exit through a combination of school district, vocational rehabilitation, and developmental disabilities funding.

TSIM was designed to combine the resources of school and postschool systems, during the last year of a student's enrollment in public education, to share the costs of a student-driven approach to transition planning, resulting in long-term adult employment in place before school exit. Most of the youth participating in TSIM have not been likely candidates to apply for standard or advertised jobs due to lack of requisite work experience and skills, and/or because of extensive or unique accommodation and support needs. However, successful employment can be achieved through job development that identifies employers who can benefit from the youth's particular attributes in alternative, customized ways (Certo & Luecking, 2006).

This approach to seamless transition has expanded from its original application for students with intellectual/developmental disabilities to a model that can be applied on behalf of any student with any disability who requires support to prepare for and achieve postschool employment success (Luecking & Luecking, 2015). The centerpiece of the seamless transition model is work experience during the secondary school years. Typically, seamless transition models feature the following components:

- *An asset-based and person-centered discovery process* that is the basis for planning for work experiences and employment and that involves working with the student to develop an inventory of skills, positive traits, interests, personal preferences, and support and accommodation requirements

- *Individualized work experiences* that potentially include a combination of informational interviews, jobsite tours, work sampling, unpaid internships, and summer youth employment opportunities

- At least one individualized *paid integrated employment* experience before school exit, defined as one where the student is paid directly by the employer and where other workers are primarily individuals without disabilities

- *Early VR case initiation* that occurs no later than the second school year prior to projected school exit

- *Interagency collaboration* represented by a cross-functional team of school and service agency professionals convened on behalf of individual students to plan for and deliver services that facilitate work experiences and paid employment

Family support and coordination with teachers and instructional staff ensure that work experiences and jobs occur with their necessary input and support. Figure 1.1 illustrates the typical progression of seamless transition service.

One feature of seamless transition worth noting is the early involvement of VR. In one study of a seamless transition model, researchers found that, compared with nonparticipants, model participants received more job-related services from VR, but fewer assessment and diagnostic services. They also achieved significantly higher employment rates at VR case closure (Luecking et al., 2018). This not only points to the strong value of work experience as a precursor to adult employment, but it also provides support for the Pre-ETS work experience provisions of WIOA as a key VR service available to transitioning students and youth. This also means that variations on the concept of seamless transition service provision can essentially be implemented in any school district in the country. Work experiences can be organized for students with disabilities anywhere transition specialists can partner with VR and other community partners. Chapter 10 includes a discussion of how to use Pre-ETS as a useful tool to facilitate work experiences. In any case—with or without the presence of highly organized work preparation programs such as Bridges or Project SEARCH, and with or without a formal seamless transition partnership model—work experiences can happen. Where there are work experiences during secondary and postsecondary education there will be more youth with disabilities who will achieve adult employment.

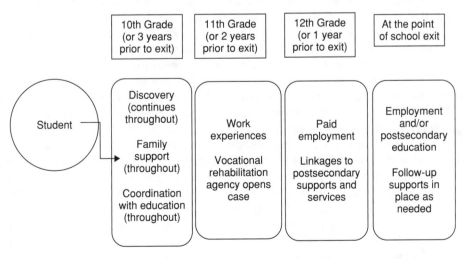

**Figure 1.1.** Seamless transition flowchart.

## IMPROVING THE QUALITY AND AVAILABILITY OF WORK EXPERIENCES

As important as work experiences are, and as clearly as research and the models described above have supported their value, there are still hurdles to implementing them on a broader scale so as to benefit all youth with disabilities currently in the nation's secondary schools, almost 400,000 of whom exit school each year (National Center for Educational Statistics, 2018). There are three general challenges to making work experiences a bigger priority in secondary and postsecondary education.

First, there is frequent tension between time at the worksite and time in the classroom because of the need to focus on academics and classroom-based instruction. This is particularly the case for students who are on track to receive a diploma. Unless there is a specific course or education-related work experience required, these students are usually only available for work experiences after school on weekends, or during summer breaks. This limits the opportunity for them to access work experience without careful planning and without schools collaborating with VR and other community programs. In addition to resources within the typical school system, potential resources for facilitating such opportunities include youth employment programs that provide work experiences for a range of youth, including those with disabilities. Also, disability-specific resources, such as those funded by state VR agencies, are important pregraduation links to jobs and work experiences that lead to eventual successful adult employment. Chapter 10 also focuses on strategies to address this need.

Second, school personnel and their community partners often struggle to find time to establish and maintain relationships with participating employers. Of course, available and willing employer partners are essential for the establishment of work experiences. Hence, the challenge becomes how to maximize the use of available time to recruit employers and to nurture relationships with them. Employers, for their part, require convenient ways to link with students that do not impede on their time or ability to operate efficiently. Thus, convenient and effective mechanisms for linking students with employers will need to be created or expanded in most school systems. Chapters 6 and 7 address this need.

Finally, there is a need to build the capacity of transition specialists to perform the tasks necessary to facilitate work experiences. Many transition specialists are thrust into their roles with little or no preparation or training. They are left to learn by trial and error or maybe through sporadically available in-service opportunities. Other transition specialists who are experienced and effective will still benefit from upgrading their skills and knowledge. Even partners in transition services who do not necessarily have direct responsibility for facilitating work experience need to know how it is best done. Indeed, it is essential that these partners understand what it takes so they can contribute to the development of work experiences and provide the ancillary services that support them. There is thus the need to create avenues for training transition specialists and their partners on how to facilitate work experiences though preservice training and in-service training. This need has been well documented for education staff (Morningstar & Clavenna-Deane, 2014), for VR counselors (Neubert, Luecking, & Fabian, 2018), and for community rehabilitation providers (Butterworth, Migliore, Nord, & Gelb, 2012).

This book is of course meant to be a resource in meeting this need. Subsequent chapters provide strategies for addressing each of these concerns while ensuring that youth with disabilities experience opportunities to receive the important exposure to work during formative education years that we know is necessary for them to achieve productive and meaningful employment in their adult lives.

## SUMMARY

Research has consistently demonstrated that education and employment outcomes for youth with disabilities can be significantly improved by frequent and systematic exposure to a variety of real work experiences. Compared to their peers without disabilities, the persistently lower employment rates of youth and young adults with disabilities suggest that these types of experiences should be integral to secondary education for students with disabilities, regardless of the nature of the disability or the need for special education services. This chapter provides a rationale for work experiences, describes the type and function of different types of work experiences, describes models that embody the best features of work as integral aspects of transition planning and service, explains indicators of quality for such experiences, and provides examples of work-based learning models that have proven effective in boosting the career development of youth with disabilities. The next chapter covers in detail the types of work experiences introduced here, when and how to use them, and ways to ensure their inclusion in transition planning.

## REFERENCES

Blackorby, J., & Wagner, M. (1996). Longitudinal postschool outcomes of youth with disabilities: Findings from the National Longitudinal Transition Study. *Exceptional Children, 65*, 399–413.

Butterworth, J., Migliore, A., Nord, D., & Gelb, A. (2012). Improving the employment outcomes of job seekers with intellectual and developmental disabilities: A training and mentoring intervention for employment consultants. *Journal of Rehabilitation, 78*, 20–29.

Carter, E. W., Austin, D., & Trainor, A. A. (2011). Predictors of postschool employment outcomes for young adults with severe disabilities. *Journal of Disability Policy Studies, 20*, 1–14.

Cease-Cook, J., Fowler, C., & Test, D. W. (2015). Strategies for creating work-based learning experiences in schools for secondary students with disabilities. *TEACHING Exceptional Children, 47*(6), 352–358.

Certo, N., & Luecking, R. (2006). Service integration and school to work transition: Customized employment as an outcome for youth with significant disabilities. *Journal of Applied Rehabilitation Counseling, 37*, 29–35.

Certo, N., Luecking, R., Murphy, S., Brown, L., Courey, S., & Belanger, D. (2009). Seamless transition and long term support for individuals with severe intellectual disabilities. *Research and Practice for Persons with Severe Disabilities, 33*, 85–95.

Dong, S., Fabian, E., & Luecking, R. (2015). The impact of school-based factors on youth employment outcomes in transition. *Rehabilitation Counseling Bulletin, 59*, 224–234.

Fabian, E., Deschamps, A., Simonsen, M., & Luecking, D. (2016). Service system collaboration in transition: An empirical exploration of its effects on rehabilitation outcomes for students with disabilities. *Journal of Rehabilitation, 82*, 3–10.

Fair Labor Standard Act (FLSA) of 1938, PL 75-718, 29 U.S.C. 201 *et seq.*

Gold, P., Fabian, E., & Luecking, R. (2013). Job acquisition by urban youth with disabilities transitioning from school to work. *Rehabilitation Counseling Bulletin, 57*, 31–45.

Haimson, J., & Bellotti, J. (2001). *Schooling in the workplace: Increasing the scale and quality of work-based learning, Final Report.* Princeton, NJ: Mathematica Policy Research, Inc.

Hoerner, J., & Wehrley, J. (1995). *Work-based learning: The key to school-to-work transition.* New York, NY: Glencoe/McGraw–Hill.

Individuals with Disabilities Education Act of 1990, PL 101-476, 20 U.S.C. 1400 *et seq.*

Individuals with Disabilities Education Improvement Act of 2004, PL 108-446, 20 U.S.C. 1400 *et seq.*

Liu, A. Y., Lacoe, J., Lipscomb, S., Haimson, J., Johnson, D. R., & Thurlow, M. L. (2018). *Preparing for life after high school: The characteristics and experiences of youth in special education. Findings from the National Longitudinal Transition Study 2012. Volume 3: Comparisons over time (Full report)* (NCEE 2018-4007). Washington, DC: U.S. Department of Education, Institute of Education Sciences, National Center for Education Evaluation and Regional Assistance.

Luecking, R., & Fabian, E. (2000). Paid internships and employment success for youth in transition. *Career Development for Exceptional Individuals, 23,* 205–221.

Luecking, R., Fabian, E., Contreary, K., Honeycutt, T., & Luecking, D. (2018). Vocational rehabilitation outcomes for students participating in a model transition program. *Rehabilitation Counseling Bulletin, 61,* 154–163.

Luecking, D., & Luecking, R. (2015). Translating research into a seamless transition model. *Career Development and Transition for Exceptional Individuals, 38,* 4–13.

Morningstar, M. E., & Clavenna-Deane, E. (2014). Preparing secondary special educators and transition specialists. In P. T. Sindelar, E. D. McCray, M. T. Brownell, & B. Lignugaris (Eds.), *Handbook of research on special education teacher preparation* (pp. 405–420). Florence, KY: Routledge.

Marriott Foundation for People with Disabilities (MFPD). (2018). *Bridges 2016 Progress Report.* Retrieved from http://www.bridgestowork.org/assets/files/1/files/bridges2016progressreport_121416-.pdf

National Center for Educational Statistics. (2018). *Children and youth with disabilities.* Retrieved from https://nces.ed.gov/programs/coe/indicator_cgg.asp

Neubert, D., Luecking, R., & Fabian, E. (2018). Transition practices of vocational rehabilitation counselors serving students and youth with disabilities in high performing state vocational rehabilitation agencies. *Rehabilitation Research, Policy & Education, 32,* 54–65.

Office of Disability Employment Policy (ODEP), U.S. Department of Labor. (2018). *U.S. Department of Labor awards $1.9 million to improve apprenticeship opportunities for youth and adults with disabilities.* Retrieved from https://www.dol.gov/newsroom/releases/odep/odep20181011

Persch, A. C., Cleary, D. S., Rutkowski, S., Malone, H., Darragh, A. R. & Case-Smith, J. D. (2015). Current practices in job matching: A Project SEARCH perspective on transition. *Journal of Vocational Rehabilitation, 43*(3), 259–273.

Project SEARCH. (2019). *Project SEARCH outcome summary.* Retrieved from https://www.projectsearch.us/outcome-summary/

Rutkowski, S., Daston, M., Van Kuiken, D., & Riehle, E. (2006). Project SEARCH: A demand-side model of high school transition. *Journal of Vocational Rehabilitation, 25,* 85–96.

Simonsen, M., Fabian, E., & Luecking, R. (2015). Employer preferences in hiring youth with disabilities. *Journal of Rehabilitation, 81,* 9–18.

Tilson, G., & Simonsen, M. (2013). The personnel factor: Exploring the personal attributes of highly successful employment specialists who work with transition-age youth. *Journal of Vocational Rehabilitation, 38*(2), 125–137.

Wehman, P. (2013). *Life beyond the classroom: Transition strategies for young people with disabilities* (5th ed.). Baltimore, MD: Paul H. Brookes Publishing Co.

Wehman, P., Sima, A., Ketchum, J., West, M., Chan, F., & Luecking, R. (2014). Predictors of successful transition from school to employment for youth with disabilities. *Journal of Occupational Rehabilitation, 25,* 223–234.

Winsor, J., Timmons, J., Butterworth, J., Shepard, J., Landa, C., Smith, F., . . . Landim, L. (2017). *StateData: The national report on employment services and outcomes.* Boston, MA: University of Massachusetts Boston, Institute for Community Inclusion.

Workforce Innovation and Opportunity Act (WIOA) of 2014, PL 113-128, 29 U.S.C. §§ *et seq.*

# Setting the Stage for Quality Work Experiences

**By completing this chapter, the reader will**

- Review work experience functions
- Understand when work experiences can be incorporated into student and youth career development
- Learn a conceptual model for the work experience process
- Examine the legal considerations when developing work experiences

Several of Eddie's high school work experiences helped him assess his career interests and skills. These experiences included a job shadowing experience during 10th grade at the offices of two different nonprofit organizations, an unpaid career assessment in 11th grade in an accounting office where he stocked deliveries of office supplies, and a paid part-time job as a copy clerk in a government agency during his final year in school. Through each of these work experiences, Eddie learned something new about what he wanted to do (office work), what he was good at (filing), and what accommodations he would need in any job (secluded work area free of distractions). When he exited his public school program, he was able to convert his part-time job in the government office into a full-time, permanent one—a seamless transition facilitated by sequential, well-organized work experiences in high school!

Cindy had a series of work experiences and one part-time job up until her last year in high school. All were difficult due to her social behavior. She was always in inclusive settings in high school, but she received a lot of what she perceived to be positive attention from her teenage peers for social behavior that was actually inappropriate—singing, speaking out, and unacceptable language. She was fired from her part-time job because of inappropriate behavior and noncompliance: When she didn't want to do something, Cindy would cross her arms and not move.

Fortunately, Cindy's school district provided a final transition-year program that linked her with additional work experiences and ultimately a job before she was scheduled to exit the school system at age 21. After 3 months of training and preparation, during which she had continual opportunities to practice and be reinforced for appropriate work behavior, Cindy got a job on a hotel housekeeping crew, and her transition specialist coached her, especially by ignoring inappropriate behavior and praising appropriate behavior. Cindy began by working 1 day a week, and within 4 months, right before she exited school, she was working 5 days a week with no personal job coach. Now Cindy wears a uniform willingly and meets the inspection standards of the housekeeping staff. Cindy has held this job for several years, learned more difficult skills, and now trains new members of the housekeeping team.

Both Eddie and Cindy were featured in the first edition of this book. After checking back on them, we learned that they are still in these jobs nearly 10 years later and they are still doing well. They continue to represent the value of work experiences that are spread out over the secondary school years. In Eddie's case, the progression of work experiences beginning in 10th grade led him to find a good vocational fit, as he began his postschool working career and as he now continues his career. For Cindy, the progression of work experiences enabled her to develop a more mature and adaptive repertoire of workplace behavior so that by the end of her educational experience, she was well on her way to what is clearly now productive adult employment.

The primary assumption of this book is that all youth—no matter the disability label or need for support—can ultimately experience self-determined and meaningful employment. Of course, as Eddie and Cindy demonstrate, the path to getting there is not always simple or straightforward, nor does it occur without continual exposure to workplace options and experiences. This chapter discusses the functions of different types of work experiences, the stages of youth career development and when they should be introduced, a conceptual model for the process of establishing and supporting quality work experiences, and legal considerations that may have an impact on how work experiences are developed and monitored.

## WORK EXPERIENCES AND CAREER PROGRESSION

Few people chart a clear and linear path to their career. Most people will experience fits and starts, multiple changes of directions, and more than a few pitfalls as they pursue adult employment and careers. While taking this into account, many career and transition experts have identified typical stages in career progression that enable all youth, including those with disabilities, to eventually craft a career direction. Many models of career development identify typical stages that are widely accepted as leading to a satisfying and productive career for youth with disabilities (Brolin, 2004; Flexer, Baer, Luft, & Simmons, 2012). These stages include

1. *Career awareness*, when students begin to develop self-awareness and learn about work values and roles in work, usually in elementary school

2. *Career exploration*, when students gather information to explore work interests, skills, and abilities, as well as the requirements of various employment options, usually starting in middle school and the early high school years

3. *Career decision making,* when students begin to select job and career areas that match interests and aptitudes, usually beginning in high school but continuing often well into adulthood

4. *Career preparation,* when students begin to understand their strengths and challenges and they make informed choices about preparation activities that will lead them to a chosen career area, usually throughout high school and after school exit

5. *Career placement,* when youth begin to responsibly and productively participate in a job and a career area

These stages may not always look the same for everyone or follow in this exact order. However, one thing is a constant—the more youth are exposed to work the more easily they can decide what they like, what they are good at, and what help they might need to establish their eventual careers.

To set the stage for quality work experiences, it is useful to consider the *National Standards and Quality Indicators for Secondary Education and Transition* (NASET, 2005) listed in Table 2.1. These standards and indicators provide a foundation for the path for youth to arrive at a chosen and productive career. They also serve as a foundation for transition specialists to help them get there.

**Table 2.1.**  Standards and indicators for career preparatory experiences

| | |
|---|---|
| **2.1** | **Youth participate in career awareness, exploration, and preparatory activities in school- and community-based settings.** |
| 2.1.1 | Schools and community partners offer courses, programs, and activities that broaden and deepen youths' knowledge of careers and allow for more informed postsecondary education and career choices. |
| 2.1.2 | Career preparatory courses, programs, and activities incorporate contextual teaching and learning. |
| 2.1.3 | Schools, employers, and community partners collaboratively plan and design career preparatory courses, programs, and activities that support quality standards, practices, and experiences. |
| 2.1.4 | Youth and families understand the relationship between postsecondary and career choices, and financial and benefits planning. |
| 2.1.5 | Youth understand how community resources, experiences, and family members can assist them in their role as workers. |
| **2.2** | **Academic and nonacademic courses and programs include integrated career development activities.** |
| 2.2.1 | Schools offer broad career curricula that allow youth to organize and select academic, career, or technical courses based on their career interests and goals. |
| 2.2.2 | With the guidance of school and/or community professionals, youth use a career planning process (e.g., assessments, career portfolio, etc.) based on career goals, interests, and abilities. |
| 2.2.3 | Career preparatory courses, programs, and activities align with labor market trends and specific job requirements. |
| 2.2.4 | Career preparatory courses, programs, and activities provide the basic skills crucial to success in a career field, further training, and professional growth. |

*(continued)*

**Table 2.1.**   *(continued)*

| | |
|---|---|
| **2.3** | **Schools and community partners provide youth with opportunities to participate in meaningful school- and community-based work experiences.** |
| 2.3.1 | Youth participate in quality work experiences that are offered to them prior to exiting school (e.g., apprenticeships, mentoring, paid and unpaid work, service learning, school-based enterprises, on-the-job training, internships, etc.). |
| 2.3.2 | Work experiences are relevant and aligned with each youth's career interests, postsecondary education plans, goals, skills, abilities, and strengths. |
| 2.3.3 | Youth participate in various on-the-job training experiences, including community service (paid or unpaid) specifically linked to school credit or program content. |
| 2.3.4 | Youth are able to access, accept, and use individually needed supports and accommodations for work experiences. |
| **2.4** | **Schools and community partners provide career preparatory activities that lead to youths' acquisition of employability and technical skills, knowledge, and behaviors.** |
| 2.4.1 | Youth have multiple opportunities to develop traditional job preparation skills through job-readiness curricula and training. |
| 2.4.2 | Youth complete career assessments to identify school and postschool preferences, interests, skills, and abilities. |
| 2.4.3 | Youth exhibit understanding of career expectations, workplace culture, and the changing nature of work and educational requirements. |
| 2.4.4 | Youth demonstrate that they understand how personal skill development (e.g., positive attitude, self-discipline, honesty, time management) affects their employability. |
| 2.4.5 | Youth demonstrate appropriate job-seeking behaviors. |

From National Alliance for Secondary Education and Transition (NASET). (2005). *National standards and quality indicators: Transition toolkit for systems improvement* (pp. 6–7). Minneapolis: University of Minnesota, National Center on Secondary Education and Transition; adapted by permission.

Standard 2.3 in the table emphasizes the importance of meaningful work experiences. To ensure that a work experience is meaningful, readers should consider the following questions:

- Is the student pursuing work experiences for the most fitting purpose?

- Are the work experiences being used at the right times in the student's career development?

- Is there a process for identifying and implementing good work experiences?

- Do the work experiences reflect quality? How?

The following sections consider these questions, offering answers on work experience functions, timing of work experiences, and processes for making them effective.

## Functions of Work Experiences

Chapter 1 provided descriptions of common types of work experiences. They span a range from cursory exposure to work and workplaces to intensive on-the-job learning and training. Although they are not always linear or experienced in a particular order, work experiences generally should be introduced at standard points in youth education and career development. Each kind of work experience serves a distinct purpose in preparing youth for eventual employment choices and employment success.

Table 2.2 outlines types of work experiences, representative examples of each, times when they should be considered, and their typical function. Although the table presents a logical progression, many youth with disabilities are not exposed to even the most basic work opportunities until late in their education (and, hence, may start later), may not experience them in any particular order, or may not

**Table 2.2.**   Types of work experiences and functions

| Type | Examples | When to consider | Function |
|---|---|---|---|
| Career exploration | Company tours/field trips<br>Talks with employers | As youth begin awareness of adult occupational opportunities | Initial exposure to jobs and careers |
| Job shadowing | Take your child to work day<br>Groundhog Job Shadow Day<br>Disability mentoring day<br>Teacher-arranged shadowing | When youth begin to sample work and workplace interests | Observation of work environment, exposure to jobs and careers |
| Work sampling | Rotation through various community workstations<br>Job task sampling<br>Career assessments<br>Any unpaid workplace experience | When youth begin exposure to workplace environments and expectations, and as preludes to more intensive work experiences | Job task sampling, sample work environments, identify potential supports and accommodations |
| Service learning | Volunteer for community and social programs<br>Formal volunteer service in a structured community service program | As adjuncts or alternatives to volunteer work experiences | Learning responsibility of following through, taking directions, community responsibility |
| Internships | Unpaid or paid student co-op<br>Formal time-limited work experience paired with course of instruction<br>Formal arrangement with an employer to learn identified work skills | As adjuncts to specific course of study, most common during late high school or in postsecondary education and training | Intensive career/job preparation, prelude to a career choice, in-depth exposure to job and workplace |
| Apprenticeships | Trade-related paid or unpaid work with a certified, skilled journeyman | As an integrated component of specific occupational training | Building occupational skills related to trade certification |
| Paid employment | Part-time jobs<br>Full-time jobs<br>Related to course of study and/or transition plan<br>Adjunctive or unrelated experiences to school and course work (e.g., after-school jobs, weekend jobs, summer jobs) | Later secondary school years and postsecondary education | Building a résumé, earning money, continuing to build work skills, identifying workplace and vocational preferences |

experience them at all (Lipscomb, Lacoe, Liu, & Haimson, 2018). Ideally, however, the work experiences will occur sequentially and build on the preceding experiences, ultimately resulting in postschool employment and careers.

## Timing of Work Experiences

Work experiences should progress across grade levels, to build a progressively expanding work experience repertoire leading to postschool careers. As discussed earlier, the order and availability of work experiences will vary considerably among school systems and youth employment systems, as well as for the individuals in these systems. A sample progression is outlined in Table 2.3.

Diploma-bound students may experience work if cooperative learning is a feature of the curriculum, such as in a career or technical education course. Or they may experience work as an unrelated adjunct to their curriculum (e.g., after school and summer work programs). Students who are seeking a certificate of completion or related nondiploma school completion option or who continue in school up to age 21 will often experience work in a slightly different chronology. They may experience volunteer and paid work throughout their final three years in school. Ideally, they will also experience paid work as one of the culminating features of their education. Similarly, youth who pursue various types of postsecondary education may also have work experiences integrated into their curriculum, depending on the type of program in which they are enrolled. Though the sequence of work experiences may vary, the progression will often be similar to that presented in Table 2.3. The further along the youth is in school, the more advanced and intensive the types of work experiences that may be introduced.

**Table 2.3.**  Sample work experience progression

| Year in school | Typical work experience pursued |
| --- | --- |
| Middle school | Career exploration<br>Job shadowing |
| 9th grade | Career exploration<br>Job shadowing |
| 10th grade | Work sampling<br>Service learning<br>Paid employment |
| 11th grade | Work sampling<br>Service learning<br>Paid employment |
| 12th grade | Service learning<br>Internships<br>Apprenticeships<br>Paid employment |
| 12th grade+ (ages 18–21) | Work sampling<br>Paid employment |
| Postsecondary education (any age) | Work sampling<br>Internships<br>Apprenticeships<br>Paid employment |

In many cases, certain work opportunities may not be available to students at some stages of their education. For example, transition specialists may be tasked with helping youth find paid work, even though those youth may have had limited or no exposure to career exploration, job shadowing, or work sampling experiences that often set the stage for later paid employment. This is a disadvantage for the youth as they consider where and under what circumstances they want to work. It also is a disadvantage for those who might be assisting the youth in pursuing work experiences. It is not a disadvantage that is insurmountable, but it is a challenging one nevertheless. To the extent possible, the array of work experiences should be available as youth move through their education experience. When this is not the case, there are still strategies to help youth best take advantage of any work experience anywhere along the continuum of possible work experience types. One way of conceptualizing how to make this happen is to have a representative model that organizes the steps to getting to the most individualized, effective, and quality work experience.

## Process for Identifying and Implementing Work Experiences

To establish work experiences of any kind, transition specialists can follow a conceptual model that progresses from identifying the goals of the work experience, to negotiating the work experience, and ultimately to supporting the youth in the work experience. Figure 2.1 represents this process from the first identification of work experience goals all the way through steps to ensure that youth have the necessary support to succeed in the work experience.

Planning for the work experience begins with identifying the goals of the work experience and the opportunities it offers. Transition specialists should consider: Is the work experience intended to expose youth to a type of work environment, a type of occupation, or merely to sample work? Will it be for pay or will it be an unpaid experience? What should the youth learn during the experience?

Once the purpose and goals of the work experience are identified, it is time to consider the youth's skills, interests, and support needs when planning for the work experience. These will be the basis for finding an employer and a workplace where the youth's characteristics are welcomed and accommodated. The ideal work experience is in a workplace where the employer's expectations and requirements overlap with the youth's goals, strengths, and support needs.

If the considerations of both the youth and the employer mesh, or at least appear to be compatible, then negotiating begins with the employer. Items to consider in these negotiations include the following.

- *Purpose of the work experience*: Is it for sampling new tasks, shadowing a particular employee, learning through an internship of limited duration, earning money, or another reason? Each of these suggest unique considerations in terms of the youth's performance, and in terms of the degree to which the employer must involve coworkers and prepare the work environment for the youth's presence.

- *Expected outcomes*: How long will it last? What is the level of mastery expected for the youth's performance of tasks? What happens when the experience ends? The answers to these questions will be different for each type of work experience, and for each youth.

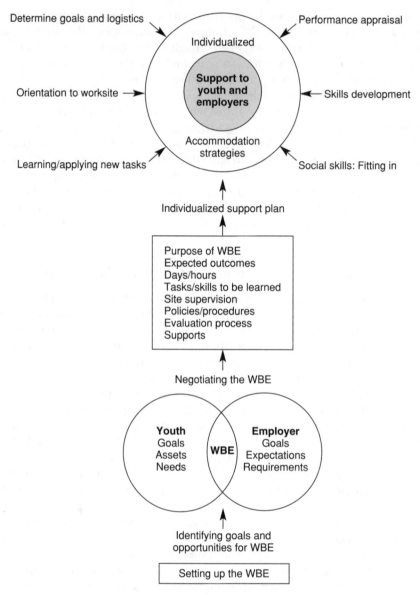

Determine goals and logistics          Performance appraisal

Individualized

**Support to
youth and
employers**

Orientation to worksite →          ← Skills development

Accommodation
strategies

Learning/applying new tasks          Social skills: Fitting in

↑

Individualized support plan

↑

Purpose of WBE
Expected outcomes
Days/hours
Tasks/skills to be learned
Site supervision
Policies/procedures
Evaluation process
Supports

↑

Negotiating the WBE

**Youth**          **Employer**
Goals          **WBE**          Goals
Assets          Expectations
Needs          Requirements

↑

Identifying goals and
opportunities for WBE

Setting up the WBE

**Figure 2.1.**   The work experience process. (*Key:* WBE, work-based experience.)

- *Conditions of work*: How many hours and/or days a week will the youth be expected to be at the worksite? Is the experience paid or unpaid? Both educational and legal implications exist for these conditions, as discussed later in this chapter.

- *Site supervision*: How involved or available will the transition specialist be? Will a coworker or mentor have supervisory responsibilities? A critical feature of a quality work experience is clear role clarification of all involved parties, and no role is more important to youth success at the workplace than that of overseeing performance.

- *Workplace policies and procedures*: What are the workplace policies and procedures? Who will make sure the student knows them? Creating an opportunity for orientation and training when students start at the workplace is critical to later performance and workplace assimilation.

- *Evaluation process*: What will the evaluation process entail? Who will contribute to evaluating the student's performance? At what intervals will performance be reviewed and by whom? Almost all work experience should have a way for youth performance to be reviewed; this maximizes the experience's contribution to the student's learning, future work, and career direction. Chapter 8 presents one template for work experience evaluation.

- *Supports and accommodations*—What supports are necessary and who will ensure they are in place? As discussed in Chapter 8, work experience success often hinges on effective, individually tailored supports and accommodations.

## Process for Promoting Work Experience Success

It is often tempting to take the path of least resistance. That is, transition specialists may be inclined to place a youth in work experience just because there is an available employer. Perhaps an employer has hosted youth in the past or has a good working relationship with the transition specialist, making them a "soft target" for work experience proposals. This might make them more inclined to accept any student presented to them. Yet easier does not necessarily mean better, especially when work experiences generated this way may not be a match for specific students. As discussed in subsequent chapters, each work experience should be driven by youth characteristics, by youth interests, and with input from the youth. That is, the work experience should serve the student's goals, not the convenience of transition specialists. Furthermore, once youth are in the workplace, much can go wrong if disability accommodations are not in place and the work experience activity is not adequately monitored. Neither the youth nor the employer benefit when youth are, as one employer put it, "dropped in my lap with no follow up."

Adequate support to both the youth and employer should be considered in every work experience. Support also will be helpful to ensure the youth is able to integrate with coworkers and in workplace activities. Finally, much can be gained from soliciting both the youth's and the employer's perspectives during the experience as well as at its conclusion. After all, transition specialists can learn as much from each work experience as the student does by careful review of the experience. This leads to ongoing quality improvement of future work experiences, that is, success at facilitating more and better work experiences.

Given these circumstances, a well-considered work experience process will include the following essential components:

1. *An asset-based youth profile* that outlines skills, positive traits, preferences, interests, and need for support

2. *Disability disclosure decisions* about if, when, and how disability is disclosed

3. *Employer outreach* driven by the asset-based youth profile

4. *Support on the job site* as necessary and as determined with youth and employer input

**Table 2.4.** Components for facilitating successful work experiences

| Component | Evidence of implementation |
|---|---|
| Asset-based youth profile | Documentation of skills, positive traits, preferences, interests, and need for support (see Chapter 3) |
| Disability disclosure decisions | Disclosure scripts (see Chapter 4) |
| Employer outreach driven by the asset-based youth profile | Work experience/job search plan (see Chapter 3) |
| Support on the job site | Individual support plan (see Chapter 8) |
| Feedback solicited from students on the work experience | Student feedback form (see Chapter 8) |
| Feedback solicited from employers on the work experience | Employer Satisfaction Questionnaire (see Chapter 7) |
| Repeat! | Quality improves in subsequent work experiences |

5. *Feedback solicited from youth* on the work experience

6. *Feedback solicited from employers* on the work experience

7. *Repeat!* Each subsequent work experience follows the same process, informed by prior work experiences.

Table 2.4 outlines these components and what might be evidence of their application. Subsequent chapters will contain strategies for implementing each of these components.

## LEGAL ASPECTS OF WORK EXPERIENCE

As planning for work experience begins, transition specialists must be aware of certain legal considerations that apply to work experiences. Three relevant laws that may affect the pursuit of work experience are the Fair Labor Standards Act (FLSA) of 1938 (PL 75-718), the Workforce Innovation and Opportunity Act (WIOA) of 2014 (PL 113-128), and the Americans with Disabilities Act (ADA) of 1990 (PL 101-336). When work experiences are unpaid, such as in career explorations and volunteer job sampling, there are provisions of the FLSA about when and under what conditions a youth can be in the workplace and not receive remuneration. When work experiences involve pay and wages, the FLSA provides guidance about conditions that must be met regarding youth age, job hazards, and wage levels. The WIOA also addresses wage level requirements for school-sponsored work and for referrals to services that sponsor or provide work. Finally, there are discrimination and accommodation provisions of the ADA that often apply to youth with disabilities in transition work experiences. One additional legal consideration is liability for injury or harm in any work experience. These situations are discussed in the remainder of this section.

### FLSA Provisions for Unpaid Work Experience

Federal policy makers and federal agencies have long recognized the importance of work-based learning and work experiences in preparing youth with disabilities for employment. They also have recognized that when youth are in the workplace for planned instruction and work experience, circumstances unique to youth may affect certain protections the law affords workers in the country (Morningstar, 2014; Simon, Cobb, Halloran, Norman, & Bourexis, 1994; Simon & Halloran, 1994). As a result, the U.S. Departments of Labor and Education adopted a joint Statement of Principle (Johnson, Sword, & Habhegger, 2005) that says,

> The U.S. Departments of Labor and Education are committed to the continued development and implementation of individual education programs, in accordance with the Individuals with Disabilities Education Act (IDEA), that will facilitate the transition of students with disabilities from school to employment within their communities. This transition must take place under conditions that will not jeopardize the protections afforded by the Fair Labor Standards Act to Program participants, employees, employers, or programs providing rehabilitation services to individuals with disabilities. (p. 8)

The FLSA establishes the guidelines for minimum wage regulations, child labor provisions, and distinguishing unpaid vocational and instructional training that may occur in the workplace from conditions that require employers to pay employees. Johnson et al. (2005) summarized how these guidelines affect the participation of youth with disabilities in unpaid work-based experiences. Students with disabilities are not considered employees of the businesses in which they engage in work experiences only if they can demonstrate compliance with all of the guidelines listed next.

- Participants will be youth with physical and/or mental disabilities for whom competitive employment at or above the minimum wage level is not immediately obtainable and who, because of their disability, will need intensive ongoing support to perform in a work setting.

- Participation will be for career exploration, career assessment, or work-related training at a worksite placement under the general supervision of public school personnel.

- Worksite placements will be clearly defined components of individualized education programs (IEPs) developed and designed for the benefit of each student. The statement of needed transition services established for the exploration, assessment, training, or cooperative work experience components will be included in the student's IEP.

- Information contained in a student's IEP will not have to be made available; however, documentation as to the student's enrollment in the work-based learning program will be made available to the Departments of Labor and Education. The student and his or her parent(s) or guardian(s) must be fully informed of the IEP and the career exploration, career assessment, or work-related training components and have indicated voluntary participation with the understanding that participation in these components does not entitle the student-participant to wages or other compensation for duties performed at the worksite placement.

- The activities of the student at the worksite do not result in an immediate advantage to the business. The Department of Labor looks at the following factors to determine if this guideline is being met:

  o There has been no displacement of employees, vacant positions have not been filled, employees have not been relieved of assigned duties, and the students are not performing services that, although not ordinarily performed by employees, clearly are of benefit to the business.

- o   The students receive continued and direct supervision by either representatives of the school or by employees of the business. The student receives ongoing instruction and close supervision at the worksite during the entire experience, resulting in any tasks the student performs being offset by the burden to the employer of providing ongoing training and supervision.

- o   Such placements are made according to the requirements of the student's IEP and not to meet the labor needs of the business.

- o   The periods of time spent by the students at any one site or in any clearly distinguishable job classification are specifically limited by the IEP.

- Students are not automatically entitled to employment at the business at the conclusion of their IEP. However, once a student has become an employee, all laws pertaining to employer/employee relationships apply.

Schools and participating businesses are responsible for ensuring that all of these guidelines are met. If any of these guidelines are not met, an employment relationship exists, and participating businesses can be held responsible for full compliance with the FLSA, meaning they must pay youth according to applicable wage laws. In short, schools must document that unpaid experiences are part of an educational program as determined by the IEP. In addition, employers must demonstrate that the students are not performing tasks that displace other workers and that do not materially benefit the employer's operation. Reports to the U.S. Department of Labor or the U.S. Department of Education are not necessary. However, adequate records documenting compliance with the guidelines for unpaid work activities must be maintained in the event the Department of Labor should ask for it.

When youth are no longer in school, there may still be legitimate purpose to unpaid work experiences and workplace training. The same considerations apply as those above, except that those guidelines regarding the IEP will not apply. In other words,

- The training is for an identified vocational preparation purpose

- The training is for the benefit of the youth, not the employer

- The youth do not displace regular employees, but work under close supervision of either a transition professional or supervisor/coworker

- The business derives no immediate advantage from the activities of the youth, and the placement may involve extra effort on the part of the employer

- The youth are not entitled to a job at the conclusion of the work experience

- The youth understand that they are not entitled to wages for the period of training

The FLSA, of course, ensures that youth are protected from unfair labor practices of employers. However, the value of unpaid work experience for youth is such that under the conditions outlined above youth have the opportunity to enjoy the advantages these experiences offer. Therefore, it is essential to plan work experiences according to the career objectives, preferences, and interests of the youth, as discussed in the next chapter, and according to the best practices of partnering with the employers who will host the youth, as discussed in Chapters 6 and 7.

## Paid Work Experiences and FLSA

When an employment relationship exists, youth must be paid the same as any employee who performs the same tasks. In cases where they are performing tasks that do not match an existing job description or if they are performing tasks that represent only a portion of an existing job description or job category, they can be paid a negotiated wage. However, the wage can be no less than the established federal legal minimum wage or the established minimum legal wage for the municipality or state in which the youth lives, whichever is more. That is, overtime pay, minimum wage provisions, and child labor provisions apply. As described next, FLSA contains several provisions addressing younger employees who are 14 and 15, employees who are 16 and 17, and employees 18 and older.

- *Youth ages 14 and 15*: These youth can work outside of school hours if they work no more than three hours on a school day with a limit of 18 hours in a school week. These youth may not work in jobs declared hazardous by the Secretary of Labor. They may work in retail stores, food service establishments, and gasoline service stations with some restrictions. A 14- or 15-year-old may not perform certain tasks in the retail and service industries, such as baking, cooking, and operating certain equipment. However, they can perform tasks like bagging and carrying customer's orders; cashiering; cleaning up; delivering items by foot, bicycle, or public transportation; and conducting grounds maintenance. For grounds maintenance, the young worker may use vacuums and floor waxers but cannot use power-driven mowers, cutters, and trimmers.

- *Youth ages 16 and 17*: Except in states that have laws limiting work hours, these youth may work anytime for unlimited hours in all jobs not declared hazardous by the Secretary of Labor.

- *Youth ages 18 and older*: These workers may perform any task, whether hazardous or not. Hazardous jobs are defined as any occupation that may be detrimental to the health and well-being of children under 18 years of age or an occupation that may jeopardize their educational opportunities.

Under certain circumstances the FLSA also contains provisions allowing employers to pay less than the federal minimum wage to students enrolled in specific full-time student programs. These programs are rare and employers must obtain a special certificate from the Department of Labor. The FLSA also allows workers with disabilities in supported employment programs to be employed at wage rates that may be below the statutory minimum, but wages paid must always be commensurate with the workers' productivity as compared to the productivity of nondisabled workers performing the same tasks. To pay a wage rate below the statutory minimum, an employer must obtain a special minimum wage certificate from the Department of Labor. Some states have, or are preparing to enact, provisions that eliminate subminimum wage. The WIOA, as discussed in the next section, also limits the circumstances under which a subminimum wage can be paid to transitioning students and youth.

Useful summary resources on the FLSA as it applies to work-based experiences are available from the National Center on Secondary Education and Transition (http://www.ncset.org). Johnson et al. (2005) also advise transition specialists to consult with the U.S. Department of Labor, Employment Standards Administration,

Wage and Hour Division Regional Office for additional guidance, as well as state and local government agencies in cases where clarification of an employment relationship might be necessary. It is important to know, however, that the U.S. Department of Labor, with the guidelines summarized above, has made it clear that it agrees that there is a valuable educational purpose to work experiences of all kinds. The guidelines for how the FLSA applies to transition programs strike an important balance between protecting workers' rights for fair compensation and allowing employers to make their workplaces available for youth to learn about working.

## Subminimum Wage Restrictions

Section 511 of the WIOA reflects the contemporary movement to limit the occasions when individuals with disabilities—especially those with complex and significant disabilities for whom job placement in the past has been limited—work in segregated settings and where they might be paid less than the prevailing minimum wage. There are two important provisions in this section that apply to youth with disabilities.

First, schools are prohibited from entering into contracts or agreements with community rehabilitation providers so that youth transition into segregated programs. This has been a common practice in some school districts when the expectation for students with disabilities was that they would transition directly into sheltered workshops as that was presumed to be the most likely vocational option. However, recent advocacy for more inclusive employment has led to new prohibitions on this practice. Past practices where schools contracted with sheltered workshops to provide subminimum wage work opportunities are no longer allowed and schools currently contracting with agencies holding subminimum wage certificates will not be able to continue. Schools can still use community rehabilitation providers to provide services in community integrated work settings. In fact, as discussed in Chapter 10, there are many potential advantages to working with these providers to facilitate work experiences.

Second, Section 511 prohibits employers from hiring youth with disabilities at a subminimum wage level, unless the youth are afforded meaningful opportunities to access vocational rehabilitation (VR) services, including pre-employment transition services (Pre-ETS). Before working at a rate below minimum wage, youth with disabilities must receive Pre-ETS and documented career counseling about their options to pursue community integrated employment.

The student's IEP can still identify an employment goal that will pay a subminimum wage, but certain requirements must be met:

- The student cannot participate in any subminimum wage employment as long as that individual is considered a student under the school district.

- The student must be referred to the state VR program.

- The student must be given the opportunity to receive Pre-ETS from VR.

- Documentation of subminimum wage needs to be completed prior to completing school services.

These provisions necessitate that schools work closely with VR agencies on behalf of those students who in the past might have been considered candidates for employment in sheltered workshops. This requirement offers the opportunity to receive useful help from VR agencies and the community rehabilitation providers who are VR vendors to facilitate work experiences and to plan for adult employment. Chapter 10 offers strategies for collaborating with these entities for work experience development.

## Nondiscrimination and Reasonable Accommodations

The Americans with Disabilities Act (ADA) of 1990 (PL 101-336) is considered a landmark civil rights law which, among other things, prohibits employment discrimination by employers against job candidates and employees with disabilities. Title I of the ADA requires private employers with 15 or more employees, as well as state and local governments (regardless of how many employees they have), to make reasonable accommodations for qualified job applicants and employees with disabilities. Under the law, "reasonable accommodations" are adjustments and modifications that range from making the physical work environment accessible to providing assistive technology to offering flexible work scheduling for "qualified" individuals. Qualified individuals are those who can perform the "essential functions" of the job, *with or without* reasonable accommodations.

Reasonable accommodations are designed to enable individuals to perform essential functions of a job, meaning those fundamental tasks required of a position, often represented in a job description. Reasonable accommodations also pertain to enabling individuals to enjoy equal benefits and privileges of employment, such as fringe benefits, office social functions, staff meetings, and so forth. An employer is not required to provide any accommodation that would constitute an undue hardship, that is, something that imposes significant difficulty or expense, or that fundamentally alters the operation of the business. This is distinctly different from education settings governed by the Individuals with Disabilities Education Improvement Act (IDEIA) of 2004 (PL 108-446), where schools must provide learning and physical accommodations if they are identified as necessary in the IEP.

In the context of youth work experiences, legally required reasonable accommodations only apply to paid employment when the youth can reasonably be expected to perform the *essential functions* of a job *and* when the cost and difficulty of providing the accommodations are not excessive. For work experiences where there is no legal employer/employee relationship, such as in many volunteer positions, unpaid internships, career explorations, and job shadowing opportunities, employers are not required to provide accommodations, reasonable or not. It should be noted, however, that there are some unpaid work situations where there are elements of the employment relationship, such as when volunteers are provided with benefits (e.g., insurance, workers' compensation), or where such work is required for or regularly leads to paid positions with the employer, as in the case of some internships. In such situations, the reasonable accommodations provisions of the ADA apply.

Many youth will be able to perform jobs with standard job descriptions with or without accommodations. Even if these accommodations might be extensive, such as wheelchair accessibility or modified keyboards, the employer must offer them if they are not an undue hardship on the company. Many individuals in transition programs, however, may only be able to perform some tasks within a standard job description. In these cases, the employer is under no obligation to provide accommodations or to hire the youth. However, as discussed throughout this book, when accommodations are presented in the context of how they will help make the work experience successful, employers are likely to accept them as minimally intrusive and ultimately beneficial to student performance on the job. Most often employers are quite willing to work with youth and transition specialists in implementing necessary accommodations, no matter the circumstance of the youth or the absence of a legal obligation, as long as they receive competent help and service from transition specialists.

The ADA directly applies to many youth in transition who are seeking and will be hired into regular jobs as part of their transition experience. It will continue to apply to youth as they seek and enter employment as adults. It is therefore important for youth to be aware of their rights if they require an accommodation. They also will need to decide how and when to disclose their disability and to ask for accommodations. Chapter 4 discusses disclosure considerations in detail.

Furthermore, the need for and type of accommodations are often part of the negotiation with employers when the youth is establishing a relationship with an employer. Considerations in negotiations with employers and considerations about establishing workplace supports and accommodations are also covered in later chapters. Ultimately, when accommodations are needed it is important to prepare or assist youth to negotiate accommodations with employers who host youth work experiences (see Chapter 4).

## What About Liability?

Often transition specialists are asked by other transition service partners or by employers about who is liable when a student or youth is injured in the workplace. There are two basic considerations, depending if the work experience is unpaid or paid. When the work experience is considered part of the IEP and does not include pay, the worksite is perceived as an extension of the school. That is, if the student is pursuing instructional objectives in a work setting, the school may be responsible for liability coverage. Generally, the same insurance and liability policies that apply to other off-site school experiences (e.g., athletic events, field trips) apply here. Each district has its own policies regarding liability. Transition specialists should check with school administration as to how liability policies apply in particular school districts. In cases where community rehabilitation providers are involved in creating and supervising work experience, the liability policies they carry will cover the activities associated with the work experience.

In unpaid work experiences, students are not employees and are not eligible for the usual workers' compensation or insurance coverage provided to employees. However, when the student is in work experience where wages are paid by the employer, pertinent insurance and liability policies that cover all employees apply to the student as well. In short, students, transition specialists, and employers almost always have liability protection one way or another in work experience situations. Transition specialists should request explanations from supervisors or administrators how this applies in their work and should be prepared to explain this to prospective employers when the question of liability comes up. The bottom line is that questions about liability should rarely be an impediment to facilitating work experiences for students and youth in transition.

## SUMMARY

This chapter reviewed work experience types and their functions, as well as how and when they may be used to prepare youth in their career development. There are many junctures throughout a youth's educational program, and even well after school exit, when youth work experiences might be introduced. Although there is an ideal and logical order in which different work experiences might be introduced to students, no hard-and-fast rule exists as to when or in what order students are exposed to work experiences. It often depends on available educational services and a host of other circumstances that may be out of the control of students and the transition specialists who are assisting them. Nevertheless, the standard is that the earlier and more often students are exposed to career and work options, the better. This chapter also introduced a conceptual model for the process of establishing and supporting work-based learning opportunities. The mechanics of this process are covered in subsequent chapters. Legal aspects of work experience relating to compensation and conditions of work were also discussed.

Overall, this chapter presented considerations for organizing activity so the greatest positive impact can be pursued for student and youth work experience. The rest of the book is devoted to strategies that will make that happen: how youth must participate in planning work experiences, considerations for disclosing disability and asking for accommodations, ways to involve families in work experience planning and implementation, recruiting and retaining employer partners, ways to support and mentor youth in the workplace, and connecting and partnering with other professionals and programs to foster and sustain work experience success. The stage has been set. Use the remainder of the book to help make work happen for students and youth!

## REFERENCES

Americans with Disabilities Act (ADA) of 1990, PL101-336, 42 U.S.C. 12101 *et seq.*

Brolin, D. (2004). *Life centered career education.* Arlington, VA: Council for Exceptional Children.

Fair Labor Standard Act (FLSA) of 1938, PL 75-718, 29 U.S.C. 201 *et seq.*

Flexer, R., Baer, R., Luft, P., & Simmons, T. (2012). *Transition planning for secondary students with disabilities* (4th ed.). Upper Saddle River, NJ: Pearson/Merrill Prentice Hall.

Individuals with Disabilities Education Improvement Act of 2004, PL 108-446, 20 U.S.C. 1400 *et seq.*

Johnson, D. R., Sword, C., & Habhagger, B. (2005). *Handbook for implementing a comprehensive work-based learning program according to the Fair Labor Standards Act* (3rd ed.). Minneapolis: University of Minnesota, Institute on Community Integration, National Center on Secondary Education and Transition.

Lipscomb, S., Lacoe, J., Liu, A., & Haimson, J. (2018). *Preparing for life after high school: The characteristics and experiences of youth in special education: A summary of key findings from the National Longitudinal Transition Study 2012* (NCEE Evaluation Brief). Washington, DC: Institute of Education Sciences, National Center for Education Evaluation and Regional Assistance.

Morningstar, M. E. (2014). *Ensuring that work based learning aligns with the Fair Labor Standards Act training agreement* [Online instructional video]. Lawrence: Transition Coalition, University of Kansas, Beach Center on Disability, Life Span Institute.

National Alliance for Secondary Education and Transition (NASET). (2005). *National standards and quality indicators: Transition toolkit for systems improvement.* Minneapolis: University of Minnesota, National Center on Secondary Education and Transition.

Simon, M., Cobb, B., Halloran, W., Norman, M., & Bourexis, P. (1994). *Meeting the needs of youth with disabilities: Handbook for implementing community-based vocational education programs according to the Fair Labor Standards Act.* Fort Collins: Colorado State University.

Simon, M., & Halloran, W. (1994). Community-based vocational education: Guidelines for complying with the Fair Labor Standards Act. *Journal of the Association for Severely Handicapped, 19,* 52–60.

Workforce Innovation and Opportunity Act (WOIA) of 2014, PL 113-128, 29 U.S.C. §§ *et seq.*

# Planning for Work Experiences

Richard G. Luecking, Amy Dwyre D'Agati, and Marie Parker Harvey

---

**By completing this chapter, the reader will**

- Discover how to gather information for planning work experiences
- Learn the guiding principles and considerations for planning work experiences
- Identify ways to use an asset-based profile as a useful tool in planning work experiences
- Complete a Learning Lab on work experience planning

---

*"I want to work. I like cars.*
*My teacher helped me find a job at the tire store."*
High school student whose work experience turned into a long-term job

Beginning at age 19, Jalen and the other students in his special education program started the same work skills training program. This included simulated settings to learn cleaning skills, basic administration tasks, and food preparation. Then the students were placed in local elementary schools to either help in the lunchroom or assist the janitorial staff. The goal was that the students would develop skills in these areas because the majority of them would be employed after school exit by an adult service provider in the area that had big food service and janitorial contracts with local hospitals and hotels. Without being consulted, Jalen was placed in a janitorial work experience because the teacher thought it could accommodate his slow pace at completing many physical tasks. Jalen needed a lot of assistance doing janitorial tasks, especially mopping. He also got very tired being on his feet for long periods. He hated this work, did not perform well, and was rated by his supervisor as "not ready to work."

Fortunately for Jalen, the story did not end there. In his final year of high school, his family moved when his dad got transferred at work. Jalen's new school had a transition program that featured work experience. The assigned transition specialist discovered that Jalen loved sports and followed the local radio announcers with a passion. He and his dad attended as many games as they could. When they could not go in person, Jalen would watch games on TV with the sound off so that he could do the announcing. Given this strong interest, the transition specialist at his new school approached the local recreation center where she and Jalen convinced the head of the basketball league to create a work experience where Jalen would be the assigned score keeper for every game. Once Jalen began scoring at games, they suggested that he could do some game announcing, especially for the younger kids. He became the game announcer and scorekeeper for the 7- to 8- and 9- to 10-year-old recreation leagues. Families commented to the commissioner that game time had become much more exciting with Jalen on the microphone! By the time he exited school, Jalen had also secured his own part of a local sports show where he did an overview of the local college circuit, and he ended each segment with a fun baseball fact he knew from his many hours of following the sport. Jalen loved these jobs—they allowed him to tap into his passion for sports and did not tire him physically. He is on his way to a sports-related career!

Pigeonholing students into a job or career path based on a disability label or easily available work experiences is never a good idea. Had Jalen not moved, he would have been a victim of this limited way of thinking. Instead, transition programs should integrate individualized planning that features informed choices by youth, driven by their particular interests, skills, and preferences. This more thoughtful approach offers a springboard to success at the workplace, as was ultimately the case for Jalen. Planning for work experiences is both a science and an art. It is a science in the sense that there are a number of well-validated assessment instruments that can help identify skills, interests, and aptitudes of youth. It is an art in that there are creative ways to augment information gathered from assessments with other useful, often more important, information about youth characteristics. All available information about youth can then be used to identify and plan for potential work experiences. In fact, it is the purposeful, and oftentimes creative, gathering of information about a youth that leads to successful work experiences in almost all cases. This chapter discusses ways of gathering information that can be used for planning for work experiences, outlines guiding principles of planning for work experiences, and shows how developing an asset-based inventory can be a useful tool to guide development of work experiences.

## GATHERING INFORMATION FOR WORK EXPERIENCE PLANNING

Since the advent of the Individuals with Disabilities Education Act of 1990 (PL 101-476), planning for transition from school to work and adult life has been a federal mandate. Transition assessment has long been a foundation of this planning (Morningstar & Clavenna-Deane, 2018; Sax & Thoma, 2002; Sitlington, Neubert, Begun, Lombard, & Leconte, 2007;). Sitlington et al. (2007) defined transition assessment as "an ongoing process of collecting information on the student's strengths, needs, preferences, and interests as they relate to the demands of current and future living, learning, and working environments" (p. 2). This type of information gathering enables students, families, special educators, transition specialists, and other people assisting youth to make decisions about educational goals, work goals, and ultimately career goals. Although transition assessment offers useful information to help plan activities for a host of important transition issues, this chapter focuses on how to use this information for a subset—albeit a very important subset—of transition activities. That is, what will this information tell us about helping youth plan for work experiences and jobs?

There are a host of formal assessments that gather various types of information about youth competencies and interests. Traditional and formal assessments include standardized tests, such as those available from commercial publishers. Many of these tests must be administered by trained professionals, whereas others can be administered by classroom teachers or career specialists either in person or through an online platform. The purposes of these tests include a range of targeted assessment areas, including general aptitude, adaptive behavior, cognitive or learning aptitude, occupational interests, personality/social skills, and learning styles. These various assessments sometimes provide useful information when planning for work experiences. Detailed information on various assessments and how they apply in transition planning is available from the National Technical Assistance Center on Transition: https://www.transitionta.org/search/google/assessments.

However, there is no one-size-fits-all transition assessment instrument. Most transition assessments lack broad applicability, and no one assessment will provide a comprehensive understanding of student potential or interests as they relate to work experience development. Moreover, traditional assessments may limit thinking about potential work experiences for individuals with significant disabilities who might require extensive support or accommodations (Morningstar & Pearson, 2015). Not only are they often less-than-perfect predictors of youth performance, but they often lead to mistaken conclusions that youth are not ready or able to work in a chosen occupational area. Such tests also do not fairly evaluate an individual's aptitude or potential if the person has trouble taking tests due to learning disabilities, cognitive comprehension, language proficiency, or a test's cultural bias (Morningstar & Clavenna-Deane, 2018). Thus, information obtained from such tests and assessments may be useful in the overall picture of the person's abilities and interests, but one should not rely solely on them as a basis for work experience planning. More direct and immediately relevant ways exist to gather useful information about youth that inform the planning for work experiences as explained in this chapter.

One valuable and obvious resource outside of formal assessments are interviews with the youths' families. Families are often indispensable contributors to work experience planning. They know the youth best and can therefore contribute valuable information about his or her traits and preferences. They often have unique insights into the youth's motivation, interpersonal behavior, idiosyncrasies, and interests. For any youth, including youth with significant disabilities who are not easily able to express their own preferences, families can be the foundation for planning and are often actively involved in the planning for work experiences. The information that families can provide is most often more valuable than any formal assessment instrument.

Additional sources of information about youth that are useful in work experience planning include school and program records, interviews and questionnaires, observations in various school and natural environments, situational assessments, and portfolio assessments (Morningstar & Clavenna-Deane, 2018). Table 3.1 summarizes various methods of gathering information for work experience planning.

Although the entire process of assessment and work experience planning is useful for a number of purposes, there is little value to the information unless there is an end goal associated with it. In the context of planning for work experiences, the aim is to determine

- What type of work experience environment is appropriate for the individual youth

- How to match individual traits of youth to potential work experience sites

- How specific barriers might need to be accommodated in a work experience

- How the work experience will point the way for career and employment planning

- And, ultimately, where to look for a work experience for individual youth

Planning for work experiences is always better served when it is driven by a youth's assets and positive traits, as opposed to perceived deficits. In addition to helping youth and transition specialists plan for the best work experience match, this provides a foundation for helping youth "put their best foot forward" when it is time to present themselves to prospective employers who will host work experiences.

**Table 3.1.**   Methods for gathering information for work experience planning

| Method | Description and function in planning |
| --- | --- |
| Formal assessments | Include standardized tests such as those available from commercial publishers, which can target a range of assessment areas, including general aptitude, adaptive behavior, cognitive or learning aptitude, occupational interests, personality/social skills, and learning styles. |
| School or program records | Courses taken, grades, test scores, attendance records, IEPs, and any documentation of the youth's participation and performance. |
| Interviews | Interviews with the youth, family members, teachers, social service professionals, counselors, or anyone who knows the youth well, to determine unique interests, traits, skills, and needs for accommodations. |
| Observations | Watching the youth in typical daily environments and activities to identify patterns of behavior, personal preferences, task performance skill, and so forth. |
| Situational assessments | Observing the youth in situations that resemble potential future work environments to determine task performance skill and potential future work site support needs. |
| Portfolio assessment | Samples of the youth's work behavior over time, such as performance reviews, functional résumé, sample supervisor recommendations, pictures of past work performed, or any other material chosen by the youth that represents his or her activities and accomplishments. |
| Asset-based profile | Information gathered through an individualized, self-determined, and positive oriented process. As the term implies, these profiles are all about helping students identify what interests them, what they prefer, what supports they might need to be successful in the workplace, and what positive traits they have on which to build a career direction. |

As illustrated in the textbox titled Turning "Negatives" into "Positives", this was the case with Matthew, whose "positive" traits were highlighted instead of perceived "negative" ones in the development of his work experience.

---

### Turning "Negatives" Into "Positives"

Matthew had been receiving special education services since elementary school. Throughout his education, his dyslexia and severe attention-deficit/hyperactive disorder (ADHD) led to difficulties paying attention in class and a tendency to be disruptive. He just could not sit still. His school records were filled with absences, detentions, and trips to the principal's office for disruptive behavior. When the transition specialist began reviewing Matthew's file in preparation for helping develop a work experience, he found a wealth of information summarizing his academic deficits and "problem" behaviors. Without another way of viewing Matthew's traits, this information's only value was to eliminate various work environments. To help Matthew find a well-matched work experience, the transition specialist needed another viewpoint.

Matthew's grades were usually above average, especially in math. One high school math teacher discovered that when Matthew is allowed to break his assignment into segments and take breaks, he does fine. He can also stay very focused when the topic interests him. And if assignments and tasks are hands-on and concrete, rather than abstract, he can stay with the task longer. The transition specialist talked extensively to the math teacher, to Matthew, and to Matthew's mom. The transition specialist discovered how well Matthew can perform when tasks are broken into "chunks," when he has a chance to take breaks, and when tasks interest him. He also learned about Matthew's interest and aptitude in mechanical equipment. The transition specialist helped Matthew get work experience with a local heating, ventilation, and air conditioning (HVAC) company that was able to provide the accommodations he needed—written task lists, no more than two duties at a time, and regular breaks. An additional feature of this experience was that Matthew was assigned a work mentor who was available for consistent check-ins. Finally, the HVAC work was such that moving around was part of the job. These circumstances all led to a successful semester-long work experience. Matthew is now enrolled in an HVAC technician certification program.

---

## GUIDING PRINCIPLES FOR PLANNING WORK EXPERIENCES

Two concepts should drive good work experience planning. First, planning should be individualized and person centered. Each student has unique interests, talents, and need for support, regardless of disability label or educational circumstance. Second, planning should feature self-determination and informed choice. Each individual has preferences and should be given an opportunity to express them. Accordingly, transition specialists should follow assessment and planning principles that incorporate these concepts and that have been espoused by many experts in transition (Morningstar & Clavenna-Deanne, 2018; Wehman, 2013; Wehmeyer & Webb, 2012). The key principles that apply to work experience planning are the following:

- All youth have unique talents and traits that can potentially benefit employers.

- Assessment should focus on these talents and traits, rather than on deficits. When challenges are identified, supports and accommodations to minimize the effects of the challenges should be considered.

- Youth should be directly involved in planning and should be empowered to provide information that reflects their interests, talents, positive traits, and need for accommodations and supports.

- A youth's family should be given opportunities to be involved in work experience planning decisions and encouraged to contribute information and suggestions about the youth's history, experiences, and traits during the planning.

- Various methods of collecting information should be used, relying less on formal assessment information and school records, and relying more on interviews with youth and those who know them well, as well as observations of youth in a natural situation.

- Youth should be given supports, modifications, and accommodations as necessary when engaging in assessment and work experience planning activities.

Self-determination is just as valuable in work experience planning as it is in any aspect of transition assessment or planning activity. One longstanding definition of self-determination comes from the Division on Career Development and Transition (DCDT) of the Council on Exceptional Children:

> Self-determination is a combination of skills, knowledge, and beliefs that enable a person to engage in goal directed, self-regulated, autonomous behavior. Self-determination is an understanding of one's strengths and limitations together with a belief in oneself as capable and effective. Then acting on the basis of these skills and attitudes, individuals have a great ability to take control of their lives and assume the roles of adults in society. (Field, Martin, Miller, Ward, & Wehmeyer, 1998, p. 113)

Youth should be encouraged to learn to be the final voice in work experience planning. Students are self-determined during the planning for work experiences when they are able to do the following, with or without support:

- List tasks that they perform well.

- List hobbies, favorite leisure opportunities, and areas of interest.

- Know what accommodations they might need and ask for them, both during the planning process and in the eventual workplace.

- Ask reasonable questions about what is expected during the work experience.

- Understand the purpose of the prospective work experience.

- Express their preferences about aspects of the work experience (e.g., location, schedules, tasks, accommodation needs), to the fullest extent possible.

- List, discuss, and identify what they learned from previous work experiences.

Youth should learn to discuss their preferences, strengths, and support needs so that they can better guide what type of work experience they have, what they learn from it, and what it does to prepare them for eventual jobs and careers.

Many youth will not have the range of life experiences that have exposed them to a variety of options from which to make choices. Indeed, in the world of career preparation, experience precedes interest. It will sometimes be difficult to determine clear preferences during work experience planning. When this is the case, given the limited information available, planning for work experience can be approached from a perspective of "let's see what we and the youth can learn from this experience." In other words, work experiences themselves may function as ways to expose students to potential new interests. After all, exposure precedes interest, as illustrated by Cordell in the textbox titled Exposure Precedes Interest. The youth, however, should be fully involved in the planning and implementation of the work experience and should be aware of what can be expected from it. Then, the work experiences themselves will often act as ways of gathering important experience from which to inform future work experience and employment planning. As articulated by Sax and Thoma (2002), we "have no right to plan for another without their participation or permission" (p. 14). Or, as many self-advocates have said, "Nothing about us without us!" (Charlton, 2000). In other words, transition specialists should not plan for work experience without youth input and consent.

---

**Exposure Precedes Interest**

One would never have guessed that Cordell would thrive as an auto glass technician. He certainly didn't. He was enrolled in a welder training program through his high school's technical education program. But Cordell has other passions. He amazes his friends with his dance moves and dreams of making a living as a dancer and rapper one day. Someone with the soul of a dancer might feel restricted and confined in the tight quarters of a welding booth. And the protective gear that welders wear— including a heavy mask—might make it hard for a dancer to move his feet. He soon learned that being a welder was not for him, but he was not sure what else he might do.

Working with his school's work study coordinator Cordell decided that he would be willing to try anything else that would enable him to move around and maybe bust a move now and then. Eventually, they located a glass shop that specializes in residential, commercial, and auto glass. They needed help and Cordell needed to try something new. With the help

---

*(continued)*

of his supervisor he soon learned the basics of cutting and installing auto glass, tabletops, mirrors, and doors. In addition to having room to move when he has the urge, a crucial piece of Cordell's work experience success is a supportive person to show him the ropes and to nudge him when he gets distracted. It has meant the difference between floundering and feeling comfortable on the shop floor.

Just as important, Cordell has now turned this experience into a post-school employment and career direction. He now works at the glass shop full time and has added the skill of making window and door screens for homes and businesses. "I finally found something I enjoy doing," he says.

## DEVELOPING AN ASSET-BASED YOUTH PROFILE

An asset-based youth profile, or an asset-based inventory, is an information-gathering tool for discovering a youth's positive attributes. Featuring individualization and self-determination, these profiles help youth identify what interests them, what they prefer, what supports they might need in the workplace to be successful, and what positive traits they have to build on. There are several types of asset-based profiles in current use. Most have their roots in a process called person-centered planning (O'Brien & Mount, 2006). As the name implies, person-centered planning's primary focus is on the person—as opposed to a disability or a service or some other particular issue. Through a process that solicits input from the individual, family members, friends, and other people who know him or her, person-centered planning creates a vision for a person's life, including employment, and describes the actions needed to move it in the direction of that vision.

One type of asset-based work experience or job-planning tool is created through a process called Discovery, which includes spending time with people, instead of testing or evaluating them, as a means of finding out what people have to offer potential employers (Callahan, 2010; Griffin, Hammis, & Geary, 2007; Inge & Graham, 2015). It is especially helpful for determining the unique contributions offered by people who might not compete for "off-the-shelf" jobs due to a need for extensive or unusual supports. In the context of transitioning youth, Discovery primarily involves spending time with the youth and family members, as well as observations of the youth in natural environments. From these encounters and observations, a narrative profile is developed and used as a guide for matching an individual to an appropriate job. Often an accompanying presentation profile, or portfolio, is also developed that documents an individual's unique traits and skills and that can be shown to prospective employers for their consideration.

Another variation of an asset-based work experience or job development planning tool is called the Positive Personal Profile (Luecking & Tilson, 2009). It has been widely used for work experience planning in school-to-work transition programs and in models that have generated positive employment outcomes for students and youth with disabilities (Luecking & Luecking, 2015; Luecking, Fabian,

Contreary, Honeycutt, & Luecking, 2018). The Positive Personal Profile is not a formal assessment but, rather, a way of gathering information about a youth and his or her traits that will be helpful in planning for and finding work experiences and jobs. The components of the Positive Personal Profile include a compilation of basic information, such as the youth's dreams and goals, interests, talents, skills, knowledge, learning styles, values, positive personality traits, environmental preferences, dislikes, life and work experiences, support system, specific challenges, creative solutions and accommodations, and creative possibilities and ideas for pursuing work experiences. Any and all of these areas may offer information useful for planning work experiences.

## Using an Asset-Based Inventory

An asset-based inventory is a practical and informal way to collect information on all the attributes of youth that will be relevant to identifying potential work experiences and jobs. It also has relevance to later job searches, job matches, job retention, and long-range career development. It is a mechanism for collecting information from a variety of sources, including traditional assessments, school records, observations, and interviews and discussions with youth and the people who know them well, including family members, teachers, youth workers, and others. An asset-based inventory ensures that the transition specialist and others helping a youth have a clear picture of his or her positive attributes, as well as areas where he or she may need support or accommodations. This information can then be used to develop a work experience plan for identifying and pursuing work experience opportunities from which to build a "way to work."

The development of an asset-based youth inventory is ideally a fluid process. Such inventories can be updated at any time, as new information is gathered about the student that is relevant to work experience and employment planning. For example, at the conclusion of a work experience, the student and transition specialist might update information about the student's preferences, new skills, support needs, and more, so that it can be useful in planning for the next work experience. The Asset-Based Inventory in Appendix 3.1 provides a format for collecting and organizing information about the youth that will be helpful to work experience planning. It can be used as a guide to interviewing the youth or individuals who know the youth. In addition, this inventory can be a way to organize and store the information collected about the youth, and can serve as a reference document for planning work experience.

The Asset-Based Inventory in Appendix 3.1 groups questions into categories that focus on youth strengths, positive traits, and skills. It also helps uncover interests and preferences. The inventory is intended to be a means for collecting information from more than one source, starting with the youth, and then incorporating input from family, teachers, and any other person who may know the youth well. The areas that follow are examples of what information might be collected during the development of a work experience or job search plan, and correspond to the inventory in the appendix.

***Interests and Preferences***     "What do you like?" is an overarching question that helps us get to know people. Exploring a youth's interests and individual preferences is often a productive place to start preparing him or her for work experiences. Consider asking the youth and those familiar with him or her the following specific questions:

- *Why do you want to work?* Knowing what motivates youth is a good place to start getting to know them. When youth don't know for sure whether they want to work, it is usually because they have not yet been exposed to work.

- *What is your dream job?* The answer to this question provides a big picture of a youth's dreams and aspirations, even if they do not seem realistic to others (e.g., basketball star, actor, doctor, rap artist). The youth's answer can uncover broad areas of interest. Dreams and interest are likely to change with experience, but they may signal a possible work experience with a connection—however remote—to that dream.

- *What are some activities you enjoy* (e.g., sports, hobbies, recreational pursuits)? Such activities may show traits and interests that suggest not only what motivates youth, but what holds their interest. These activities also might suggest other positive personal traits that translate well in a workplace, such as commitment to a task, how well they interact with others, or what they are really good at. Such traits are not always apparent in traditional vocational assessments.

- *Who do you like to spend time with, and what do you do together?* Answers to this question also will help uncover youths' traits and interests, not to mention what support systems may be available when planning and engaging in work experiences.

- *In what environmental conditions do you do best* (e.g., outdoors/indoors, noisy/quiet, many/few people, slow/fast pace, time of day)? Everyone has a unique rhythm when responding to different situations and environments that might suggest how he or she would best perform in the workplace. Does the youth crave routine, predictable tasks? Does he or she like variety? Is a youth's temperament suited to a fast-paced work environment where things change rapidly? Does he or she like to be in a quiet cubicle to avoid distraction or outdoors? Does the youth favor a noisy environment with lots of activity? Considering these preferences will help make the work experience successful.

**Life and Work Experiences**     To consider life and work experience, transition specialists should ask "What have you done?" Everyone has previous experiences that might usefully inform work experience planning. These may include not only previous actual work experiences, but also household chores, community activities, or social pastimes. For instance, experience with basic household chores might tell us something about the student's capabilities, as might basic activities outside the home where interests may have been developed and skills learned. In addition, information about other, nonwork, activities can also inform work experience planning. The answers to the following questions will help uncover useful information.

- *Have you had any previous paid or unpaid work experiences? What tasks did you perform in these experiences?* For youth who have had previous work experiences, it is useful to know where and what they did there. Was it a good experience? Were there particular tasks they loved or hated? Did they perform these tasks well or poorly? Did they learn new skills? Was there anything they would like to learn to do better, or to avoid in future experiences? Were accommodations provided during that experience? Such questions can help transition specialists mine important details from youth, to inform future work experience planning.

- *What types of household chores do you complete regularly (both assigned and voluntary)?* This question is especially helpful when youth have had no previous work experience. Perhaps they have vacuumed, done dishes, or set the table. Although these may not be the types of things they want to do in a work experience, experience with chores can provide insight into work exposure, task performance, follow through, and current skills upon which to build during work experiences.

- *In what community or social activities do you participate?* These types of activities often reveal a number of interests, as well as traits and attributes. Is the student active in a faith community? Does he or she play recreational sports? Is the youth a member of any clubs or interest organizations? How often does he or she attend/participate? What does the student like best about these activities?

**Skills, Knowledge, and Abilities**      The asset-based inventory also prompts transition specialists to ask, "What can you do?" Everyone has certain "natural gifts," talents, or things that they simply have a knack for. Often youth skills can be identified simply by asking, "What do people compliment you about?" Of course, formal and informal assessments (discussed earlier) can be a good source of information about youth talents and skills, as long as the focus is on aptitudes and skills rather than deficits. In all work experience planning, the objective is to help students put their best foot forward. Thus, a youth's inventory should list as many of these skills and talents as possible. Remember that if the list of skills and abilities is not long for some youth, it doesn't mean they lack aptitude or potential. It just means we have to help them acquire these traits. That's what work experiences are for, after all. Questions to consider asking to discover information about a student's skills, knowledge, and abilities include the following:

- *What are some of your talents and things you do well? What do people compliment you about?* This can be as basic as having a friendly disposition or nice smile, or as involved as being computer savvy or playing a musical instrument. It could be as seemingly unrelated to work as assembling complicated puzzles. In any case, answers to this question highlight the best features of all youth and that information can be used to help them "put their best foot forward."

- *Describe your abilities and academic skills.* Lifting, standing, and dexterity are physical traits that help identify areas of potential performance in a work experience or job. Similarly, math, reading, and writing are academic skills that will have implications for potential work experiences. Does the youth have money skills or computer skills? What about social skills? Other talents or abilities—whether they are school- or work-related?

- *Have you been involved in any specific vocational training?* Whether such training was successful, discussing training experiences shows what the youth has been exposed to, what he or she learned how to do, and in what environments he or she has learned.

**Dislikes and Preferences**      Transition specialists should ask "What don't you like?" to learn of situations that may need to be avoided in a work experience. Everyone has dislikes that would make a work experience miserable if they had to be endured at a workplace. These may not always be clear to a student until he or she has had actual experience in workplaces. Yet, youth, their family, their teachers, or others who know them may have a good idea about what they really dislike—for instance, getting dirty, being bored, being exposed to loud noises, having frequent changes in routine, or sitting for long periods. These questions might help uncover dislikes:

- *Are there particular situations you recommend we avoid when searching for work experiences or job opportunities?*

- *What is a job or job setting that you do NOT want to do?*

- *Are there particular activities that the youth is "known" to dislike?*

**Accommodations and Support Needs**      This section of the asset-based inventory asks, "What help do you need to do well?" The types of accommodations and support that students might need to succeed in the workplace are as individual as the students themselves. Notably, it is the effects of the student's disability, not the disability itself, that need to be considered. For example, knowing that a student has a learning disability is not as useful as knowing how it specifically impacts them. Does the individual learn best hearing the information, reading it, or being shown how to do it? Does the student need more time with a task if reading is required? The question is not about the disability, but the accommodations: Do certain students require assistive technology? Do they need on-the-job coaching? Do they need a quiet environment? Do they need specific cues for social interactions? The straightforward approach to getting the information needed for work experience planning is to simply ask the following:

- *What accommodations or supports are currently being provided in school or other settings?*

- *What accommodations might be needed in the workplace (e.g., physical accessibility, assistive technology, special schedules, job coaching)?*

- *What supports might need to be maintained beyond the initial placement?*

- *What do I need to know about you so I can help you identify necessary support to succeed at work?*

Of course, some support needs are not apparent until the youth is in the actual workplace, so another question might be, *What do I need to know about you so that I can help you identify necessary support to succeed at work?*

***Transportation Resources***    Next, transition specialists can ask "How do you get around?" Transportation is the perennial challenge for getting to the workplace. Most youth will not have their own vehicle or even a driver's license. In many communities, public transportation or paratransit services (if needed) are limited or nonexistent. Resources to pay for taxis or other commercial transportation may be limited or unavailable. Thus, getting to and from work will often require creative solutions. To get an idea of what it might take for youth to get to work experience locations, use the following probes:

- *How do you get to places you want to go (e.g., bus, ride from a relative or neighbor, car service)?*

- *Do you have a bus pass, mobility sharing pass, or access to other public transportation?*

- *Have you had training to use public transportation? Is it necessary? Available?*

- *Does the school or employment agency provide transportation to work experience locations?*

- *What needs to be considered in planning how to get to work? Family member schedules? Accessibility? Proximity to home?*

***Other Available Support***    Another important consideration is "Who helps and provides encouragement at home and at school?" Does the youth have people who can provide support, encouragement, and resources for planning, developing, and successfully engaging in work experience? This may include family, friends, neighbors, acquaintances, teachers, job coaches, personal assistants, and social service agencies and personnel. Any or all of these people may perform various roles, such as providing advocacy, getting the youth to the worksite, offering a service that makes work experience possible, or simply standing on the sidelines cheering the youth on. The youth's support system may include unpaid family members and friends who simply have the youth's best interest at heart. Or it may involve paid professionals who offer a service the youth may need, such as those described in Chapter 10. In some cases, the system of support will be extensive and offer a host of help to the youth; in others, such support may be scarce. In any case, planning for work experience should take into account how much or how little support there will be for the youth as he or she pursues work experience opportunities.

***Searching for the Work Experience and Other General Provisions***    Armed with all of the previous information, the transition specialist is nearly ready to begin the work experience search. Final questions to determine what else we need to know include the following:

- *Do you have any geographical preferences (e.g., certain areas of the community, close to home)?*

- *Do you have a preference or a need to work certain days or hours? What is an ideal work schedule?*

- *Do you have any ideas about employers or types of employers we should talk to?*

- *Do you know people who might suggest particular employers or types of employers?*

- *Is there any other information that would be useful to know? For example, temperament (e.g., easy going, easily frustrated, easily distracted), habits, or idiosyncrasies?*

**Possibilities and Ideas**     The Possibilities and Ideas section of Appendix 3.1 is a place to brainstorm and record any thoughts on work possibilities or on any other work-planning matters, no matter how random or unrealistic they may seem. These notes may include ideas for employer leads, things to explore, actions to take, or simply reminders of what to consider. There will be plenty of opportunities to refine these ideas and thoughts as a work experience or job search plan is developed. In the meantime, consider these ideas as potential insights that might help get the most complete picture of the youth and that add direction to the pursuit of a work experience or job.

## Next Step: The Work Experience Plan

Information collected through a tool such as the Asset-Based Inventory is only useful if it translates directly into a plan to conduct the search for work experiences or jobs. Appendix 3.2, the Work Experience Plan, offers a tool for organizing the search. This form is provided as a sample that can be adapted by the reader as desired. Through our extensive work in the field, we and our colleagues have found it to be very useful in framing the search for a well-matched work experience—a search that takes into account positive youth characteristics and the need for accommodation and support that will help bring out the best in the youth during the work experience.

The Work Experience Plan is a direct extension of the Asset-Based Inventory. It summarizes the career strengths and most marketable features of the youth from the inventory. It also identifies the logistics that are important to a successful work experience, such as geography, schedule, transportation, supports, and so forth. Ultimately, it helps organize the development of a work experience, including the initial identification of prospective employers that might be contacted to begin identifying how youth traits will match employer needs.

Developing a work experience plan gives transition specialists a structure and guide for what to do with all the important information gathered through the Asset-Based Inventory. In using the plan, the youth's positive attributes are always the basis for negotiating the work experience. Then, the accommodation and supports that will be necessary at the worksite can be negotiated based on what the youth has to offer. Of course, work experiences do not materialize out of thin air. We have to work to find employers who may have work experience opportunities that match youth characteristics and who are willing to consider bringing youth into their workplaces. One illustrative example is featured in the text box titled Using an Asset-Based Approach to Work Experience Development. The accompanying Asset-Based Inventory and Work Experience Plan are included in the Chapter 3 appendix forms.

## Using an Asset-Based Approach to Work Experience Development

Michael is a junior in high school. He has an older brother in college, who is majoring in computer science. His dad is a software engineer and his mom is an attorney. In a family of high achievers, expectations are high. However, according to Michael's individualized education program (IEP), he needs extended time to complete school work and tests, as well as a reader to help with comprehension. Even with these supports, his school performance is significantly below grade level.

He has never had a paid job, but he is very interested in working with computers like his father and brother. However, he has limited experience or skill, even though he has taken classes in school. If asked, he would say he has great knowledge of Microsoft Word and Excel, as well as Google's G Suite. The truth is, other than classes in school and attempts to work with G Suite in class, he is not able to manipulate software applications independently. Here are a few things his transition specialist learned when talking to Michael and his mom:

- He is able to type accurately at a slow and consistent pace.

- He is good with working with his hands.

- He learns best through step-by-step instructions, modeling, or demonstration.

- He usually needs a checklist for working through a task, and he needs help with breaking down tasks and organizing his thoughts.

- Once he understands the task after a bit of practice, he has a great memory for it.

- His dream job would be computer programmer or video game developer.

- He loves to play video games with his brother, especially Super Mario Brothers.

- He will need travel training and has never ridden public transportation independently.

In fact, the transition specialist learned a great deal more as she filled out an Asset-Based Inventory (see Appendix 3.3). This became the basis for a Work Experience Plan (see Appendix 3.4). Both documents illustrate how these two tools were used to help identify Michael's traits and circumstances that would form the background for identifying a well-matched work experience.

*(continued)*

With the help of the transition specialist, Michael found a work experience he loves at a nonprofit organization, Project Reboot, that refurbishes computers for distribution to low-income families. With initial on-site job coaching and step-by step instruction he has learned how to remove the hard drive from each donated computer. When asked what his job is, Michael says, "Computer repair!" He plans to continue his work through the summer and into his senior year. He now has a basis on which to build an adult career.

Chapters 6 and 7 will detail strategies for recruiting employers to provide work experiences, and for keeping them happy when they agree to host youth. But first, Chapters 4 and 5 discuss two key things to consider before knocking on employers' doors: if, when, and how to disclose disability to prospective employers; and how to help families support work experiences.

## SUMMARY

This chapter outlined important considerations in planning for youth work experiences and jobs. There are a host of ways of gathering information that will assist in this planning, including formal assessments, observations, and interviews. The chapter introduced principles that should guide the planning process. Among these principles is the concept of individualized and self-determined planning. Youth who are able to assume a greater responsibility for their actions related to work experience planning and behavior in the workplace will learn from the experience, will be able to use the experience to continue to build a career path and will continue to achieve greater levels of independence in their work life and careers.

This chapter also provided a tool, the Asset-Based Inventory, to organize information about youth that will help them put their best foot forward when pursuing work and help identify considerations for personal preferences and needs for support and accommodations. This tool can be used for planning and for organizing the actual work experience or job search.

One final word about planning for and facilitating work experiences: Just do it! The most important thing is for youth to experience work. Work experiences are ways of adding to the inventory of information available to the youth in making decisions about subsequent work experiences, future jobs, and—ultimately—careers. Transition specialists should avoid getting so involved or bogged down in the planning and process of planning that the next step of actually getting the work experience never happens. Planning is useful only to the extent that it leads to the goal. Get out there and do it! Not all work experiences will be ideal, but each work experience will be a chance for youth to learn more about work, how to work, and where to work.

## LEARNING LAB:
## Using the Planning Tools

1. Refer to Appendix 3.1, the Asset-Based Inventory, and answer the questions as if you were planning for yourself. After completing it, identify how closely the answers match up to the job that you now do and the working conditions associated with it. This will allow you to reflect on how well items in your own Asset-Based Inventory might have influenced your choice of jobs and choice of career.

2. Use Appendix 3.1, the Asset-Based Inventory, in gathering information about a youth you know. Chart out a work experience plan for that youth using Appendix 3.2, the sample Work Experience Plan.

## REFERENCES

Callahan, M. (2010). *Using alternatives to traditional vocational assessment: The why and how of exploration strategies such as Discovery.* Gautier, MS: Mark Gold and Associates.

Charlton, J. (2000). *Nothing about us without us: Disability oppression and empowerment.* Berkeley: University of California Press.

Field, S., Martin, J., Miller, R., Ward, M., & Wehmeyer, M. (1998). Self-determination for persons with disabilities: A position statement of the Division on Career Development and Transition, Council for Exceptional Children. *Career Development for Exceptional Individuals, 21,* 113–128.

Griffin, C., Hammis, D., & Geary, T. (2007). The job developer's handbook: Practical tactics for customized employment. Baltimore, MD: Paul H. Brookes Publishing Co.

Individuals with Disabilities Education Act of 1990 (IDEA), P.L. 101-476, 20 U.S.C. 1400 *et seq.*

Inge, K., & Graham, C. (2015). *What is Discovery?* (Research Brief). Richmond: Virginia Commonwealth University, Rehabilitation Research and Training Center (RRTC) on Employment of People with Physical Disabilities.

Luecking, D., & Luecking, R. (2015). Translating research into a seamless transition model. *Career Development and Transition for Exceptional Individuals, 38,* 4–13.

Luecking, R., Fabian, E., Contreary, K., Honeycutt, T., & Luecking, D. (2018). Vocational rehabilitation outcomes for students participating in a model transition program. *Rehabilitation Counseling Bulletin, 61,* 154–163.

Luecking, R., & Tilson, G. (2009). Planning for work experiences. In R. Luecking (Ed.), *The way to work: How to facilitate work experiences for youth in transition* (pp. 41–64). Baltimore, MD: Paul H. Brookes Publishing Co.

Morningstar, M., & Clavenna-Deane, B. (2018). *Your complete guide to transition planning and services.* Baltimore, MD: Paul H. Brookes Publishing Co.

Morningstar, M., & Pearson, M. (2015). *Transition assessments for students with significant disabilities.* Lawrence: University of Kansas, Transition Coalition.

O'Brien, J., & Mount, B. (2006). *Make a difference: A guidebook for person-centered direct support.* Toronto, Canada: Inclusion Press.

Sax, C., & Thoma, C. (2002). *Transition assessment: Wise practices for quality lives.* Baltimore, MD: Paul H. Brookes Publishing Co.

Sitlington, P., Neubert, D., Begun, W., Lombard, R., & Leconte, P. (2007). *Assess for success: A practitioner's handbook on transition assessment* (2nd ed.). Thousand Oaks, CA: Corwin Press.

Wehman, P. (2013). *Life beyond the classroom: Transition strategies for young people with disabilities* (5th ed.). Baltimore, MD: Paul H. Brookes Publishing Co.

Wehmeyer, M., & Webb, K. (2012). *Handbook of transition education for youth with disabilities.* New York, NY: Routledge, Taylor and Francis.

# Chapter 3 Appendices

- Appendix 3.1: Asset-Based Inventory
- Appendix 3.2: Work Experience Plan
- Appendix 3.3: Completed Asset-Based Inventory for Michael
- Appendix 3.4: Completed Work Experience Plan for Michael

# Asset-Based Inventory

Youth: _____  Transition Specialist: _____  Date: _____

Interviewee: _____  Relationship to Youth: _____

| What do you like? | |
|---|---|
| **Interests and Preferences**<br><br>*This section allows you to get to know and learn about what motivates the youth. You learn about the youth's dreams and aspirations, about what holds his or her interest, and how he or she responds to different situations.* | *Why do you (does the youth) want to work?* |
| | *What is your (the youth's) dream job?* |
| | *What are some activities you (the youth) enjoy (e.g., sports, hobbies, passions)? What do you (does the youth do) in your (his or her) free time?* |
| | *Who do you (does the youth) spend time with and what do you (the youth) do together?* |
| | *In what environmental conditions do you (does the youth) do best (e.g., indoors/outdoors, noisy/quiet, many people/few people, slow/fast pace, time of day, routine tasks/variety)?* |
| | *How do you (does the youth) best learn a new task (e.g., model/ demonstrate, step-by-step, written check list)?* |

Notes:

*(continued)*

| What have you done? | |
|---|---|
| **Life and Work Experiences**<br><br>*This section allows you to learn about social activities and experiences the youth has enjoyed or disliked and through which has learned transferrable skills that can be used at a well-matched work experience.* | *Are you (is the youth) currently employed and earning wages? If so, where? What accommodations are in place, if any?* |
| | *Have you (the youth) had any previous paid or unpaid work experiences? What tasks did you (the youth) perform in these experiences? What accommodations were needed?* |
| | *What types of household chores are completed regularly (both assigned and voluntary)?* |
| | *In what community or social activities do you (does the youth) participate (e.g., sports, clubs, church, interest organizations)?* |
| Notes: | |

*(continued)*

| What can you do? | | |
|---|---|---|
| **Skills, Knowledge, and Abilities**<br><br>*This section allows you to learn about the youth's natural and current skills. You will learn about the things he or she is naturally good at, which will give you a baseline of the youth's skills and abilities for a starting point when negotiating tasks and duties.* | *What are some of your (the youth's) talents, things you (the youth) do well?* | |
| | **Describe your (the youth's) abilities and academic skills:** | |
| | Dexterity | |
| | Lifting | |
| | Standing | |
| | Math | |
| | Money | |
| | Reading | |
| | Writing | |
| | Computers (data entry, software programs, formatting, social media) | |
| | Basic Office Skills (ability to file, alphabetical, numeric indexing, scanning) | |
| | Customer Service and Social Skills | |
| | Communication/Speech | |
| | Other? | |
| | *Have you (the youth) been involved in any specific vocational training? If so, where and when?* | |

*(continued)*

| What don't you like? | |
|---|---|
| **Dislikes and Preferences**<br><br>*This section allows you to learn about situations that would make a work experience miserable for the youth. Through learning about dislikes, you will learn the youth's true preferences.* | *Are there particular situations you recommend we avoid when searching for work experiences and job opportunities?* |
| | *What is a job or job setting that you do (the youth does) NOT want to do?* |
| | *Are there particular activities that the youth is known to dislike?* |
| Notes: | |

*(continued)*

| What help do you need to do well? | |
|---|---|
| **Accommodations and Support Needs**<br><br>*This section will allow you to learn and understand what the youth should have in place to be successful on the job. Learning if the youth needs a distraction-free work space or assistive technology will paint a picture of the day-to-day work environment.* | *What accommodations or supports are currently being provided in school or other settings?* |
| | *What accommodations might be needed in the workplace (e.g., physical accessibility, assistive technology, special schedule, job coaching)?* |
| | *What supports might need to be maintained beyond the initial placement?* |
| | *What do I need to know about you (the youth) so I can help you (the youth) identify necessary supports once in the workplace?* |
| Notes: | |

*(continued)*

| How do you get around? | |
|---|---|
| **Transportation Resources**<br><br><br><br>*This section will allow you to learn about the transportation resources that are in place for the youth and what is needed.* | *How do you (does the youth) get to places you want (he or she wants) to go (e.g., bus, ride from a relative or neighbor, car service)?* |
| | *Do you (does the youth) have a bus pass, mobility sharing pass, or access to other public transportation?* |
| | *Have you (has the youth) had travel training? Is it necessary? Available?* |
| | *Does the school or employment agency provide transportation to work experience locations?* |
| | *What needs to be considered in planning how to get to work (e.g., family schedules, accessibility, proximity to home)?* |
| Notes: | |

*(continued)*

| Who helps and encourages you at home and at school? | |
|---|---|
| **Other Available Supports**<br><br>*This section will allow you to learn about other people who can provide support, encouragement, and resources for the youth as they look for and succeed in their work experience.* | *Are there people who support and encourage you (the youth)? How do they provide support and encouragement?*<br><br>❐ Family member: _____<br>_____<br>_____<br><br>❐ Friend: _____<br>_____<br>_____<br><br>❐ Neighbor: _____<br>_____<br>_____<br><br>❐ Teacher: _____<br>_____<br>_____<br><br>❐ Job Coach: _____<br>_____<br>_____<br><br>❐ Social Service Agency or personnel: _____<br>_____<br>_____<br><br>❐ Other: _____<br>_____<br>_____ |
| Notes: | |

*(continued)*

| | **What else should we know?** |
|---|---|
| | *Do you (does the youth) have any geographical preferences (e.g., certain areas of the community, close to home)?* |
| | *Do you (does the youth) have a preference or need to work certain days or hours? An ideal work schedule?*<br><br>❒ Part time ❒ Full time ❒ Mornings ❒ Afternoons ❒ Evenings<br>❒ Ideal work schedule: _____<br><br>❒ Days not available: _____ ❒ Hours not available: _____ |
| **Searching for the Work Experience and Other General Observations** | *Do you (does the youth) have any ideas about the employers or types of employers we should talk to?* |
| *This section provides any additional information about logistical preferences and general observations that may be helpful in planning and pursing a work experience.* | *How would you describe your (the youth's) temperament (e.g., easy going, easily frustrated, easily distracted)?* |
| | *Can you describe any habits, routines or idiosyncrasies you have (the youth has) that may stand out to others?* |
| | *Do you (does the youth) have any ideas about employers or types of employers we should talk to? Contacts in your (the youth's) network who may be open to creating a work experience?* |
| | *Do you (does the youth) know people who might suggest or have contacts with particular employers or types of employers?* |

*(continued)*

| Where should we look? | |
|---|---|
| **Possibilities and Ideas**<br><br><br>*This section will allow you to brainstorm and record your thoughts on work possibilities or any matter related to planning for the work experience.* | *Employer leads?* |
| | *Things to explore?* |
| | *Action steps?* |
| Notes: | |

# Work Experience Plan

| Date: ___ _____Initial _____Subsequent | Youth: |
|---|---|
| Staff: | Phone: |

Information on file: ❏ Asset-Based Inventory ❏ Résumé ❏ Student Information Form
❏ Authorization/General Release Form ❏ Photo/Media Release ❏ State Photo ID

| **Summary of Asset-Based Inventory** | |
|---|---|
| Interests and Preferences: | Dislikes, Issues, or Concerns: |

Position(s) desired:

Geographical location preferred:

Environmental preferences:

Schedule preferred: Part time/Full time

❏ Morning ❏ Afternoon ❏ Evening ❏ Hours not available: _____
❏ Ideal Shift: _____

Transportation resources:

Potential accommodations needed:

Potential supports or resources (e.g., benefits management, financial education):

Additional training or assessment needed/provided:

*(continued)*

| To do: | |
|---|---|
| Staff | Youth |
| | |
| | |
| | |

| Employers to Contact | Date Contacted | Outcome |
|---|---|---|
| 1. | | |
| 2. | | |
| 3. | | |
| 4. | | |
| 5. | | |

| Placement Information | | | |
|---|---|---|---|
| Employer | Start Date | Position/Duties | Shift/Schedule |
| | | | |

# Asset-Based Inventory

Youth: _Michael Young_  Transition Specialist: _Nadia Smith_  Date: _9/25_

Interviewee: _Michael and mother_  Relationship to Youth: _____

| What do you like? | |
|---|---|
| **Interests and Preferences**<br><br>*This section allows you to get to know and learn about what motivates the youth. You learn about the youth's dreams and aspirations, about what holds his or her interest, and how he or she responds to different situations.* | *Why do you (does the youth) want to work?*<br><br>Mom said I have to<br>Get money<br>Gain some experience |
| | *What is your (the youth's) dream job?*<br><br>Anything with computers<br>Create video games |
| | *What are some activities you (the youth) enjoy (e.g., sports, hobbies, passions)? What do you (does the youth do) in your (his or her) free time?*<br><br>Playing video games, watching videos on YouTube (cartoons), watching The Wheel of Fortune |
| | *Who do you (does the youth) spend time with and what do you (the youth) do together?*<br><br>Family, video games (Super Mario Brothers) with my brother, church group |
| | *In what environmental conditions do you (does the youth) do best (e.g., indoors/outdoors, noisy/quiet, many people/few people, slow/fast pace, time of day, routine tasks/variety)?*<br><br>Indoors, quiet area to work so I can focus and not be distracted, few people—no strangers, slow to medium pace; I do better with routine tasks—but with a little variety—concrete tasks |
| | *How do you (does the youth) best learn a new task (e.g., model/ demonstrate, step-by-step, written check list)?*<br><br>Step-by-step, hands on; it helps if someone writes the instructions or a checklist for me, breaks it down in small pieces |

Notes:

*(continued)*

| What have you done? | |
|---|---|
| **Life and Work Experiences**<br><br>*This section allows you to learn about social activities and experiences the youth has enjoyed or disliked and through which has learned transferrable skills that can be used at a well-matched work experience.* | *Are you (is the youth) currently employed and earning wages? If so, where? What accommodations are in place, if any?*<br><br>No, I've never had a paid job |
| | *Have you (the youth) had any previous paid or unpaid work experiences? What tasks did you (the youth) perform in these experiences? What accommodations were needed?*<br><br>Service learning experience at Project Reboot—learned step by step how to remove the hard drive and was eventually able to remove the hard drives independently after a fair amount of job coaching; sorted power cords and computer parts; used checklist to help me remember what to do; had a job coach when I started |
| | *What types of household chores are completed regularly (both assigned and voluntary)?*<br><br>Clean my room; take out the trash; set the table |
| | *In what community or social activities do you (does the youth) participate (e.g., sports, clubs, church, interest organizations)?*<br><br>Church on Sunday<br>I don't belong to any groups |
| Notes: | |

*(continued)*

| | What can you do? |
|---|---|
| | **What are some of your (the youth's) talents, things you (the youth) do well?** <br> *Good with numbers; good at organizing things in spreadsheets; very good with dates* |

| | **Describe your (the youth's) abilities and academic skills:** | |
|---|---|---|
| **Skills, Knowledge, and Abilities** <br><br> *This section allows you to learn about the youth's natural and current skills. You will learn about the things he or she is naturally good at, which will give you a baseline of the youth's skills and abilities for a starting point when negotiating tasks and duties.* | Dexterity | |
| | Lifting | *Can lift 20 lbs. if necessary* |
| | Standing | *Okay* |
| | Math | *Good at basic math and remembering numbers and dates* |
| | Money | *I know if I have the correct change; I have never worked as a cashier before; would not be comfortable being a cashier* |
| | Reading | *Basic reading* |
| | Writing | *Can write but prefer to type—I write and type very slowly* |
| | Computers (data entry, software programs, formatting, social media) | *No social media; can type in an existing Excel spreadsheet; cannot do formulas; used Google Sheets at school; can type at a slow pace—usually accurate; can use Word; learned Power Point in school but I have never done a presentation* |
| | Basic Office Skills (ability to file, alphabetical, numeric indexing, scanning) | *Can file with a letter strip and do numeric filing; never scanned before; I don't like talking on the phone* |
| | Customer Service and Social Skills | *I prefer not to do customer service* |
| | Communication/Speech | *Need to speak slowly; can be initially hard to understand* |
| | Other? | |
| | **Have you (the youth) been involved in any specific vocational training? If so, where and when?** <br> *No* | |

*(continued)*

| What don't you like? | |
|---|---|
| **Dislikes and Preferences**<br><br>*This section allows you to learn about situations that would make a work experience miserable for the youth. Through learning about dislikes, you will learn the youth's true preferences.* | *Are there particular situations you recommend we avoid when searching for work experiences and job opportunities?*<br><br>I don't like crowds or talking to strangers<br>I don't know if there is anything else |
| | *What is a job or job setting that you do (the youth does) NOT want to do?*<br><br>No cleaning<br>No retail<br>No animals |
| | *Are there particular activities that the youth is known to dislike?*<br><br>I don't like cleaning or talking to strangers |

Notes:

*(continued)*

| What help do you need to do well? | |
|---|---|
| **Accommodations and Support Needs**<br><br>*This section will allow you to learn and understand what the youth should have in place to be successful on the job. Learning if the youth needs a distraction-free work space or assistive technology will paint a picture of the day-to-day work environment.* | *What accommodations or supports are currently being provided in school or other settings?*<br><br>*I get written instructions and modeling or step-by-step instruction* |
| | *What accommodations might be needed in the workplace (e.g., physical accessibility, assistive technology, special schedule, job coaching)?*<br><br>*Job coach; checklist; written instructions* |
| | *What supports might need to be maintained beyond the initial placement?*<br><br>*Initial on-site job coach; check ins; checklist* |
| | *What do I need to know about you (the youth) so I can help you (the youth) identify necessary supports once in the workplace?*<br><br>*I don't know* |
| Notes: | |

*(continued)*

| How do you get around? | |
|---|---|
| **Transportation Resources**<br><br><br><br>*This section will allow you to learn about the transportation resources that are in place for the youth and what is needed.* | *How do you (does the youth) get to places you want (he or she wants) to go (e.g., bus, ride from a relative or neighbor, car service)?*<br><br>Mom; sometimes Dad |
| | *Do you (does the youth) have a bus pass, mobility sharing pass, or access to other public transportation?*<br><br>No |
| | *Have you (has the youth) had travel training? Is it necessary? Available?*<br><br>No. I have never been on a bus or train before; I think I can learn if someone helps me |
| | *Does the school or employment agency provide transportation to work experience locations?*<br><br>I think school can take me if I go during school, but we need to ask my teacher |
| | *What needs to be considered in planning how to get to work (e.g., family schedules, accessibility, proximity to home)?*<br><br>No work on Sunday; need to check with Mom for her schedule |
| Notes: | |

*(continued)*

| | |
|---|---|
| **Who helps and encourages you at home and at school?** | |
| **Other Available Supports**<br><br>*This section will allow you to learn about other people who can provide support, encouragement, and resources for the youth as they look for and succeed in their work experience.* | *Are there people who support and encourage you (the youth)? How do they provide support and encouragement?*<br><br>☑ Family member: *Mom helps me and thinks I can do anything; Dad drives me sometimes*<br><br>☐ Friend: _____<br><br>☐ Neighbor: _____<br><br>☑ Teacher: *Ms. Jones helped me get my service learning experience; she is nice*<br><br>☐ Job Coach: _____<br><br>☑ Social Service Agency or personnel: *VR counselor*<br><br>☐ Other: _____ |
| Notes: | |

*(continued)*

| | **What else should we know?** |
|---|---|
| **Searching for the Work Experience and Other General Observations**<br><br>*This section provides any additional information about logistical preferences and general observations that may be helpful in planning and pursing a work experience.* | *Do you (does the youth) have any geographical preferences (e.g., certain areas of the community, close to home)?*<br><br>*Close to home* |
| | *Do you (does the youth) have a preference or need to work certain days or hours? An ideal work schedule?*<br><br>☑ Part time   ☐ Full time   ☐ Mornings   ☑ Afternoons   ☐ Evenings<br>☐ Ideal work schedule: _____<br><br>☑ Days not available: *Sunday*     ☑ Hours not available: *Not after 7pm* |
| | *Do you (does the youth) have any ideas about the employers or types of employers we should talk to?*<br><br>*Computer company; gaming company; office setting; data entry* |
| | *How would you describe your (the youth's) temperament (e.g., easy going, easily frustrated, easily distracted)?*<br><br>*Easy going; distracted when there are a lot of people around; frustrated when I can't figure something out* |
| | *Can you describe any habits, routines or idiosyncrasies you have (the youth has) that may stand out to others?*<br><br>*None* |
| | *Do you (does the youth) have any ideas about employers or types of employers we should talk to? Contacts in your (the youth's) network who may be open to creating a work experience?*<br><br>*No* |
| | *Do you (does the youth) know people who might suggest or have contacts with particular employers or types of employers?*<br><br>*Teacher (Ms. Jones)* |

*(continued)*

| Where should we look? |
|---|

| | **Employer leads?**<br><br>*Computer Fix (need to learn)*<br>*Office work—data entry; numeric filing*<br>*Sort computer parts*<br>*Stock video games* |
|---|---|
| **Possibilities and Ideas**<br><br><br>*This section will allow you to brainstorm and record your thoughts on work possibilities or any matter related to planning for the work experience.* | **Things to explore?**<br><br>*Office job—data entry; gaming company; something working with numbers; sorting* |
| | **Action steps?**<br><br>*Transition teacher: contact Computer Fix and similar companies for an informational interview; career exploration at gaming company* |

| Notes: |
|---|
| |

# Work Experience Plan

| | |
|---|---|
| Date: _10/3_ _____Initial _____Subsequent | Youth: *Michael Young* |
| Staff: *Nadia Smith* | Phone: *240-555-1234* |

Information on file:  ☑ Asset-Based Inventory  ☐ Résumé  ☐ Student Information Form
☑ Authorization/General Release Form  ☑ Photo/Media Release  ☐ State Photo ID

## Summary of Asset-Based Inventory

| Interests and Preferences: | Dislikes, Issues, or Concerns: |
|---|---|
| • *Video games* <br> • *Watching videos on YouTube* <br> • *Office setting—data entry* <br> • *Cartoons* | • *Cleaning* <br> • *Animals* <br> • *Using the phone* <br> • *Crowds, customer service* |

Position(s) desired: *Working with computers; doing data entry; maybe a stock position; something concrete and routine; working at a gaming company*

Geographical location preferred: *Close to home*

Environmental preferences: *Small work environment with few people; co-workers are okay, but not customers*

Schedule preferred: *Part time*/Full time

☐ Morning  ☑ Afternoon  ☑ Evening  ☑ Hours not available: _*No Sundays; not after 7 p.m.*_
☑ Ideal Shift:  _*3:30 p.m.–7 p.m.*_

Transportation resources: *Mom can help to transport; need travel training*

Potential accommodations needed: *On-site job coaching and follow along; checklist; written instruction; customized position*

Potential supports or resources (e.g., benefits management, financial education):
*N/A*

Additional training or assessment needed/provided: *Travel training*

*(continued)*

| To do: | |
|---|---|
| Staff | Youth |
| Set up informational interview with gaming company, Computer Fix, Geek Squad, and Project Reboot | Send three places of interest to the transition teacher—name, address, and phone number |
| Research office positions near Michael's home | |
| Research gaming companies like Bethesda Softworks or BreakAway Games | |

| Employers to Contact | Date Contacted | Outcome |
|---|---|---|
| 1. Geek Squad | | |
| 2. Bethesda Softworks | | |
| 3. Computer Fix | | |
| 4. Project Reboot | | |
| 5. | | |

| Placement Information | | | |
|---|---|---|---|
| Employer | Start Date | Position/Duties | Shift/Schedule |
| | | | |

# Navigating Work Experience and Disability Disclosure

**By completing this chapter, the reader will**

- Understand considerations for when youth might or might not disclose disability
- Determine what youth might disclose about disability and accommodations
- Learn how to help youth disclose disability and need for accommodations
- Complete a Learning Lab on disability disclosure

*"Nothing about us without us!"*
James I. Charlton, disability advocate and author

*"No one knows more about how my disability affects me than me."*
Kirsten Davidson, self-advocate

Joy is a 17-year-old student who is planning her first work experience with the help of a transition specialist. She is a very fast worker, and has the ability to deeply focus on the task at hand. Joy experiences difficulty in social interactions because she is literal in her communications. She doesn't understand jokes or subtle wordplay, as when someone uses figures of speech such as "stop horsing around" or "fit as a fiddle." She also gets very upset when she is in a noisy area. These traits may make it difficult for Joy to succeed in the workplace, if accommodations are not made.

Joy worked with her transition specialist to identify ways to present her skills and her accommodation needs to potential employers. She agreed to disclose that she has autism spectrum disorder by first presenting what she was very good at—speedy computer work. Then she would explain about how literal communication helped her, how supervisors and coworkers would need to learn this, and how a quiet work area would be necessary. For Joy, disclosing manifestations of her disability did not cost her a shot at a work experience she wanted. Rather, it helped the employer understand that accommodating the disability could help the company gain a productive worker. After a 2-month work internship at the company, she was hired as a regular part-time employee while she finished school.

Another student, David, was interested in becoming an electrician; he worked with his transition specialist to find a work experience with a company that installs electric charging stations. He was certain that the employer and his coworkers would think he was "dumb" and make fun of him if he disclosed his learning disability. He chose not to disclose it. This nearly turned out to be an unfortunate decision because he often makes mistakes when given verbal instructions. After several days with this company, the employer approached David and said if he kept making these mistakes he would have to ask him to leave. It was at this point that David asked his transition specialist to help him explain to the employer his need for written prompts as an accommodation. A process for this was negotiated and David's performance dramatically improved. For David, not disclosing his disability could have been an opportunity lost.

Doreen put together a resume detailing her educational accomplishments, her extracurricular activities in high school, and her involvement in recreation programs for people who are blind or visually impaired. In effect, she was disclosing her disability on the resume. Despite her high grade-point average and obvious talents, she never received a response from employers to whom she sent her resume. There is no way of knowing if this lack of response is due to her disability. However, the fact is she is still looking for that first job.

Marvin is in a special education class for youth with intellectual disabilities. He cannot read or perform basic math functions, but he can recognize numbers. He has basic communication skills and can follow directions with occasional prompts. His transition specialist worked with him and his parents to complete an asset-based profile which identified one thing he was really good at: organizing and sorting items. His room at home was as neat as a pin! Since he has no personal network to identify work opportunities, Marvin agreed to have his transition specialist represent him to prospective employers. Also, since he needed several job accommodations, including coaching to learn new work tasks, he agreed that his transition specialist could explain to potential employers about his disabilities and his need for initial coaching at the workplace. After several interviews where he and his transition specialist met with employers, he was hired by a large department store to work in the shoe area where he was tasked with stocking and organizing shoes by sizes and types in the storage area. Disclosing his disability was necessary in Marvin's case because of his need for representation in negotiating with employers and his need for on-site coaching. Otherwise, he would likely never become employed.

The decision to disclose a disability is not always an easy one, but it is always a very personal one. It is also one that has many ramifications—some useful, others problematic. It could mean succeeding in a workplace where accommodations and supports can be provided, as in Joy's and Marvin's cases, or failing because an effective accommodation for the disability was not made, as was initially the case for David. Some youth, like Marvin, will require help disclosing their disability so that the necessary accommodations and supports are provided for their workplace success. Disclosure may be the reason for not getting a job, as in Doreen's case. The latter is subtle discrimination, but it happens—and there is usually no way to prove it.

Youth, therefore, have many important questions to consider: Disclose or not? When? To whom? By whom? How? Getting the answers to these questions is an important prerequisite to youth pursuing work experiences and for transition specialists who will be helping them. This chapter provides considerations for deciding how best to answer each of these questions.

## DECIDING WHETHER TO DISCLOSE

For youth with visible disabilities, the decision to disclose is much easier. They most often will not need to disclose because it is clear that they have a disability. However, they will have to decide how and in what context to discuss with prospective and current employers and coworkers how their disabilities affect their work, which is discussed later in the chapter. For youth with learning, intellectual, emotional, or certain health-related disabilities, the decision becomes more complicated because their disabilities are not always readily apparent. These youth may understandably be reluctant to disclose information about the presence or the nature of their disability for fear of discrimination or negative perceptions.

Chapter 3 discusses ways to ensure that youth participate in and lead the planning for their work experiences. The concepts of self-determination and person-centered planning are equally paramount in decisions about disability disclosure as they are in planning for work experiences. Indeed, disclosure decisions are an important part of work experience planning. Like any other facet of work experience planning, youth need to lead the decision making. The choice about when and how to disclose personal information about a disability, as well as any need for accommodation and support, should always be made by the youth.

The youth's decision to disclose may change with circumstance. Disclosure may be necessary to ensure adequate accommodation in one situation, such as to a supervisor who can approve a flexible schedule. In another case, it may not be a good idea to disclose a disability to coworkers who do not need to know about it. Whatever the circumstance, the youth needs to make informed decisions about disclosure.

Guidance is often necessary to help youth decide whether to disclose a disability, as well as in their management of the decision. David's situation is a good example. He initially decided not to disclose his disability. It almost cost him the work experience. However, when his work performance became problematic, he asked the transition specialist to help him. Together they explained to the employer that he has a learning disability that makes processing oral instructions difficult. With explanations and help organizing David's daily work tasks through brief written instructions, the employer was willing to continue the work experience. He was ultimately pleased with the arrangement and David's performance. But throughout the process it was always David's choice about whether to disclose and how to do it.

Many factors can influence the ultimate decision of whether disclosure is the best course of action in a given circumstance. As the previous examples illustrate, youth will often need guidance in making sound judgments regarding disclosure.

Ultimately, youth who can articulate their needs and goals, and who have been coached on the selective sharing of personal information, enjoy greater control over disclosure decisions. To make these decisions, youth and their transition specialists need to understand the advantages and disadvantages of disclosing personal information about a disability.

## Advantages of Disclosure

Disability disclosure can create opportunities that may not otherwise be available without accommodations to minimize barriers to workplace participation. Proper accommodation and workplace support can make the difference between succeeding in the workplace and failing miserably. The following are advantages to disclosing information about a disability.

- Disclosure ensures that youth get the help they need to perform well in the workplace. In fact, it is often necessary. For example, Marvin needed a transition specialist to coach him in learning tasks in every new work experience. He gave his transition specialist permission to tell prospective employers about this accommodation so that the transition specialist could negotiate with employers about it.

- Disclosure gives youth the opportunity to fully present their abilities under conditions of effective accommodation. For example, when interviewing for her job, Joy detailed her fast and accurate abilities in computer data entry. She asserted her likelihood for high productivity and quality of work. To do so, she articulated her need, because of her disability, for direct and nonambiguous directions from her boss, literal communications with her coworkers, and a quiet place to concentrate on her work. A few easy accommodations helped her have a very successful internship experience.

- Disclosure provides the groundwork for advocating for additional accommodations and supports when task assignments change or when new coworkers or supervisors interact with the youth. For example, Caitlin's new boss wondered why she got an extra break in the afternoon, but no one else did. Caitlin was able to explain that stamina was often an issue because of her neurological condition. An extra break enabled her to complete her assignments in the same time frame as the other staff members.

- Disclosure improves the youth's ability to advocate for him- or herself and to improve his or her self-image, as in Joy's internship experience.

- Disclosure can create a comfortable work environment in which the youth does not have to worry about keeping the disability a secret. For example, if a student in a work experience has epilepsy, he or she may want supervisors and coworkers to know how to respond in the event that of a seizure.

- Disclosure makes it possible to receive reasonable accommodations under the Americans with Disabilities Act (ADA) (PL 101-336). If an employer hires someone who is qualified to perform the essential functions of the job, the employer must provide reasonable accommodations, but only if the employer is aware of a disability. For example, because D'onte has regularly scheduled sessions with a counselor because of a mental health disability, he needs to flex his work schedule one day a week. He is really competent in his job at the electronics store and he can catch up with his work after he returns from his counseling session. His boss had no problem granting D'onte's request for flexing his schedule accordingly.

It is useful to note that employment protections under the ADA only apply to paid work as discussed in more detail in Chapter 2. With or without legal protections, the decision to disclose disability still rests with the youth. In other unpaid work experience situations, and even most paid work experiences, the decision to disclose is based more on practical considerations than on legal ones, as the several examples provided in this chapter and the sample disclosure scripts illustrate. Employers are almost always willing to make accommodations when shown how accommodations will benefit the youth's participation and performance in the workplace and when given help to implement them.

## Disadvantages to Disclosure

For various reasons, youth may decide that disclosure is not necessary or that it will create discomfort, stigma, or rejection. The following are some potential disadvantages to disclosing a disability.

- Disclosure can result in discrimination in consideration for a work experience or a job. For example, many youth with emotional disabilities may feel stigmatized by the label and choose not to tell anyone outside of school, especially employers who, because of misperceptions, might be reluctant to hire them if the employers knew about the disability.

- Disclosure can result in stereotyping or inaccurate perceptions of the youth's ability. For example, Taylor knows that his learning disability is accommodated well in school, but he doesn't want people to think he is "stupid," as he had occasionally been called as a child. Consequently, he decided not to share with his work experience supervisor or his coworkers that he has received special education services.

- Disclosure can lead to disparate treatment—either overly solicitous attention or exclusion. In either case, the youth is being treated differently than others. For example, Marcella told a coworker that she has to take insulin shots every day for her diabetes. After that, her supervisor was reluctant to give her anything to do because he was afraid she would go into insulin shock. In another case, Michael feared that if any of his coworkers knew about his hospitalizations, he would never be accepted by them or included in any of their social activities.

- Disclosure can be difficult or embarrassing for the youth. For example, Nicholas takes antiseizure medication but has not had a seizure for more than a year. Still, he is very sensitive about the fact that he has had seizures and has opted to not tell anyone at his worksite.

- Disclosure can lead to ill treatment or suspicion from coworkers. For example, Gregory was teased by coworkers at his last part-time job when one of them discovered that Gregory had special education services for a reading disability. He is determined to keep his disability a secret from people at his next job.

**Table 4.1.**   Deciding whether to disclose disability

| It helps to disclose disability when it | It may not be a good idea to disclose disability when it |
| --- | --- |
| Is necessary in order to receive legally available accommodations | Can cause discrimination to occur |
| Enables supports for better workplace performance | Leads to stereotyped reactions or misperceptions about the youth's ability |
| Allows additional accommodations when job duties or supervisors change | Results in the youth being treated differently or unfairly |
| Improves self-advocacy skills | Makes the youth feel embarrassment or sensitivity |
| Promotes comfortable interactions with coworkers when they understand disability | Is possible that coworkers resent accommodations as special treatment |

Table 4.1 summarizes considerations for helping youth to decide when to disclose personal information about their disability. It is important to reiterate that the decision to disclose is ultimately and appropriately up to the youth; however, a transition specialist may need to prepare the youth not only to decide whether to disclose the disability, but also when, how, and to whom. The youth may need preparation, perhaps through self-advocacy and self-determination training, as well as through opportunities to practice disclosure. The purpose of these activities is to increase comfort with and knowledge of the youth's disability. An excellent and timeless resource for helping youth navigate the disclosure decision process is the *411 on Disability Disclosure: A Workbook for Youth with Disabilities* produced by the National Collaborative on Workforce and Disability for Youth (NCWD/Youth; 2005). It contains several lessons and worksheets that help youth learn about disability disclosure and making decisions about it. Especially useful is a self-examination questionnaire for youth as a prelude to deciding whether to disclose. The workbook can be accessed on the NCWD/ Youth web site at http://www.ncwd-youth.info/wp-content/uploads/2016/10/411 _Disability_Disclosure_complete.pdf

## WHEN TO DISCLOSE

There are several possible junctures at which youth may have an opportunity to disclose their disabilities, including

- During the initial contact with an employer, such as in a request for an interview or the scheduling of an interview

- During the interview itself

- After the interview or acceptance into a work experience

- Any time after the work experience begins

Alternatively, the youth may decide to never disclose. No single right time or way to disclose disability exists, but there are important contexts to consider. When a youth has decided that disclosing a disability is necessary, helpful, or simply an empowering way to take proactive control of his or her life, certain settings and circumstances are more appropriate than others for disclosure.

When youth are pursuing unpaid work experiences, such as job shadowing, work sampling, or unpaid internships, the issue of disclosure is different than when they are seeking a paid job. For example, less is at stake in a volunteer situation because there are theoretically fewer expectations on the part of the employer for productivity. Also, a company may have fewer legal considerations in volunteer situations as opposed to when it is considering compensating the youth. Nevertheless, accommodation needs will often necessitate disclosure at various times in the work experience. The need for wheelchair access, for example, may have to be discussed on the telephone with a company prior to a volunteer experience for a particular youth. A youth who is deaf may require an interpreter, in which case disclosure will be not only useful but necessary. A different student may require a transition specialist to accompany him or her to the worksite; disclosure about such a need may best be done during the initial contact with the company.

Alternatively, the youth may not want anyone at the worksite to know about the disability—or at least certain aspects of it. Youth may choose not to disclose at any juncture of the experience, whether it is while applying for it, at the first contact with the company, at the interview, or after the experience begins. Youth, however, can change their minds at any of these junctures for reasons both personal and practical. For example, they may become comfortable with certain supervisors or coworkers and feel safe disclosing their disabilities. Or, youth may find that asking for an accommodation, such as written rather than verbal instructions, is necessary to keep up with assignments, as was the case with David at the beginning of this chapter. The choice to disclose is personal, but it is helpful to have someone available to counsel the youth on these decisions.

If a youth is applying for a paid job, the stakes may be a little higher—both for the youth, who benefits from the compensation, and for the employer, who has job performance expectations. For paid employment experiences, the decision about when to disclose varies with the phase of the job search or employment experience. When looking for a job, the considerations are different than when the youth has already started working. Ultimately, it is important to remember that accommodations in the workplace are only provided when a worker discloses his or her disability and requests job accommodations from the employer. Table 4.2 provides contexts and examples about when youth may want to disclose their disabilities.

## HOW AND WHAT TO DISCLOSE

Building self-awareness is critical. Each youth who is contemplating a work experience should be fully prepared to identify strengths, skills, and accommodation requirements. Whether the student decides to disclose a disability, a discussion of relevant accommodations or alternative methods for completing work can take place. Employers are already arranging accommodations such as job restructuring, job sharing, and alternative methods of providing instruction and training to workers without disabilities. If such accommodations facilitate employee productivity, they are usually readily made. Thus, it is especially useful to present the need for accommodation in such a way that the company sees the benefit far more readily than they see the disability. Encourage youth to consider the following points when deciding what personal disability information to disclose and how to disclose it.

**Table 4.2.**   When to disclose a disability

| Circumstance | Example |
| --- | --- |
| In a third-party phone call or reference | Transition specialists may need to make direct connections with local employers on behalf of youth. Youth should be counseled to decide whether they want the transition specialist to disclose the disability and, if so, how to represent it. |
| In a letter of application or résumé | Some individuals choose to disclose their disability in their résumé or letter of application. Having a disability may be viewed as a positive trait by some companies with disability recruitment programs. However, counseling a youth against this practice generally is recommended, as it may cause an employer to decide not to interview the youth. |
| Preinterview | Disclosure prior to the interview is encouraged only when an accommodation is needed for the actual interview (e.g., wheelchair accessibility, a sign language interpreter, a job coach to accompany the youth). |
| At the interview | A youth may or may not decide to disclose his or her disability during an interview. If the disability is visible, the youth may want to discuss the disability in the context of how it will not be a barrier to doing a good job, especially with proper accommodations. If the disability is not apparent, the youth will need to decide whether to disclose based on comfort level and confidence in his or her ability to be articulate about it and potential accommodations. |
| After the work experience or job offer | Some youth will choose to disclose their disability after they have been offered the position. They want to be selected for their skills and positive attributes and worry that disclosure prior to selection may influence an interviewer's decision. Once hired, however, they may need accommodations to do essential functions of the job, so disclosure is necessary. Also, if the job requires medical or drug testing and the youth is taking medication that will show up in a screening, it will be an important time to disclose this to the employer. |
| During the course of employment | Sometimes youth will not recognize that aspects of their disability will negatively affect job performance without accommodations. This is especially true of youth with little job experience. It is always better to ask for an accommodation before job performance is questioned. However, sometimes after discussion with the employer, and maybe a transition specialist, an accommodation might be jointly identified that will improve the youth's ability to meet employers' performance requirements. |
| Never | If youth are able to perform job tasks to the satisfaction of the employer without accommodations or supports, it is not necessary to disclose disability. |

From National Collaborative on Workforce and Disability for Youth. (2005). *The 411 on disability disclosure workbook*. Washington, DC: Institute for Educational Leadership; adapted by permission.

- Prepare ahead of time. Youth will need to understand and be comfortable with their disabilities and accommodation needs so that they are prepared to discuss how these needs translate into what companies need to do to make it work for all involved.

- Be honest, be straightforward, and give factual information to make it easy for employers or coworkers to understand what the disability means for the youth and what it means for interactions with the youth.

- Relate comments to the immediate situation, such as how the youth's disability will affect (or not affect) the tasks assigned to the youth—not what it means in school or at home.

- Decide if it is necessary to name the disability or just identify accommodations. For example, the youth can say either, "My learning disability makes it hard for me to understand written directions" or "I learn better when I hear the directions than when someone writes them."

Often, it is useful to help youth develop a script they can practice with friends, teachers, relatives, or mentors. Most people find it easier to talk about the impact of a disability and how it will relate to a particular situation if they can practice it with people they know and trust. To prepare a disclosure script, youth can write or orally list positive attributes or strengths, identify challenges that they might expect at work or have experienced in the past at work, identify accommodations that have worked in the past and why, and consider how disclosing a disability can help the business or coworkers. The script should begin and end with positive points about the youth or the requested accommodation. That way the need for accommodation is always presented in a way that minimizes the perceived barriers presented by the disability and that highlights the youth's assets. A disclosure script should also be brief and avoid using technical terms that might be intimidating or confusing, as illustrated in the textbox titled Examples of Disclosure Scripts. The textbox titled Practice Disclosure Script Activity presents a five-step guide for helping youth prepare and practice a disability disclosure script.

---

### Examples of Disclosure Scripts

- "I'm really looking forward to this interview. I've heard so much about your company. I am checking to make sure the interview room can accommodate my wheelchair. That way I can more comfortably present my qualifications for this work experience."

- "I like to stay busy, but I learn new jobs slowly. If my teacher comes with me to the job the first few times, I can learn what I need to do and stay busy at it."

- "I am a very fast worker and get along with people well. In spite of my hearing impairment, I can lipread in face-to-face interaction. But I will need to communicate with my coworkers using e-mail frequently and use TTY services and devices when using the phone."

- "My energy and attention to detail would make me good at this job, and I would be very productive. I have an oral processing disability, which means that it helps when instructions are in writing rather than verbal. With this small accommodation, I know I can do the job quickly and then make myself available to help out others with their tasks."

- "I really like this job, but I get anxious when there is so much noise. I work best in a more isolated area. I know I can do it better if I can move my workstation to another part of the office."

## Practice Disclosure Script Activity

To help youth practice explaining their disabilities, it helps to have them write out, or memorize, a script. The script should say what a youth wants to communicate in a way that someone who knows very little about disabilities will understand. Here are some steps to follow to help youth prepare and practice a script:

**Step 1.** Have the youth write or say things about his or her positive attributes. Examples:

> "I am friendly."

> "I work fast."

> "I am organized."

**Step 2.** Have the youth identify the limitations or challenges he or she faces because of the disability. Examples:

> "I need help learning new tasks."

> "I need to work in a quiet place."

> "I need more breaks."

> "I need wheelchair access."

> "I type with one hand."

**Step 3.** Help the youth identify which accommodations have worked best in the past. Examples:

> "When my teacher shows me how to do a new job, I do well."

> "Written instructions help me remember what I'm supposed to do next."

> "When a keyboard is placed higher on the desk, I can reach it from my wheelchair."

**Step 4.** Help the youth put him- or herself in the employer's shoes, and consider how disclosing will make it easier or better for the company. Examples:

> "I will work faster if I have a quiet workstation."

> "I will not get tired if I get a short break every hour."

> "If I can show you how I work with my own keyboard, you will get an idea of how well I can type."

**Step 5.** Help the youth create a script and practice it!

## TO WHOM TO DISCLOSE

To whom people choose to disclose their disabilities may depend a great deal on the position or role of the individual who will be the recipient of that information. Youth may choose or need to tell a prospective employer, a workplace supervisor, a workplace mentor, or a coworker. When deciding to whom to disclose a disability, youth should consider the following questions.

- Does the person have the power or authority to help implement an accommodation?

- Can the person provide the accommodation?

- Is the person responsible for hiring, promoting, or evaluating workplace performance?

- Is the person someone who can help provide support at the workplace?

- Can the person be trusted to keep disclosed information confidential?

If the answer is yes to any of these questions, then the person is likely someone to whom youth can consider disclosing disability information. Even if the answer is yes, however, youth may still choose not to disclose for reasons discussed previously.

A youth may also choose or need to disclose through a third party such as a job coach, teacher, or other transition professional who might act as an intermediary or "agent" when the youth cannot or is not prepared to do it for him- or herself. The next section outlines how this might be pursued.

## REPRESENTING A YOUTH'S DISABILITY TO EMPLOYERS

Many youth will decide that it is necessary or desirable for someone to represent them in finding and negotiating work experiences because of communication challenges, significant support needs, or simply lack of confidence. By virtue of being a special education, transition, employment, or rehabilitation professional, many transition specialists are already readily identified as disability professionals. Thus, anyone to whom these professionals introduce themselves already knows that they represent youth with disabilities. In that sense, any youth represented by these professionals are already "outed" as having a disability, and some measure of disclosure has taken place. Therefore, a youth's association with a transition, school, or employment service may, however indirectly, identify him or her as having a disability.

Youth, however, should still be empowered to exercise control over what, how, by whom, and to whom information about their disability should be disclosed, as discussed in previous sections. It is important to note that transition specialists who represent youth in the pursuit, negotiation, and support of work experiences have an obligation to disclose information about a youth's disabilities in a manner that is both respectful and appropriately presented. Just as in any disclosure scenario, third-party disclosure—that is, disclosure via a transition specialist—should always start with a positive rendering of the youth's traits, such as, "Cordell is a fast worker when he gets the hang of a job," "Sheldon is really interested in technology and is well versed in computer applications," or "Carla can stay on task for long periods of time." Then, challenges that youth might expect at work or have experienced in the past are presented in the context of how they can be accommodated while sharing successful solutions. "Cordell needs a job coach at the worksite to help him learn his tasks," "Sheldon needs a special keyboard for his computer," or "Carla will need a quiet place to work."

It helps to show how these accommodations or supports have worked in the past, as well as why and how these accommodations can be implemented to provide minimum intrusion on the company's operation, such as, "I will be Cordell's job coach and will work with him to learn the work tasks," "Sheldon will bring his own keyboard, and I will help him set it up at his workstation," or "Carla knows when to ask for help." Transition specialists who represent youth can prepare and practice their own disclosure script to help with this exchange.

Remember that the disability label does not define the youth. For example, it is not useful to say, "James has an intellectual disability and can't read." Instead, one should say, "James will take time to learn new tasks, but once he learns them he performs them well. And I will help teach him." It might be necessary or useful to explain the disability in terms of how to interact with youth—for instance, "Matthew has autism. Often people with autism have trouble with social interactions, particularly subtle meanings or metaphors. It is most effective to avoid teasing and to be direct in your communication with him."

Whether representing the youth or helping youth learn how to represent themselves when making disclosure about a disability, there are some general considerations for transition specialists to keep in mind, as first presented by Buchanan (2003) as "do's and don'ts" and adapted next.

**Do**

- Link discussion of disclosure to self-determination and self-advocacy—that is, helping youth get to know and speak up for themselves

- Get to know the youth well enough to be aware of accommodation needs, such as through the development of an asset-based inventory (see Chapter 3)

- Engage the youth in a discussion regarding thoughts and feelings on disclosing personal information

- Determine the reason and need for disclosure

- Weigh advantages and disadvantages of disclosing and not disclosing

- Determine who needs to know about the disability: The boss? Coworkers? Nobody?

- Determine why they need to know: So accommodations can be made? So work assignments and tasks are effectively followed? So the youth will be included in workplace communication and social functions?

- Limit information sharing to essential individuals; beware of providing too much information and providing it to people who don't need to know

- Assure the youth that both written and verbal information will be maintained in a confidential manner

- Get the permission of the youth (and parent or guardian, if necessary) to share personal information before disclosing to an employer or anyone else

- Relate disclosure comments to the actual situation—for example, in the context of how it will affect specific work situations or accommodations

- Discuss private information in a private setting

- Plan and/or practice with youth on how to disclose personal information—that is, help youth develop a script, and develop one for yourself if you are representing the youth

**Don't**

- Share personal information about the youth without his or her consent (or the consent of parent or guardians when the youth is a minor)

- Discuss personal information about the youth with people who are not involved in his or her transition planning or service

- Ask personal questions in a group or public setting

- Leave written information in an area where it may be read by others not involved in delivering services to the youth

- Use confidential information for any reason other than the purpose for which it was collected, disclosed, and indicated to the youth or his or her parent or guardian

## COUNSELING YOUTH ABOUT THEIR DISCLOSURE RIGHTS AND RESPONSIBILITIES

It is worth adding a final word about helping youth to decide if, when, and how to disclose personal disability information to employers or anyone else. The law provides certain rights designed to prevent discrimination, and widely accepted good transition practice provides guidance to professionals about ensuring that youth have a self-determined voice in disclosure decisions. Youth, however, must assume certain responsibilities to make effective decisions regarding disclosure. Transition professionals will find it useful to counsel youth on not only their rights, but also their responsibilities to themselves and their employers, supervisors, mentors, and coworkers. The National Collaborative on Workforce and Disability for Youth (2005) provided guidance on this issue, as summarized in Table 4.3.

**Table 4.3.**   Rights and responsibilities

| Youth have the right to | Youth have the responsibility to |
|---|---|
| Have information about their disability treated confidentially and respectfully | Disclose their need for accommodations if they desire any work-related adjustments |
| Seek information about hiring practices from any organization | Search for jobs that match skills and interests |
| Choose to disclose their disability at any time during the employment process | Inform hiring managers or interviewers about the need for interview accommodations prior to an interview |
| Receive appropriate accommodations in an interview in order to demonstrate skills and competencies | Identify appropriate and reasonable accommodations for an interview |

*(continued)*

**Table 4.3.**   *(continued)*

| Youth have the right to | Youth have the responsibility to |
| --- | --- |
| Be considered for job positions based on skill and merit | Negotiate accommodations with an employer at the point of job offer and any time after beginning work |
| Have respectful questioning about their disability for the purpose of reasonable accommodation | Demonstrate their skills and merits |
| Be self-determined and proactive in disability disclosure decisions | Be truthful, self-determined, and proactive |

*Source:* National Collaborative on Workforce and Disability for Youth (2005).

## SUMMARY

This chapter presented considerations about whether and under what circumstances youth may disclose personal information related to a disability. It also provided considerations and activities that transition specialists may use to help prepare youth to make disclosures of disability information. In all of these interactions, youth self-determination and self-advocacy should drive disclosure decisions. In addition, when it is important for employers and coworkers to know about a youth's disability and accommodation needs, it is the youth who should determine the method of disclosure.

The issue of disclosure is pertinent to any work experience, but more is at stake if disclosure decisions are related to a paid job. As discussed throughout this book, practice and research has taught us that employer decisions about bringing youth into their workplaces are less likely to be influenced by the presence or absence of disability than by potential contribution of youth to the company (Luecking, 2008; Simonsen, Fabian, & Luecking, 2015). This has significant implications for planning for if, when, and how disability is disclosed. Disclosure decisions will influence work experience and job searches, identification of supports and accommodations, managing job tasks, and producing on the job to the satisfaction of future employers (MacDonald-Wilson et al., 2011). In other words, it can make the difference between success and failure in the workplace. A youth's awareness of his or her strengths and support needs can significantly enhance the pursuit of the right work experience and related advocacy for accommodations. The importance of this self-awareness extends well beyond the youth's initial exposure to work experiences into future jobs and adult life.

## LEARNING LAB:
### Disclosure or No Disclosure?

Read the following examples and consider how youth may be counseled to respond to the questions about disclosure. First consider the issues that might determine whether to disclose the disability. Then, consider why, when, what, to whom, and how. There are no right or wrong answers in this exercise, but use the information presented in this chapter when considering possible answers. (Adapted from National Collaborative on Workforce and Disability for Youth, 2005.)

1.   Brittany's anxiety has recently worsened around people, and it has affected her ability to concentrate on aspects of her work experience. Her psychiatrist has

changed her medications and has given her some recommendations regarding changes in her schedule.

Disclose?

Why?

When?

What?

To whom?

How?

2.  Gola has arranged an interview with the supervisor of a large department store to discuss a position as a sales clerk. She wonders how much her learning disability in math will affect her ability to run the cash register and make change.

Disclose?

Why?

When?

What?

To whom?

How?

3.  Manuel has scheduled an interview for an internship at a small technology company. He wonders if the building and the interview room will be accessible for his wheelchair.

Disclose?

Why?

When?

What?

To whom?

How?

4.  Kim has seizures that are mostly controlled by medication. She has mild cerebral palsy that affects her gait. She also has a mild speech impairment. Her coworkers have started to imitate her walk and her speech.

Disclose?

Why?

When?

What?

To whom?

How?

# REFERENCES

Americans with Disabilities Act of 1990, PL 101-336, 42 U.S.C. 12101 *et seq.*

Buchanan, L. (2003). *The disclosure dilemma for advocates.* Washington, DC: George Washington University HEATH Resource Center.

Luecking, R. (2008). Emerging employer views of people with disabilities and the future of job development. *Journal of Vocational Rehabilitation, 29,* 3–13.

MacDonald-Wilson, K., Zlatka, E., Rogers, S., Chia Huei, L., Ferguson, T., Dong, S., & MacDonald, M. (2011). Disclosure of mental health disabilities in the workplace. In I. Schultz & E. Rogers (Eds.), *Work accommodation and retention in mental health.* New York, NY: Springer.

National Collaborative on Workforce and Disability for Youth. (2005). *The 411 on disability disclosure: A workbook for youth with disabilities.* Washington, DC: Institute for Educational Leadership.

Simonsen, M., Fabian, E., & Luecking, R. (2015). Employer preferences in hiring youth with disabilities. *Journal of Rehabilitation, 81,* 9–18.

# Supporting Families to Support Work Experience

Richard G. Luecking and Amy Dwyre D'Agati

> **By completing this chapter, the reader will**
>
> - Identify common challenges for families of youth in transition
> - Learn strategies for involving families in preparing and planning for work experiences
> - Learn strategies for helping families support transition work experiences and employment
> - Complete a Learning Lab on supporting families to support transition work experiences

*"It is really important for Jalen to learn both what he does and doesn't like to do while he is still in high school so he can make the right decisions after high school."*

Mom of a high school student in his second work experience

*"Giving our kids the chance to go out and try real jobs is really the best way to learn—it certainly helped our kid make plans for after high school."*

Father of a high school senior planning for college

Isabella is the youngest child of a big and close-knit family. Her parents were very hesitant about her working outside of a protected environment. She is mostly nonverbal and has difficulty with simple tasks such as crossing the street safely. Her parents were afraid that she would be taken advantage of in a work setting. They would not allow her to participate in a work experience program until her final year in school, when a transition specialist met with the family to discuss what they might be comfortable with her trying. Isabella's sister, who worked at a local gym, suggested she might know of tasks there that would match Isabella's skills. In the beginning of a work experience that was arranged at the gym, Isabella's parents only felt comfortable letting Isabella go to work at the same time as her sister. Over time, their parents became more comfortable with Isabella having her own schedule, separate from her sister's, if support staff from the school was also there.

As a prompt on the job, the transition specialist developed a picture book of all of Isabella's tasks, which included wiping down workout machines, cleaning the mirrors, restocking the towels, and directing customers around the gym. Isabella's parents had the chance to watch her working independently after they dropped her off at the gym. In addition to seeing her perform her tasks, Isabella's parents noticed that so many of the customers knew and greeted her. For her parents, seeing was believing! Isabella kept the job after her sister went off to college.

Harrison's mom insisted that he get the chance to try out job tasks outside of the sheltered work center that he and his classmates sometimes attended during the school day. The school agreed, and a transition specialist interviewed Harrison and his parents to brainstorm ideas. The transition specialist learned that Harrison was in his best mood when they were planning a trip and when the family travelled. Harrison keeps a file cabinet in his room with all the brochures that he has collected from their travels—hotels, restaurants, amusement parks, rental car companies, bus tours, anything! Harrison's dad connected the transition specialist with a travel agent the family has used for years. After an informational interview, they came up with a list of tasks that Harrison could do to help the office: open shipments of brochures and organize them, put together travel packets and folders for presentations, file special-deal e-mails by topic (e.g., rental cars, hotels, cruises). This family's expectation of real work, its input into the work experience process, and its family connection resulted in a part-time job for Harrison.

The family—meaning broadly anyone living under the same roof, whether they are parents, siblings, other relatives, or unrelated persons—can significantly influence transition-age youth. It would be an understatement to say that families can have a significant positive impact on the success of youth as they pursue and participate in work-based learning experiences in the earlier years of secondary school, as they obtain employment, and as they leave school and pursue their careers. As in the cases of Isabella and Harrison, the ways in which families support youth in work experience may vary, as will the ways in which families are supported by transition specialists.

This chapter principally addresses the roles of the primary adults in the youth's life. It also includes a discussion of the roles that siblings may play and the influence they can have on youth with disabilities. Of course, parents and families are as diverse as the transitioning youth. As emphasized by the National Parent Teacher Association (2009), school professionals work with "families from all races, ethnicities, cultures, religions, family structures, and economic levels" (p. 9).

Therefore, the term *family* throughout this chapter will refer to any people who may exert influence on the youth, recognizing that the makeup of families encompasses a wide spectrum of possibilities, including traditional two-parent households; single-parent families; homes where grandparents, guardians, or other adults have the primary responsibility for a youth's development; and homes that may have any number of siblings or other extended family members living in the home. This chapter highlights the opportunities and challenges that families experience and the critical roles they play in supporting youth work experiences. It also discusses how transition specialists can promote family involvement in a way that is respectful and considerate of this supportive role and the diversity of the people who fill this role.

## WHY FAMILY SUPPORT IS IMPORTANT

Family support of youth in transition is critical to youth work success for several reasons. First, the family knows the youth best—an obvious but often underappreciated fact. The family is an important source of information about a youth's attributes and traits, talents, preferences, and accommodation needs. They are also likely to be a key source of support—however modest or intense—long after the youth has made the transition to adulthood. Most families will at the very least remain in contact and will have some influence over the youth indefinitely after school exit. The preparation of youth for transition from secondary school to adulthood is an important time to build relationships with families so that they can positively influence youths' long-term career development.

Most families are positioned to help. Emerging evidence suggests that schools and transition programs are more effective in achieving their goals when there is a presumed importance of families in educational service delivery (Elbaum, Blatz, & Rodriquez, 2016; Wandry & Pleet, 2009) and when the families have expectations of adult employment (Carter, Austin, & Trainor, 2011; Wehman et al., 2014). This means schools and transition specialists should work in partnership with families, rather than dictating how families should support their children's education and transition. The paradigm is shifting from mere "parent involvement" to a concept of "shared responsibility" through school, family, and community partnerships (Epstein, 2019). In the context of transition and work experience, families are best viewed as critical partners who are not simply informed, but also contribute to the planning for work experiences.

Transition specialists' efforts to involve families are at least as important for transition success as family background variables such as race or ethnicity, social class, income, and marital status (Pleet-Odle et al., 2016). That is, when transition specialists reach out to families and include them in planning for transition activities, the results should be uniformly improved, regardless of family background. Evidence also suggests that family expectations influence the achievements of youth with disabilities, regardless of the nature of their disabilities (Wehman et al., 2014). Elevating and cultivating these expectations are therefore important to a youth's workplace success. Transition specialists can play a significant role in shaping family expectations as well as family influence on work experience.

Furthermore, the law supports this approach. The Individuals with Disabilities Education Improvement Act of 2004 (PL 108-440) requires state special education plans to ensure parents' rights for input; provide joint trainings of education personnel, parents, and related service providers; and use parents' feedback to monitor local school systems and student placement. Special education administrators must show how parent involvement was obtained and used in evaluation and improvement plans. Most important to transition specialists, provisions mandate parent involvement in and approval of students' individualized education programs (IEPs). These requirements illustrate recognition of the important role of families as educational partners.

Thus, practice, research, and the law all reflect the importance of the family–educator partnership. In the end, the most compelling reason to promote family participation is that transition activities, especially work experiences, are well served by intentional partnerships between families and practitioners. This chapter explores many of the ways to enhance and encourage these partnership activities.

## KEY ISSUES FOR FAMILIES IN SUPPORTING YOUTH WORK EXPERIENCES

It is universal for family members to worry about their child's future, regardless of whether the child has a disability. For families of youth with disabilities who are in transition, these concerns may be more intense and be the result of more challenging circumstances. These challenges will influence the planning for and the success of youth in work experiences. For families of youth with disabilities, common challenges include the following (Grigal & Neubert, 2004; Hall, Bose, Winsor, and Migliore, 2014; NCWD/Youth, 2011; Wandry & Pleet, 2009).

- *Balancing expectations*: Low expectations about work are common, especially among families of youth with low-incidence disabilities, because of lingering traditional disability stereotypes that focus on deficits. On the other hand, unrealistically high expectations are not unusual due to such circumstances as misunderstanding the nature of the disability or the presence of high-achieving siblings who set a standard for expected achievement. One of the best ways to achieve a balance is for families to learn from the work experience of the youth. Learning what kinds of work environments, tasks, and supports the youth needs is just as valuable for families as it is for the youth.

- *Finding time and energy*: The demands of parenting, jobs, and myriad other family issues may tax the ability of family members to be available for planning and supporting work experiences. In these situations, transition specialists need to be prepared to facilitate family involvement in such a way as to minimize the demands on family time and resources, while maximizing family input. In addition, other complications such as poverty, low educational levels, illness, and substance abuse can adversely affect the capacity for some families to focus on youth work experience support.

- *Understanding and gaining access to resources and services*: Many families are unaware of the array of services that exist during school and after school exit. Moreover, the complexity of many of the service systems is overwhelming to some families. These families will need considerable assistance in navigating necessary transition and postschool services and programs, which will support or affect the ability to pursue work experience and employment goals. At various times, youth may need or benefit from services such as vocational rehabilitation, youth employment programs, developmental disabilities and mental health programs, and various other social and health services. Even the savviest family members may struggle to understand and obtain these services without help from transition professionals.

- *Understanding the role of transition professionals*: Many families will passively defer to teachers and transition professionals, thinking that professionals "know best." On the other hand, some families have experienced disagreements and conflicts with the school system. It will take some time under these circumstances to gain the trust of these families so that they see the role of transition specialists as partners rather than adversaries. In either case, communication is necessary to build trust and understanding of how the family and professionals can work in partnership to promote work experience success.

- *Navigating diversity*: Families from various cultural, ethnic, and racial groups and speakers of English as a second language may bring different expectations or concerns when dealing with school systems and transition professionals. They may possess cultural values that conflict with usual approaches taken by schools and professionals. Transition specialists must practice cultural responsiveness and consider family circumstances to ensure that youth can successfully participate in and benefit from work experiences.

## STRATEGIES FOR INVOLVING FAMILIES IN PREPARATION AND PLANNING

The work experience schemata introduced in Chapter 2 featured three phases of work experiences, namely

1. Identifying goals and objectives for work experiences

2. Negotiating the work experience

3. Implementing an individualized support plan

Families should play a key role in all three of these phases of implementing work experiences. In fact, it is never too early for families to promote career- and work-focused activities, and it is never too late for families to reinforce the value of work experience.

In the first phase, families can provide knowledge and experiences that facilitate planning. For example, family members can be encouraged to

- Bring the youth along to visit them at their jobs

- Give the youth tasks and household chores to do at home

- Help the youth to pursue volunteering opportunities, as these opportunities provide experience in soft skills (e.g., dependability, appearance and behavior on the job, following directions, attitude)

- Help the youth to decide what type of job and work environment he or she really wants

- Talk to the youth about his or her dreams, as this helps to identify areas of interest and ways to draw the youth into making decisions about and planning for
work experiences

The transition specialist should speak positively about the youth as a future
worker to draw families into the planning process. This helps to minimize discussions about the youth that focus on a deficit-based lens of disability. The specialist
should talk as much as possible in a positive context about the youth's positive
personality traits, notable skills, and expressed interests. For instance, one family
was dismissive about their son's dream to pursue a job in professional sports. The
transition specialist told the family that this interest could be a key facet of planning for work experiences. The family's dismissiveness turned into enthusiasm
when his transition specialist helped him to land a part-time job as an equipment
manager's assistant with a minor league baseball team. From October to March,
the youth works part-time sorting and delivering mail, labeling donation request
cards, recording the inventory of autographed balls and jerseys, and filling goody
bags for fans. From April to September, the youth is living his dream: working
right in the dugout, polishing and preparing helmets and bats, getting towels and
Gatorade, and making sure there are enough balls for practice. This family now
regularly speaks to other families about elevating expectations about their youths'
career plans.

Chapter 3 discussed various strategies and methods for gathering information
on youths' preferences, traits, skills, and needs for support through an asset-based
inventory. Not only can families help to gather this information, but they can also
be significant partners in using this information to plan for work experience. In
most cases, families will be interested and willing to participate in this process.
Beyond the development of an IEP, families can contribute to any planning that
takes place to identify directions for a work experience plan.

Families can make valuable contributions by

- Identifying preferences, hobbies, and leisure activities that might point to a possible career or job interest for the youth

- Identifying tasks that the youth performs at home that illustrate potential work
skills and work behavior

- Identifying networks of relatives, friends, and neighbors who might help in finding a potential employer to host an identified type of work experience, as with
Harrison at the beginning of this chapter

- Identifying accommodations and supports the youth will need at work, including supports with which the family may assist (e.g., transportation to and from
the work experience)

- Communicating work expectations, as the father quoted in the textbox titled
One Dad's Approach did.

Given how busy most families are, family participation in the planning process
can be best facilitated by holding discussions at times (e.g., before or after school)
and places (e.g., family home, nearby public meeting place) that are most convenient for the family.

**One Dad's Approach**

Brian Wall is a dad who has high expectations for his son, Tim. He shared the following about using work experiences as springboards to adult employment.

"As soon as Tim was a sophomore, we had regular conversations about planning for his future—what he liked to do, what he was good at, and about getting a job. We tried to create a sense of urgency about working so he would have a better idea what he wants to do with his life. Once we started working with a transition specialist, we encouraged Tim to tell her all his ideas.

"We supported the idea of work experiences—to open the door for a potential career.

"Once Tim got his job, we encouraged his independence and asked him a lot about his day at work. We told him we were proud of him all the time.

"Once Tim realized he really enjoyed working in a small business and may want to start his own one day, we helped him enroll at the local community college to take coursework that supported that dream. Kids these days need guidance—parents need to stress the importance of working, and then a transition specialist can connect them to good jobs."

## STRATEGIES FOR INVOLVING FAMILIES IN NEGOTIATING AND ORGANIZING WORK EXPERIENCES

When prospective worksites are identified, family input is useful—and often essential—to negotiating with employers and organizing the schedules, tasks, supports, and other important features of the work experience. The work experience is likely to be more successful if transition specialists are careful to communicate with families, solicit their input, and involve them in decisions before the youth begins the work experience. Recommended activities for transition specialists to solicit the highest level of family support in organizing work experiences include to

- Inform families of schedules and work expectations about prospective worksites

- Work with families to plan ways they can support prospective work experiences, such as making sure the youth has the proper clothes and is ready on time

- Inform families about the status of conversations with prospective worksites so that they are not surprised by any development, are ready to support the work experience when it starts, and are ready to support the continued search if necessary

- Be prepared to fully explain to families the advantages and disadvantages of prospective worksites (e.g., location, type of tasks, accommodation possibilities)

- Be prepared to fully explain the reasons a particular worksite is targeted for the youth (e.g., what it offers in terms of potential tasks that are matched to the youth's skills, what can be learned from the experience, what features are suited for the youth's circumstances, the level of employer interest)

- Seek family feedback about and input into what supports and accommodations might be needed at a particular prospective worksite

- Make sure families are fully aware of attendance expectations for a prospective worksite so that their support in getting youth to the site is assured

## STRATEGIES FOR INVOLVING FAMILIES IN IMPLEMENTING WORK EXPERIENCE SUPPORT

Once a worksite is identified and it is time to begin the work experience, families can be strong influencers of the success of the work experience. They can provide ideas about how to improve the experience, ensure proper support and accommodations, and evaluate and assess the benefit of the work experience. Transition specialists can seek family input throughout the work experience, recognizing that some families will expect more involvement or be able to contribute more than others. In any case, there are several ways family support will help the success of the work experience. To solicit and use this support, transition professionals can

- Ask family members to identify accommodations and supports that work at home and that might be useful in the workplace (see Chapter 8 for a detailed discussion of workplace supports)

- Communicate regularly with families about progress at the worksite by telephone, text, e-mail, or even written notes—whichever is most convenient for the family

- Invite family input for solving problems related to accommodations or other issues that arise during the work experience

- Help link the youth and family to services and supports necessary for the youth to continue to pursue work (e.g., health and social services, vocational rehabilitation)

- Help link the youth and family to resources that can explain the effects of earnings on income support, such as Supplemental Security Income, and that can assist with the reporting and management of work experience income when necessary

- Support families to encourage youth to speak up for themselves. Promoting youth self-advocacy encourages youth to exercise informed choice over their work experience planning and implementation.

- Conduct meetings with families at times and places that are convenient and comfortable to families.

- Celebrate success: nothing gives parents and family members more pride—and nothing better sets the stage for ongoing collaboration about work experience—than providing information and elaborating on a youth's successes

### Mom Helps Son Aim High and in the Right Direction

Seema Hammaker knew her son, Keith, would need the right kind of guidance and experience to pursue a career because of the uncertain expectations that come with managing his disability. When asked her how she approached this need, she said,

"We told Keith that as he got older, it would be beneficial for him to get some work experience to help him decide on a career field. Keith thought he wanted to work in a lab, so a transition specialist helped him get a summer internship working in a lab. Turns out he really didn't like it and wanted to quit. We encouraged him to stick it out until the end and then immediately try something else so he wouldn't lose momentum. We knew he had always been interested in engineering as well. His transition specialist helped him find the next internship in an engineering firm, which he loves. When Keith comes home with challenges at work, we sit down and talk through those challenges with him to help him come up with a plan of what to do at work next. At home, we helped him with staying on top of his schedule and with organization for the job—what he needed to bring, ask about, etc. He was thinking about going to college for engineering, and now this convinced him to do that."

in the workplace. Make special calls to the family to report workplace gains and successes, mark successes with special occasions (however small) to celebrate them, and send notes and texts telling of particular gains made by the youth at the workplace.

The textbox Mom Helps Son Aim High and in the Right Direction shows how one parent supported her son's career pursuits.

## PARENT-TO-PARENT SUGGESTIONS FOR SUCCESSFUL WORK EXPERIENCES

One of the most useful strategies for promoting family support of work experiences is to facilitate opportunities for families to talk to each other for support, information, and guidance. Few experiences have more immediate influence than when other families who "have been there" lend advice to families who are seeing their youth go to a worksite for the first time—or even the second, third, or fourth time! One transition teacher keeps the names and telephone numbers of the families of previous students who agree to be available to talk to other families of students who are new to her class each year. She begins each school year by sharing these names and contact information with new students' families. She often tries to purposefully match new families to experienced families with similar backgrounds or to youth with similar circumstances and disabilities. She asks the experienced families to share information about what to expect from the work experiences that are a major part of the year's curriculum. This information runs the gamut: how to help youth dress for work, identifying alternative transportation ideas, preparing for unique scheduling due to work hours, what to expect from the transition specialist, where to go to report earnings to the Social Security office, and many more areas of greater or lesser importance. Many times, the families develop a mutual bond as a result. The result is a group of families who are extremely supportive of their working youth. It is no surprise to the teacher that almost all of the students who exit her program have paid employment at the end of their secondary school education.

The following are activities that transition specialists might be encouraging families to do but are even more powerful when other families who have already experienced the process share them with those families who are new to supporting youth's work experiences.

- Help build a résumé that includes volunteer and work experience, skills, and strengths.

- Know the youth's strengths, interests, and preferences.

- Help the youth to speak for him- or herself.

- Network with friends, neighbors, and colleagues, and let them know that the youth is looking for a certain kind of work opportunity.

- Don't expect to find the one perfect job that will last a lifetime—everyone changes jobs at some point.

- Talk early and often about the benefits of working.

- Seek information on what factors the youth should consider in deciding when or how to disclose a particular disability when planning for a work experience.

- Avoid being "helicopter parents," hovering nearby while the youth attempts to work.

- Model, discuss, and share soft skills with the youth (e.g., appropriate attitudes and dress on the job, showing up on time, taking directions, working with coworkers, eagerness to work and to learn skills).

- Be creative and take advantage of as many learning opportunities as possible— you never know when one might lead to a work experience.

Other strategies for supporting families include formal and informal parent-to-parent support groups where family members talk about shared experiences, lessons learned, helpful resources, and other pieces of useful information and advice about how to support work experiences and employment. Transition seminars and fairs are also occasions for families to convene for mutual learning about what to expect as youth prepare for and engage in work experiences. Finally, it is often useful to individually link experienced families with families who are new to transition issues and to the prospect of their youth working. The textbox Setting the Stage for Family Support illustrates one transition specialist's approach to getting families together to communicate about work experiences.

**Setting the Stage for Family Support**

A transition specialist from a local school district holds a group meeting with students' families at the beginning of each school year. The purpose of the meeting is to inform the families about how work experience will be incorporated into each student's schedule. The specialist has the following agenda for the meeting:

- Introductions

- Review of the importance of the work experiences and how they have helped previous students (usually a family member of a previous student also speaks)

- Overview of the process for arranging the work experiences, including how family members can support and participate in the process

- Discussion on communicating information about the work experiences

- Suggestions on how families can contribute to student success in the work experience

- Questions and answers

- Contact information and wrap-up

This transition specialist reports that this meeting sets the stage for strong family support of the work experience throughout the school year. In all but the rarest circumstances, she has found family members to be extremely cooperative and helpful as a result.

## SIBLINGS

The role of siblings may not be as prominent as that of adult family members, but they can have influential impact on work experience planning, development, and support. When a young person with a disability has a sibling, he or she often is a role model for the youth. This can drive expectations that the youth has for him- or herself and can help the parents understand expectations better. If a sibling gets a job during high school, for example, the young person with a disability might have a stronger desire to work based on the family experience. If a sibling goes to college, the young person with a disability has a greater chance of recognizing that opportunity—and at least asking the questions: Can I get a job? Can I go to college?

The world of special education and disability supports sometimes creates a separate path of opportunities for young people with disabilities. A family that has typically developing children as well as a child with a disability has the experience of accessing the full realm of opportunities—going to community schools, playing sports, joining clubs, getting a job, having relationships, going to college or training programs, and starting a career. Siblings can be a normalizing guide through the real world, helping families recognize that all their children can access that same path by just adding extra supports where needed.

Siblings also can be very helpful in the discovery and assessment process as well. Siblings are each other's first social network and have their own unique relationships. When a transition specialist needs to understand a student's strengths, support needs, talents, and desires, siblings are a rich source of information. Often, siblings know things about each other that parents don't even know—particularly interests and desires, and understanding what motivates them. In addition, siblings who are out working already may also have contacts to help with leads for work experiences, as in Isabella's example at the beginning of this chapter. They may be able to network on behalf of their siblings.

## RESPECTING FAMILY CULTURE

Transition professionals should consider the family's ethnic and/or cultural background throughout transition planning, relationship building, and transition implementation. Notably, family culture often affects views of youth independence and pursuit of work (Kalyanpur & Harry, 2012). Some cultures respond to disability by extended family support, which may provide a great deal of caring support; at the same time, some family members may be reluctant to support work goals or independent living (Wandry & Pleet, 2009). Others will see a youth's disability through the lens of culturally influenced stigma and thus will not believe that work is a suitable goal. Still others will have to cope with ethnic, racial, and linguistic inequities that make access to information about work and disability more difficult. It is therefore important for transition professionals to be sensitive to and respect the cultural values of families of transitioning youth. Professionals should adapt supports to meet the family's needs as they begin to identify work goals and expectations for their youth.

Strategies for accommodating culturally and linguistically diverse families in the planning and implementation of work experiences include the following:

- Identify and use people from diverse cultural backgrounds in trainings and meetings.

- When possible, assign staff who have personal experience with the family's language and culture to work with the youth and family.

- Provide information in the family's native language so as to ensure greater ease of communication with families who are less fluent in English.

- Arrange meetings and contacts so that they are held in familiar community settings rather than in school buildings.

- Match family members of successful youth from the same cultural background to provide family-to-family support, encouragement, and information about the value of work and the impact it has had on their youth and family.

- Respect disagreements about work goals (see the comments on cultural reciprocity later in this chapter).

- Don't hesitate to promote the value of work in the context of the family's culture. For example, assure protective families that you will initially accompany the youth to ensure the safety of transportation and work arrangements.

When it is not practical to pursue many of these strategies, transition specialists can still be very effective when working with culturally and linguistically diverse families. Kalyanpur and Harry (2012) discuss three levels of cultural awareness that lead to successively more responsiveness to family culture and therefore higher likelihoods of effective relationships with diverse families. They refer to the lowest intensity of cultural awareness as the *overt level*, in which professionals are aware of clear external differences such as the way people dress, the color of their skin, or the fact that they speak a language other than English. This level of awareness is superficial and therefore limited in its helpfulness because stereotypes might be common. Thus, judgments made about the families and communications with them are based on limited understanding of the culture. The resulting misperceptions will then create difficulties in establishing a productive partnership with the families, complicating the likelihood that the families will effectively support the youth's work experience.

The next level of cultural awareness is called *covert awareness*. At this level, professionals have more background knowledge of a culture and observe individual differences, such as communication styles. They may even ask families to explain the differences or they may acknowledge wishes of families as they make plans for work experiences. This background knowledge, however, is still often based on common stereotypes; professionals may still not be sensitive to cultural differences and how they affect a family's willingness to support work experiences.

The highest level of cultural awareness is called *subtle awareness*, when transition specialists understand that work and disability each mean different things to different cultures. These cultural values sometimes differ from those of the schools or transition programs. Without judging the families' motives, beliefs, or values, the transition professional operating at a subtle level of cultural awareness will find ways to communicate necessary information in the context of the families' cultural value system and accept that a family may not want to do things exactly the way they are generally done.

One transition professional made arrangements to meet a family at their home to communicate about a prospective work experience. This not only made the family more comfortable with the professional in spite of the language differences, but it gave the professional an opportunity to observe the youth and family interacting. In addition, for every visit, the youth's mother would prepare food, a gesture this family's culture makes to every visitor to the home. The professional quickly realized that turning down the food would be insulting to the family, so she ate all that was offered. During the meal, they would talk informally about the work opportunities she was helping the youth to pursue. It was during these discussions that the youth's mother came to trust the transition professional. A once reluctant mother became a strong supporter of her son's work experience as a result of the professional's cultural awareness.

## Cultural Reciprocity

In the interaction and collaboration between professionals and families from culturally or linguistically diverse backgrounds, Kalyanpur and Harry (2012) recommend adopting an approach they call cultural reciprocity. Cultural reciprocity is the process of becoming aware of and understanding entrenched, and often subtle, values in one's own professional beliefs and practice so that we can explain them to families from culturally and linguistically diverse backgrounds who might not share these same values. From this perspective, it is not sufficient to simply be aware of a family's culture. Professionals also must be prepared to help families understand the values and processes embedded in the system of educational and transition services. For example, for some cultures, the concept of a person with a significant disability working in a paid job is not compatible with cultural norms they know and value. Thus, it may take time and explanation to help families understand how approaches such as supported employment, for example, fit with larger societal values of the dignity of work, the right to work, and the right to earn money. Transition specialists cannot always assume that the goals they hold for people with disabilities are the "right" goals, without recognizing that they resulted from a particular set of values and a particular societal or economic context.

For example, cultural reciprocity in the context of work experiences means that it is not sufficient to understand that punctuality is not part of a particular culture's orientation, as important and respectful as that may be. Transition specialists may also need to explain to families that most employers expect youth to be on time for work. Thus, if a youth is to succeed in the workplace the families will need to help the youth get ready in time. Or, alternatively, work experiences may need to be arranged that allow a flexible schedule where punctuality is less important. Negotiation might be necessary to strike a balance that is compatible with cultural values and the expectations embedded in the system of transition services. It is useful for transition specialists to remember that the values they hold about work are also cultural and not necessarily universal.

## RECOGNIZING SUCCESSFUL FAMILY–PROFESSIONAL PARTNERSHIPS

How do we know when we are successful at engaging families? How do we know when there is a true partnership between families and transition specialists as youth pursue work experiences and jobs? And, as important as any aspect of family–professional partnership, how do we know whether families are satisfied with the partnership or if they view it as a successful relationship?

Several useful indicators will show that families are involved, satisfied, and engaged in transition services that focus on work experience (NCWD/Youth, 2011; Pleet-Odle et al., 2016). From a family's perspective, an effective partnership between a family and a transition specialist will likely include the following components:

- A transition specialist who listens to the family's perspectives and concerns and then cooperatively identifies supports that are needed for the family in its efforts to support the youth's pursuit of work experiences.

- Meetings that are held at times and places that are convenient to the family and considerate of its circumstances (e.g., in the home, with child care provided, at a faith community, in their native language).

- A transition specialist who demonstrates a belief that youth can achieve work experience goals.

- A transition specialist who suspends judgment of family status or past actions. He or she avoids blaming the family when there are problems at the worksite or external problems that affect the work experience.

- The family trusts that the transition specialist has the best interest of the youth in mind.

- A transition specialist who uses family feedback when planning for, implementing, and evaluating the work experience.

These components are useful barometers for how effective transition specialists are when working with families. Consequently, transition specialists can ask themselves the following questions when evaluating their own ability to engage families:

- Do I solicit and am I receptive to family feedback?

- Do I give families all of the necessary information to make decisions about youth in the workplace?

- Do I let families function as experts on their child's disability and their child's talents? That is, do they contribute to the planning, implementation, and evaluation of work experience?

- Do I provide regular communication about the status of the youth's work experience?

- Do I provide regular structured as well as informal opportunities for families to review the youth's progress?

- Do I consider the youth and his or her family as full team members when planning for and implementing work experiences?

## SUMMARY

This chapter outlined many of the challenges that families face as they are engaged to help plan and support youth work experiences. The importance of a family's influence on the transition process is well documented. Transition specialists have the opportunity to make this influence as useful as possible for successful work experiences. This requires a shared partnership in which families and transition specialists have a shared responsibility for the youth's pursuit of work experience and employment.

Strategies were presented that help transition specialists involve and accommodate families so that relationships are nurtured and families become partners in supporting work experience pursuits. Families are as unique and diverse as youth in transition. Thus, transition specialists are encouraged to develop a strong understanding and keen sensitivity to diverse family cultures and family circumstances. Ultimately, success in the workplace will be enhanced and reinforced when families, including siblings, are active supporters of the efforts involved in the youth's work experiences. Therefore, transition specialists are well advised to understand how families may view the partnership with transition professionals; in other words, see the relationship through the families' eyes.

Transition specialists cannot be all things to all families. On many occasions, family needs will be considerable, and it is not practical to solve every issue that might affect the youth's ability to participate in a work experience or to hold a job. The family's support of the youth's work experience may not be optimal or may simply not be feasible because of factors outside the control of transition specialists. Some families will be able to provide only minimal input into work experience support. Some families will need gentle prodding, and others will need to be coaxed into partnering for the work experience effort. Still other families will require help to moderate their input, but all families will be somehow involved as youth pursue work experience. One way or another, families are almost always important influencers of a youth's workplace success. This chapter offered strategies to take advantage of and nurture the family support that will contribute to this success.

## LEARNING LAB:
### Seeing Work Experience Through Family Eyes

Imagine you are the parent of a child with a significant disability.

1.  List the traits you would want in a transition specialist who is facilitating a work experience for your child.

2.  Role-play with another professional or write a brief dialogue for one of the following situations, in which you initiate a conversation about the possibility of a part-time job or volunteer work experience for your child with the following people.

    a.  A neighbor who works in a local, medium-sized private business

    b.  An acquaintance in your faith community who works for a government agency

    c.  A leader in an organization or company in an area of interest for your child (e.g., sports team, theater, law enforcement, retail)

## REFERENCES

Carter, E. W., Austin, D., & Trainor, A. A. (2011). Predictors of postschool employment outcomes for young adults with severe disabilities. *Journal of Disability Policy Studies, 20*, 1–14.

Elbaum, B., Blatz, E., & Rodriguez, R. (2016). Parents' experiences as predictors of state accountability measures of schools' facilitation of parent involvement. *Remedial and Special Education, 37*, 115–127.

Epstein, J. (2019). *School, family, and school partnerships: Your handbook for action* (4th ed.). Thousand Oaks, CA: Corwin.

Grigal, M., & Neubert, D. (2004). Parents' in-school values and post-school expectations for transition aged youth with disabilities. *Career Development for Exceptional Individuals, 27*, 65–85.

Hall, A., Bose, J., Winsor, J., & Migliore, A. (2014). Knowledge translation in job development: Strategies for involving families. *Journal of Applied Research in Intellectual Disabilities, 27*, 489–492.

Individuals with Disabilities Education Improvement Act of 2004, PL 108-446, 20 U.S.C. §§ 1400 *et seq.*

Kalyanpur, M., & Harry, B. (2012). *Cultural reciprocity in special education: Building family–professional relationships.* Baltimore, MD: Paul H. Brookes Publishing Co.

National Collaborative on Workforce and Disability for Youth (NCWD/Youth). (2011). *Tapping into the power of families: How families of youth with disabilities can assist in job search and retention* (Info Brief). Washington, DC: Institute for Educational Leadership.

National Parent Teacher Association. (2009). *National standards for parent/family involvement programs.* Alexandria, VA: Author.

Pleet-Odle, A., Aspel, N., Leuchovious, D., Roy, S., Hawkins, C., Jennings, D., . . . Test, D. (2016). Promoting high expectations for postschool success by family members: A "to-do" list for professionals. *Career Development and Transition for Exceptional Individuals, 39,* 249–255.

Wandry, D. L., & Pleet, A. M. (Eds.). (2009). *Engaging and empowering families in secondary transition: A practitioner's guide.* Arlington, VA: Council for Exceptional Children.

Wehman, P., Sima, A., Ketchum, J., West, M., Chan, F., & Luecking, R. (2014). Predictors of successful transition from school to employment for youth with disabilities. *Journal of Occupational Rehabilitation, 25,* 223–234.

# Finding
# Workplace Partners

Strategies for Recruiting Employers

**By completing this chapter, the reader will**

- Identify reasons why employers might consider bringing youth with disabilities into their workplaces

- Learn strategies for meeting employer expectations when recruiting them to provide work experiences

- Learn complementary strategies for finding and recruiting employers

- Complete a Learning Lab on employer recruitment

*"The transition specialist seemed to know my needs
and responded quickly and directly to help me meet them"*
An employer who agreed to host youth work experiences

*"Not only did the project staff help [employee],
but they helped the company."*
Owner of a fulfillment company who hired a youth intern

Networking is all about who you know. One transition specialist stopped in a neighborhood bakery nearly every morning for a pastry and coffee. Over time, she got to know the owner, who always met her with a friendly greeting. The owner got to know her as a loyal customer who always had a friendly greeting in return. When the transition specialist began working with a student who was interested in learning more about baking, it was logical that she would talk to the bakery owner about how his business operated and what daily tasks needed to be done. After several conversations, she learned that things would go faster if someone assisted with scooping and measuring ingredients the day before baking. Not long after, she negotiated a paid work experience at the bakery for the student, who performed several bakery preparation tasks.

Sometimes the best way to market a transition program is providing excellent customer service. One transition program has developed a strong reputation for competent and responsive assistance to a large grocery store chain. The chain especially has a high regard for the ability of the transition program to match youth with assignments in the many stores the chain operates in the community. As a result, the grocery store chain not only provides numerous paid work experiences in its various stores to youth served by the transition program, but it regularly solicits referrals from the program. This partnership meets an ongoing need of the chain to keep certain departments fully staffed, and it helps the chain to identify future employees. And, of course, these work experiences have provided numerous benefits to youth who learn work skills and valuable work behaviors useful in their employment and career development.

An often-asked question when anyone considers entering a partnership is "what's in it for me?" One large children's museum found one answer when it teamed with a local transition program to build its cadre of volunteers. The transition program agreed to do two helpful tasks. One was to help identify various volunteer assignments throughout the museum that might match individual youth's interests. The other was to support and coach youth through the mandatory volunteer training and during the volunteer assignments. As a result, the museum has more volunteers to fill regular shifts while providing multiple work experiences for youth each year for students in the transition program.

The previous chapters established that work experiences are critical to the career development of youth with disabilities. Yet, these experiences can only happen if there are available and interested employers who are willing to include youth in their workplaces. Without cooperating employers, everything else discussed in this book will be of limited value to the career development of youth. As such, finding, recruiting, and partnering with employers should be a top priority and key skill for transition specialists.

This chapter discusses how to attract employers to host work experiences. It provides specific strategies to recruit and appeal to employers so that work experiences are as plentiful and as varied as youth's interests and circumstances require. Chapter 7 expands on the discussion in this chapter, exploring how to maintain effective employer relationships and how to keep employers interested in working with transitioning youth and transition programs.

## WHAT EMPLOYERS WANT

Under the right conditions, employers should benefit from programs that put them in contact with youth with disabilities. The success of these programs can be their successes. Regardless of how they come in contact with transition programs or their motivations for hosting youth work experiences, employers still have to do one or more of these three things: make money, save money, and operate as smoothly as possible. Thus, to develop and maintain employer relationships, it is essential to understand employers' needs, circumstances, and perspectives.

Over the years, employers who have successfully brought youth with disabilities into their workplaces continue to cite three key reasons for doing so (Luecking, 2004; Simonsen, Fabian, & Luecking, 2015). In order of importance, these reasons are

1. To meet a specific company need, such as filling a job opening or addressing a production or service need

2. To meet an industrywide need, such as preparing potential new workers in a technology industry

3. To meet a community need, such as helping youth become productive citizens

Although many employers are willing and interested in hosting youth in the workplace out of good citizenship, the order of these reasons suggests that it is more effective to appeal to employers' self-interest than it is to appeal to their potential altruistic interest in helping youth. The fact is that no company or employer is in the business of hiring individuals with disabilities. It is therefore best to avoid appeals to an employer's benevolence by trying to convince employers of the value of helping youth with disabilities. It is more important to find out what employers want and then determine how an individual youth can help the employers.

Employers typically do not have the time or resources to seek out youth on their own. However, with proper information, support, and access, employers can be recruited effectively for partnerships with transition programs and professionals. Generally, employers identify four key factors that contribute both to their decisions to bring youth with disabilities into their workplaces and to their satisfaction with the contribution youth make in the workplace (Luecking & Buchanan, 2012; Simonsen et al., 2015).

1. Competent and convenient assistance in receiving youth referrals. Transition specialists earn employer trust when they exhibit professionalism and responsiveness when interacting with employers. Although this seems intuitive and self-evident, employers have long been known to complain about disability program representatives who do not respect business needs and who do not present themselves as reliable professionals (Luecking, Cuozzo, & Buchanan, 2006; Simonsen, Fabian, Buchanan, & Luecking, 2011). Conversely, employer confidence in transition specialists is a key reason for them to bring youth into the workplace (Simonsen et al., 2015). In addition, for busy employers to react positively to solicitations and involvement with transition programs, the arrangement must be easy to manage and not interfere with the pressing demands of their workplace.

2. Matching of youth skills and interests to job tasks and documenting their capacity to perform them. Although it is often tempting to guide a youth into the first workplace where there is a willing employer partner, it can be a disaster if the youth is not matched well to what the workplace has to offer. If the asset-based approaches discussed in Chapter 3 are used as a basis for identifying potential workplaces for individual youth, then the likelihood of making that good match increases. At the same time, if care is taken to fully understand the operation and the culture of the workplace, then the likelihood increases that the employer will be happy to consider being matched with a youth whose interests and skills fit with that workplace.

This also means showing the employer that the youth can perform at the workplace, complete specific tasks, or otherwise address specific unmet business needs. In other words, how will this youth add value to the business's bottom line, rather than how well will this applicant fill an existing position. This runs counter to the notion of using help wanted ads and job opening postings to develop work experience for youth with disabilities. Rather, the transition specialist's direct contact and interaction with employers to learn of business operational needs are far more useful strategies. Nothing beats first-hand contact to get to know an employer's operations. Experience has shown that employers often discover work experience options in their companies that they didn't even know existed until they were shown by a transition specialist (Luecking & Buchanan, 2012).

3.   Support in training and monitoring the youth at the worksite. Employers do not appreciate what one manager described to the author as a "drop off and see you later program." If transition professionals truly understand that employers are partners, then they will deliver whatever follow-up support the employer wants and needs to provide an effective work experience for the youth. This support is related to the time-tested concept in business that is called *service after the sale*. In the context of arranging work experiences, making sure the employer is comfortable and happy with the arrangement is a necessary aspect of the service provided to the employer after the youth is situated in the workplace. How to offer ongoing support is discussed further in Chapter 7.

4.   Formal and informal disability awareness and training for the youth's coworkers (when the youth chooses to disclose a disability). As discussed in Chapter 4, the decision on whether or how disability is disclosed is a personal one. However, when the youth gives permission to disclose and is involved in the disclosure process, it is often important for the youth's coworkers to receive at least a basic orientation on how best to interact and communicate with the youth. More is also said about this in Chapter 7.

The section that follows outlines key strategies that are useful in addressing each of these factors so that employers become willing participants in programs and services that help youth pave the way to work.

## HOW TO GIVE EMPLOYERS WHAT THEY WANT

There is an old business marketing maxim that says, "It is better to find out what your customer needs and wants and then match it to what you have to offer than it is to try to get them to buy what you are selling." Transition specialists can think of employers as customers of the transition programs, and act on this wise advice. First, transition specialists should avoid appealing exclusively to employer altruism by selling employers on helping youth with disabilities. Not only is this strategy ineffective, but it creates an image of youth with disabilities that does not do justice to their individuality and potential competence as workers. Rather, specialists should promote the youth's competence, positive traits, and skills.

Second, neither the youth's nor the employers' needs can be met without first getting to know employers and their operations. It is far easier to negotiate work experience placement when employers know you are looking out for their needs.

Finally, long-term relationships with employers depend on making sure they get what they want from the arrangement; otherwise, they will bail out at the first sign of trouble.

Table 6.1 provides a list of strategies that can be incorporated to meet each of the four employer expectations. This chapter discusses the first nine of these strategies, which are designed to find and recruit employers. Chapter 7 discusses the remainder of the strategies, which address ways to keep employers happy that they "signed on," satisfied with the service from the transition program, and willing to stay involved for as long as they are needed. After all, satisfied customers are repeat customers!

Armed with information about what types of workplaces and work experiences individual youth are seeking (see Appendix 3.2, Work Experience Plan), the transition specialist should now be ready to contact prospective employers to find out about their staffing and operational needs. Below are proven strategies to make that happen and to use that knowledge to negotiate work experiences for transitioning youth.

## Competent and Convenient Assistance in Receiving Youth Referrals

To provide competent and convenient assistance in receiving youth referrals, transition specialists can use the following strategies.

**Table 6.1.** Strategies to address employer expectations

| Employer expectation | Strategies |
|---|---|
| Competent and convenient assistance in receiving youth referrals | 1. Conduct informational interviews.<br>2. Use business language.<br>3. Establish a single point of contact.<br>4. Maintain professional and responsive contact.<br>5. Underpromise and overdeliver. |
| Matching of youth skills and interests to job tasks and documenting their ability to perform them | 6. Know both the youth's capabilities and interests and the employer's circumstances thoroughly.<br>7. Identify tasks that are important to both the youth and the employer.<br>8. Customize assignments as necessary.<br>9. Propose and negotiate task assignments. |
| Support in training and monitoring the youth at the worksite | 10. Clarify employer expectations about job training, coaching, and follow up.<br>11. Follow through on agreed follow-up procedures.<br>12. Solicit employers' feedback on service from the transition program.<br>13. Adjust support and service to employers based on their feedback. |
| Formal and informal disability awareness (when the youth chooses to disclose a disability) | 14. Deliver information about specific accommodations required by the youth.<br>15. Ask what further information and help the employer desires.<br>16. Provide disability awareness information based on what the employer requests.<br>17. Model interaction and support appropriate for the youth.<br>18. Provide periodic guidance and information as necessary. |

**STRATEGY 1**
**Conduct informational interviews.**

Informational interviews are likely the most effective tool in the transition specialist's toolbox. They are easy and effective ways for transition specialists to show
interest in potential employers, as well as to identify opportunities for work-based
experiences that may exist in their workplaces. In fact, they are a great way to meet
new employers and learn their needs without the pressure of trying to convince
them to make a work experience placement. Few employers will refuse a request
for a meeting to share what they do if they are approached with a genuine sincerity
to get to know them better—as opposed to an approach that feels like a sales call.
Consider the following tips on how to conduct such interviews.

- Ask to meet with a knowledgeable person in the business. This might be someone who has been recommended by a friend or acquaintance, someone you
  meet through networking contacts, or simply someone you learn about by contacting the company and asking who is responsible for hiring.

- Make the meeting request easy to fulfill. For example, you might say, "I would
  like to find out more about your business so that I can better understand the
  human resource needs in your industry." Alternatively, you could say, "Many of
  my students are really interested in [industry type]. Is it possible for me to visit
  briefly and get more information?" Do not say, "I want to find out about opportunities for people with disabilities." The initial contact should be strictly focused
  on learning about the employer.

- Be prepared. Thoroughly research the business and prepare questions for the
  meeting, such as: What are the most pressing production or business operation
  challenges? What are some of the biggest staffing challenges? What kinds of
  skills do your workers need? What are anticipated future workforce requirements? What are the ways in which you like to be approached by applicants or
  by schools and programs representing youth?

- Indicate an interest in understanding the staffing and operational needs of the
  business and learning how you may be able to help meet them. Request a tour.
  During the tour, be conversational, asking questions about how things get done
  and about what you observe.

- Keep it short. Respect the employer's time; 15–20 minutes should be more than
  enough.

- Thank the employer for his or her time. When you get back to your office, send
  an e-mail or text message acknowledging the employer's time and interest.

Not every informational interview will directly yield work experience opportunities. At the very least, however, each interview adds to increasing numbers of
contacts for future reference, as well as a growing knowledge of what employers are
looking for and how they operate (see the textbox Informational Interview Leads
to Work Experiences). It is important that your foot has been in the door of another
workplace. If the informational interview seems to indicate that there are opportunities that may match a particular youth's asset-based profile, the negotiations

**Informational Interview Leads to Work Experience**

Justin liked cars and often helped his dad tinker with his car, so the transition specialist began researching car repair shops near Justin's home. She then arranged informational interviews with select car repair shops, to learn more about their staffing and operational needs. At one informational interview, the transition specialist learned that the repair shop often had a backlog with its car repairs. This resulted in occasional customer complaints about how long it took to get their cars back. In addition, the transition specialist learned that skilled mechanics often had to be assigned simple oil changes and tire rotations. This took them away from the more involved repairs that took more time, adding to the backlog problem.

The transition specialist negotiated a work experience that allowed Justin to learn how to perform a basic oil change and to rotate tires. Once a skilled mechanic "showed him the ropes," Justin became quick and efficient at those tasks. Justin's part-time work experience turned into a full-time job when he finished high school. Just as important, the repair shop has increased the number of oil changes delivered, completes car repairs in a timelier manner, and has seen a pick-up in business overall at the shop.

for a work opportunity can begin (see Strategy 9). In any case, it always helps to document the contact for future reference. A sample Employer Contact Sheet is included in Appendix 6.1.

## STRATEGY 2
## Use business language.

Education or transition jargon is likely to generate confusion when used to describe professional roles or transition programs. Transition specialists should talk about what their program can do in terms that the target employer will understand. For example, specialists could say that they help with *recruitment assistance* or *prescreened applicants*, or *access to an expanded labor pool*, or *preparing the future workforce*, rather than promoting their work as helping youth with disabilities achieve employment. Phrases such as *customized responses to human resource needs*, *recruiting assistance*, and *help in managing a diverse workforce* are much more meaningful ways to describe the value to employers, rather than trying to sell them on the importance of youth work experience or disability employment initiatives.

Finally, avoid using language, terms, and acronyms such as *vocational experience*, *work-based learning*, *IEPs*, *WIOA*, *supported employment*, *customized employment*, *job carving*, *work study*, or *cooperative learning*. Not only are they usually meaningless to people outside of the education or transition field, but they also tend to take the focus off the needs of the employer.

**STRATEGY 3**
**Establish a single point of contact.**

Convenience and easy access to youth is important to employers who have hosted youth with disabilities in their workplaces. Transition specialists should minimize the number of school or community professionals that employers interact with. A single individual should be designated to act as an account representative for each employer contact established, to prevent the employer from having to navigate schools and transition programs independently. This allows the transition specialist to become thoroughly acquainted with the employer's needs and circumstances and thus to be more responsive to these needs. It is easier and more convenient for employers when one representative handles all youth referrals to each company, which avoids duplicative and time-consuming interactions. For employers, having a single point of contact also considerably decreases the confusion and duplication that typically occur when multiple people from one school, organization, or program come in and out of an employer's operation to place and supervise youth on the job.

 **STRATEGY 4**
**Maintain professional and responsive contact.**

Transition specialists should observe basic courtesies such as keeping appointments and being on time; dressing professionally; and returning telephone calls, e-mails, and text messages promptly. It is especially important to always thank employers for their time. Not only do these courtesies make a good impression, but they also indicate ongoing regard and respect for employers that will keep them interested in working with transition specialists. In fact, ongoing responsiveness to any employer request is important for maintaining productive relationships, as Chapter 7 discusses. For instance, after an initial informational interview, one transition professional sent occasional notes and even a holiday card to one employer with whom she had a particularly informative and pleasant conversation during the interview. Although there was no immediate job opening for youth at the first meeting, this responsive contact resulted in the employer calling the transition professional 9 months later to tell her of a job opening. Needless to say, it was filled by a youth she represented.

Again, Appendix 6.1 provides a form for organizing and maintaining information on employer contacts.

 **STRATEGY 5**
**Underpromise and overdeliver.**

"Underpromise and overdeliver" is a longstanding hallmark of customer service in any business relationship. It simply refers to giving customers more than they expect to ensure they come back for more. They are also likely to tell others about the service. In the context of youth transition activities, prospective employers should receive service that is over and above what was promised. It can be a simple matter, such as filling an employer's request before an agreed-upon deadline, or it can be more involved, such as helping an employer recruit employees from another source such as another program or agency if the transition specialist cannot provide applicants for a specific position. For example, one employer told a transition specialist of an immediate need to hire an inventory clerk. The transition specialist did not know of a youth to fill this position but referred the employer to a professional in another employment service program who was able to link a candidate to the job opening.

In the figurative sense, such additional service essentially acts to build credit with the employer. That is, the employer feels grateful to the point that it is easy to later make a request of the employer—to consider a particular youth for a work experience, for example. One transition professional helped an employer implement an application process for applicants who could not read English but were fluent in another language. Although this process applied to other people besides youth with disabilities, the assistance was very helpful to the employer and built good will. Guess who the employer called first whenever there was an opening in the company? Another transition specialist brought cookies she baked for the whole staff on a youth's first day on the job. This thoughtful gesture opened many doors to youth with disabilities who had a first shot at future work experience opportunities. These transition specialists delivered more than promised to the employers, and the result in each case was a long-time partnership, which brought many youth with disabilities into the workplace over the years.

## Matching of Youth Skills and Interests to Job Tasks and Documenting Their Ability to Perform Them

The remaining strategies help to ensure that the youth is well matched to the prospective job and will be supported in learning and performing the tasks to which they are assigned.

## STRATEGY 6
## Know both the youth's capabilities and interests and the employer's circumstances thoroughly.

It can be tempting to immediately place a youth in a workplace to fill the employer's interest or need. However, as discussed in earlier chapters, it is essential to first fully understand what the youth and what the employer require. The short-term expediency of a quick placement can lead to dire consequences if the match is not a good one. Never try to force the match.

A well-done, asset-based inventory (see Chapter 3) will yield a thorough knowledge of the youth's interests, skills, preferences, and needs for accommodation. Indeed, this should be the basis for the employer contact in the first place. Informational interviews as described above will be more useful when they are driven by youth interests and circumstances. For example, informational interviews with sporting goods store managers are in order if a youth has strong interest in that area, or with a veterinarian when a youth is interested in animals, or with an office manager when a youth wants to sample administrative support tasks, and so forth. An informational interview should yield a thorough knowledge of an employer's operation so that matching is considered well before a youth is presented for an employer's consideration.

## STRATEGY 7
### Identify tasks that are important to both the youth and the employer.

To ensure that both the youth and employer stay interested and engaged after the placement, transition specialists should clearly identify and outline the possible assignments and likely performance expectations before the work experience begins. This closely follows the previous strategy and represents an important next step after knowing the youth's interests and employer's needs. Regardless of the type of work experience a transition professional is seeking for a youth, it is important to look simultaneously at the youth's interests and the employer's tasks. (See the textbox Mutual Benefit in Proposing an Employer–Youth Match for an example.) "Make-work" situations are not likely to keep employers any more interested than the youth.

Tasks that may be identified in a workplace run the gamut from simple, such as shredding paper, to complicated, such as operating high-tech equipment. Regardless of the relative complexity of the task, transition specialists should ensure that youth are performing a task that will teach something of value. As important, and especially if the employer is to become and remain a partner in transition work experiences, the employer must see the youth performing tasks that either need to be done or that will eventually produce the kinds of skills that will ultimately benefit the employer's operation.

Appendix 6.2 provides a tool for identifying and taking an inventory of an employer's needs, which can be used to match to a youth's circumstances.

---

### Mutual Benefit in Proposing an Employer–Youth Match

Peyton likes to use his computer, which is adapted for voice recognition because he is blind. He is a proficient braille user. He also has a charismatic personality and has been described as a born "schmoozer." Clearly, he would thrive in a people-oriented work experience. After meeting an established realtor at an unrelated community event, Peyton's transition specialist arranged to meet with the realtor later for an informational interview. The transition specialist learned that the realtor hoped to increase business through direct contacts with potential customers. He had developed a script for direct phone contacts, but had little time to implement a customer contact approach. The transition specialist and Peyton proposed that the script be written in braille and that Peyton use it to make the contacts. He would then keep track of the contacts in a database and communicate to the realtor contact information for follow up when potential customers expressed an interest. The realtor agreed to give it a try.

Many customers commented on the pleasant exchanges they had with Peyton. Peyton represented the realty company so well in these contacts that business increased. The company was pleased, and the work experience proved valuable to Peyton's career interests. He now wants to be a telemarketer.

## STRATEGY 8
### Customize assignments as necessary.

The availability of employer resources will be an important determinant of how youth assignments are organized. For example, the transition specialist will need to determine: Will a coworker mentor be available to be assigned to the youth (see Chapter 9)? How much supervisor time will be available? Will the youth need to receive standard in-house training? What are the employer's preferences for onsite support, such as job coaching, from the transition program?

Determine how the tasks can be monitored most effectively through any combination of employer and transition professional oversight so that youth receive effective task training and performance feedback once they are at the workplace. It will be different for each youth and each employer. Again, success of the future work experience is more likely when as much of this as possible can be determined before a youth is presented to an employer for consideration. See the textbox Customizing Assignments for an illustration of this strategy.

---

**Customizing Assignments**

After an in-depth informational interview and tour of a nationally known retail chain store, a transition specialist was able to recognize areas of operation that needed significant improvement. The most crucial problem areas included the mismatching of sizing tags on clothing with the size nubs on hangers (the local store was fined by national headquarters 3 months in a row after failing secret tests), the disorganization of the toy department (the only department to go down in sales profits since last quarter), and disorganization in the stock room (requiring personnel to work overtime at least once a week).

Based on this information, the transition specialist proposed a list of tasks that would address these key problems:

- Weekly accuracy checks of tags to size nubs to reduce incidence of fines and make shopping easier for customers

- Weekly cleanup and organization of the toy department to make it more accessible and appealing to shoppers and therefore increase sales

- Evening cleanup and preparation in the stockroom for the morning shift to make all employees' jobs run more smoothly and to reduce unnecessary overtime

The transition specialist further proposed that these tasks be done by Natasha, who liked to work with people and excelled in detail work. After organizing the necessary supports to train her to do these tasks, Natasha began work. The manager is very pleased and has noticed the increased sales as well as reduced fines and overtime pay.

---

## STRATEGY 9
### Propose and negotiate task assignments.

As all of the previous strategies are pursued, transition specialists should always keep an eye on the end goal: closing the deal for individual youth work experiences. Negotiating a work experience placement is obviously a critical step in the employer recruitment process. Ultimately, the negotiation with employers will hinge on proposing and negotiating task assignments based on how they will help the employer. Typical steps in such negotiation include the following:

1. Presenting tasks that might be performed by the youth in the workplace

2. Outlining how these tasks might be assigned to the youth

3. Highlighting how the tasks match the circumstances of the youth (e.g., interests, previous experience, skills)

4. Presenting the possible benefits to the employer of assigning a job or tasks to the youth (e.g., getting the job done if a paid job, preparing the future workforce if a career exploration experience)

5. Clearly describing the role of the program in supporting the youth (e.g., training, coaching, follow up)

6. Making the "ask," such as

   "Does this look like it will work for you?"

   "Do you have any more questions?"

   "Is there anything else I can do to make this work for you?"

   "Can we set a start date?"

7. Reiterating the potential benefits to the employer. In the end, this will be what "sells" the employer on the relationship.

   Each youth—including those requiring significant support from transition specialists—brings a range of competencies to any given workplace. Almost always, tasks can be identified that offer some benefit to an employer when performed by a youth worker. Employers may get involved with transition programs because they see it as an important means of addressing a community need, but most often employers' involvement is based on addressing an immediate or projected workforce need. Negotiating with employers for a youth placement is most successful when employers see a clear advantage for participating—that is, "what's in it for them." Wise transition specialists will keep this in mind during all stages of their relationships with employers.

   Proposals to employers are most often informal, verbal presentations. However, sometimes it helps to have a prepared format to make a proposal to an employer. This can help organize one's thoughts about what to say to the employer or can serve as a formal adjunct to the "ask" that is given to the employer. Appendix 6.3 provides a sample work experience proposal template.

## COMPLEMENTARY STRATEGIES FOR FINDING AND RECRUITING EMPLOYERS

In addition to the strategies provided, there are a host of other strategies that transition specialists can draw on to help in their search for potential employers. Networking and developing an effective "elevator speech" are two of the most common and useful.

### Networking

Nothing beats having a large network of connections. As the old saying goes, it is not what you know, but who you know. In fact, the task of finding employers who are willing to offer their workplaces to youth with disabilities involves, if nothing else, "prospecting" for potentially interested employers. Networking is essential to finding leads for potential youth work experience (Fabian, Simonsen, Buchanan, & Luecking, 2011; Griffin, Hammis, & Geary, 2007). In fact, many seasoned transition specialists would say the strategies outlined previously are only useful as complements to networks of potential employer contacts. Still others would say that having a network of people who can put you in contact with employers trumps all other methods for identifying potential work experiences and jobs.

When thinking about networking, transition specialists should ask themselves:

- Who do I know who can identify an employer contact?

- Who do my friends know?

- Who do the youth and the youth's family and friends know?

- Who do my colleagues know?

- Who do my transition partners know?

- Who do employers with whom I have already worked know?

- What business organizations might I join to help me build my network?

In effect, *everyone* you know is part of the network that can put you in touch with potential employers (see the textbox Networking Opportunities Are Everywhere). Research has consistently shown that the larger the network, the more likely that work opportunities can be found (Arbex, O'Dea, & Wiczer, 2018; Granovetter, 1995; Hagner, 2003). It is not just who you know, but also how many people you know.

Therefore, the task is to always be on the lookout for opportunities to expand your network and meet new people, no matter the venue. Joining business organizations such as the Chamber of Commerce is useful; they provide a place to meet more people outside the usual circle of transition specialists. Your network is also expanded when you meet people at your place of worship, at the grocery store, at the gym, at cocktail parties—basically everywhere.

### The Elevator Speech

When you meet new people, will you be ready to answer the inevitable question of what you do for a living? Transition specialists need to be ready with a concise

---

**Networking Opportunities Are Everywhere**

One transition specialist, when she was buying a house, established an excellent relationship with the law office that handled the settlement. After several meetings there, she noticed the busy activity in the office and the many tasks being performed by the staff. She thought such an office would be a great place for youth to find out about jobs in the legal profession specifically, but also to find out about the types of tasks and responsibilities that office jobs entail generally. She mentioned this to the lawyer during the settlement and asked if the lawyer knew of places like his office where this might be possible and where there might be some interest in hosting youth for work experiences.

Not only did the lawyer introduce the transition specialist to lawyers in two other law firms, but the lawyer also arranged for his office manager to help the transition specialist identify tasks in his office. Eventually, this office and another became active partners in providing work internships for youth in the transition specialist's school.

---

explanation that represents what they do in an interesting yet brief way—something that is suitable for any encounter with each new member of their network. Effective transition specialists need to have an *elevator speech.*

Can you explain your work with youth concisely and compellingly enough to get your message across to a stranger in the time it takes to ride an elevator a few floors—using language that puts you and the youth in the best possible light, and in a way that causes people to want to learn more? If you can, then the world waits to become your network! The concept of an elevator speech is simply that it is useful to have a straightforward way to get a message across to a new acquaintance in any spontaneous encounter. When you have someone's attention and exchange information, there is a chance to follow up with another contact. The person becomes someone transition specialists might call on later as they add to their network. This person might know someone they can contact, who might know someone else they can contact, and so on.

Below are examples from colleagues who have used elevator speeches to great effect:

- *"Our school is working to really improve the ability of the students to be good workers. I work together with many of the community's employers so that youth have the opportunity to learn good work skills and so that employers find good people to fill their jobs."*

- *"I love it when young people grow up and become responsible employees! At my school I spend a lot of time helping them to learn on the job."*

- *"I work with area companies to identify ways to meet their future workforce needs by linking them with youth. It's exciting to see youth perform and to see companies happy about it!"*

There is no exact formula for the best elevator speech, but there are three basic rules: keep it short, keep it concise, and keep it positive. The speech should be one that you are comfortable with and that communicates positively what your work is all about. You can introduce the fact that you work with youth with disabilities, but it should not be the main thing emphasized. It may not be useful to do it at all during a very brief, first-time encounter.

If you do mention that you work with youth with disabilities or in special education and you get a response such as, "It must be *sooo* rewarding," you may have given the wrong impression. You should phrase it so that you create a positive image—or at least prevent a negative or stereotyped one: "Many of the youth I work with require some modifications to the workplace or to work assignments because of a disability. My school is really good at matching their skills to an employer's needs to make them and the youth's coworkers as productive as possible." This communicates competence and professionalism. Remember, you never get a second chance to make a good first impression. Use a good elevator speech to make that impression.

## SUMMARY

This chapter introduced the importance of focusing on employer needs as work experience and jobs are pursued with and on behalf of youth with disabilities. It discussed reasons why employers might consider participating as partners with transition programs and what they want from these partnerships. Employers are motivated mostly by their self-interest to find people to fill their present jobs or to help develop the workforce that will meet their future needs. They are least motivated by opportunities to meet a community need to improve youth circumstances. The implications of these motivations are that appeals to employers to host youth in their workplace must emphasize how the partnership will benefit the employers. We also saw that employers want competent and convenient ways to receive youth referrals, and they want youth who are well matched to their tasks and workplaces. Based on these factors, several proven strategies to interact with and recruit employers were introduced. The strategies discussed in this chapter are basic to developing relationships with employers.

Transition specialists must elevate their level of professionalism when interacting with employers and must increase the opportunities for interactions with employers, no matter the strategies used. Ultimately, success linking youth with work is as much about meeting employers' needs as it is about serving youth. Otherwise, the entry of youth with disabilities into the labor market will continue to be only sporadically successful and characterized by low-wage, low-skill jobs. Therefore, greater emphasis needs to be placed on making transition programs for youth with disabilities more attractive and friendly to employers. Chapter 7 continues this discussion about meeting employer needs and keeping employers involved.

## LEARNING LAB:
### Becoming an Employer Recruitment Pro

1. *Introducing yourself*—Can you grab the attention of strangers when they ask what you do? Compose an elevator speech that you can use to describe your work with youth. Remember to keep it short, keep it concise, and keep it positive!

2. *Expanding your network*—The opportunity to recruit employers grows with the number of people you know who can put you in touch with persons in their line of work. Make a list of people you know in each of the following types of industries:

Animal care

Automotive

Construction

Finance

Government

Hospitality

Information technology

Legal

Manufacturing

Medical and health care

Recreation

Retail

Science and technology

Security

Social services

Other

3. *Contacting someone from the list*—Schedule and conduct an informational interview using the questions presented in the discussion of Strategy 1. Record your experience on the Employer Contact Sheet in Appendix 6.1, and file the form away for future reference!

## REFERENCES

Arbex, M., O'Dea, D., & Wiczer, D. (2018). *Network search: Climbing the job ladder faster* (Working Paper 2016-009B). Federal Reserve Bank of St. Louis Working Paper Series. Retrieved from https://s3.amazonaws.com/real.stlouisfed.org/wp/2016/2016-009.pdf

Fabian, E., Simonsen, M., Buchanan, L., & Luecking, R. (2011). *Attitudes and beliefs of job developers toward employers* (Technical Report 1). New Brunswick, NJ: Rutgers University, John J. Heldrich Center for Workforce Development.

Granovetter, M. (1995). *Getting a job: A study of contacts and careers* (2nd ed.). Chicago, IL: University of Chicago Press.

Griffin, C., Hammis, D., & Geary, T. (2007). *The job developer's handbook: Practical tactics for customized employment.* Baltimore, MD: Paul H. Brookes Publishing Co.

Hagner, D. (2003). Job development and job search assistance. In E. M. Szymanski & R. M. Parker (Eds.), *Work and disability: Issues and strategies in career development and job placement* (2nd ed., pp. 343–373). Austin, TX: PRO-ED.

Luecking, R. (Ed.). (2004). *Essential tools: In their own words: Employer perspectives on youth with disabilities in the workplace.* Minneapolis: University of Minnesota, Institute on Community Integration, National Center on Secondary Education and Transition.

Luecking, R. (2011). Connecting employers with people who have intellectual disability. *Intellectual and Developmental Disabilities, 49,* 261–273.

Luecking, R., & Buchanan, L. (2012). Job development and placement in youth transition education services. In M. Wehmeyer & K. Webb (Eds.). *Handbook of transition education for youth with disabilities.* New York, NY: Routledge, Taylor and Francis.

Luecking, R., Cuozzo, L., & Buchanan, L. (2006). Demand-side workforce needs and the potential for job customization. *Journal of Applied Rehabilitation Counseling, 37,* 5–13.

Simonsen, M., Fabian, E., Buchanan, L., & Luecking, R. (2011). *How well are employment service providers responding to business in the job development process?* (Technical Report 2). New Brunswick, NJ: Rutgers University, John J. Heldrich Center for Workforce Development.

Simonsen, M., Fabian, E., & Luecking, R. (2015). Employer preferences in hiring youth with disabilities. *Journal of Rehabilitation, 81,* 9–18.

# Chapter 6 Appendices

- Appendix 6.1: Employer Contact Sheet
- Appendix 6.2: Inventory of Employer's Needs and Tasks
- Appendix 6.3: Work Experience Proposal Template

# Employer Contact Sheet

Name of company/employer: _____

Date of contact: _____

Company contact person: _____

Address: _____

_____

Telephone number: _____

E-mail address: _____


**Nature of contact**

☐   Telephone call

☐   Informational interview

☐   Company tour

☐   Other _____


Describe contact: _____

_____

_____

_____


Next steps: _____

_____

_____

_____


_____    _____

Transition specialist's signature               Date

# Inventory of Employer's Needs and Tasks

Name of company/employer: _____

Address: _____

_____

Description of business: _____

Contact person: _____

Telephone number: _____

E-mail address: _____

**Are there?**

| | | | |
|---|---|---|---|
| *Logjams in work areas* | Yes ☐ | No ☐ | Explain: |
| *Backlogs of unfinished work* | Yes ☐ | No ☐ | Explain: |
| *Rush times* | Yes ☐ | No ☐ | Explain: |
| *Seasonal fluctuations* | Yes ☐ | No ☐ | Explain: |
| *Highly paid employees doing administrative tasks* | Yes ☐ | No ☐ | Explain: |
| *Sporadic but important tasks* | Yes ☐ | No ☐ | Explain: |
| *Areas of staff turnover* | Yes ☐ | No ☐ | Explain: |
| *Future workforce needs* | Yes ☐ | No ☐ | Explain: |

*(continued)*

**Potential tasks that youth interns/workers could do**

1. _____

2. _____

3. _____

4. _____

5. _____

6. _____

7. _____

8. _____

9. _____

10. _____

**Additional comments**

_____

_____

_____

_____

_____

_____        _____
Transition specialist's signature                                Date

# Work Experience Proposal Template

| | |
|---|---|
| **1** | *Recap visits or contacts*<br><br>"Thank you for the time you took to show me your operations last week. It was interesting to observe your employees at work!" |
| **2** | *What did you see?*<br><br>"During my visit, I heard several of your colleagues say that there were often backlogs due to increased customer orders." |
| **3** | *Tasks that could be assigned to youth*<br><br>"I realized that there are tasks such as delivering documents across departments, assembling customer packets, copying documents, and sorting incoming mail that people are spending a lot of time doing." |
| **4** | *How the tasks match the youth intern*<br><br>"One of my students, Joseph, is good at clearly organized tasks and would love to work in an office." |
| **5** | *How would this help the company*<br><br>"If Joseph assembles and delivers the packets to each department, workers could attend to other tasks. This might help reduce the backlog of work." |
| **6** | *How will you help?*<br><br>"I will accompany Joseph to get him oriented to his new tasks and check in every day to see how he is doing." |
| **7** | *Make the "ask"*<br><br>"Can I bring Joseph in for an interview?" |
| **8** | *Reiterate the benefits to the company*<br><br>"With my help, Joseph can learn these tasks and the other employees will not have to worry about their tasks. He can help move the work along." |

# Retaining
# Workplace Partners

Strategies for Ensuring Effective Employer Participation

---

**By completing this chapter, the reader will**

- Learn strategies for helping employers to provide effective work experiences for youth
- Learn strategies for keeping employers pleased and willing to continue hosting youth in the workplace
- Learn strategies and resources for helping employers to accept and understand disability and accommodations
- Complete a Learning Lab on managing employer partnerships

---

*"I never worked with job seekers like this before.
But I am happy I did because [the transition specialist]
was so interested in making it work for me and my company."*

An employer who has partnered with transition programs for many years

*"[The transition specialist] couldn't be more
responsive. She was always there when I needed her."*

Comments from an employer surveyed about experience with a transition program

Like in many small companies, workers in The Computer Guy, a computer repair company, had many job functions. In addition to the actual computer repairs, several of the employees also rotated the responsibilities associated with taking customer calls, filing repair orders, ordering repair parts, and handling other general office tasks. This company hired a student from a local high school transition program to be the receptionist and to monitor e-mail requests from customers. The student's transition specialist not only agreed to help coach the student during her first week on the job, but she also helped the company develop a script for the student to use during initial customer interactions. The script was a template for explaining the company services and the process for setting up repairs. The script turned out to be so helpful that every other employee at the company used the template when the student was not there and when it was their turn to interact directly with new customers. This transition specialist says that ever since she helped the company to put this new process in place, she has been treated as part of the workplace "family."

Another transition program employs transition specialists to facilitate and support work experiences for students receiving special education services. It has adopted several standard procedures that are designed to be especially responsive to the employers who host the program's students in their workplaces. These procedures in include

- Responding to phone, e-mail, and text messages within 24 hours

- Showing up in person whenever the employer asks for help or advice about a student

- Contacting the employer directly a minimum of once a week to ask two things— how the student is doing in the workplace and what can the transition specialist do to help with the placement

- When the work experience ends, surveying the employer about satisfaction with the transition program

The transition program staff meets once a week to review employer contact and feedback, using this information to look for ways to improve their interactions with employers. As a result of these strategies, this transition program has an exceedingly high success rate in both work experience placement and work experience retention.

When employers are treated like customers of transition programs, opportunities for work experiences can be plentiful and successful, as in these two examples. After all, getting employers interested in hosting youth in the workplace, as discussed in the previous chapter, is only half the battle. Keeping them interested is just as important. As with any partnership, the best partnerships with employers are those characterized by trust, mutual benefit, and durability. In other words, can the partners count on each other to do what they say they will do? Will both partners get something out of it? Will the partnership last beyond the initial relationship? Having these features built into the partnership can mean the difference between employers going away mad or raving about how great the experience was. Whereas Chapter 6 offered strategies to attract employers, this chapter focuses on strategies that promote ongoing employer partnerships after the initial relationship is established.

## REVISITING EMPLOYER EXPECTATIONS

Employers are primarily motivated by their self-interest when choosing to partner with transition programs. As discussed in Chapter 6, everything employers do is to either make a profit, save money, or make their enterprise operate as efficiently as possible. This applies to all employers, whether they are in the private, government, or nonprofit sector. Interest in having youth in the workplace may come from the need to fill immediate job openings, to deal with future workforce shortages, or to address a perceived community need such as promoting constructive development of its citizens—in this case, youth with disabilities. Even in the latter situation, in which employers want to become good corporate citizens, it is still self-interest that drives their participation. Whatever the reason, strategies that show respect for employers' needs and interests are necessary to convince them to enter into and maintain partnerships with transition programs that represent youth with disabilities.

Chapter 6 discussed four expectations that employers have when deciding to host youth in their workplaces:

1. Competent and convenient assistance in receiving youth referrals

2. Matching of youth skills and interests to job tasks and documenting their capacity to perform them

3. Support in training and monitoring the youth at the worksite

4. Formal or informal disability awareness (when the youth chooses to disclose a disability)

Years of experience of colleagues around the county working with employer partners on behalf of youth with disabilities bear out the validity of these expectations. More important, employers themselves who have successfully hosted youth in their workplaces have expressed these expectations in their own words (Luecking, 2004; Simonsen, Fabian, & Luecking, 2011; Luecking & Fabian, 2015).

Chapter 6 introduced strategies to address these expectations, as summarized in Table 7.1. This chapter details those strategies not covered in the last chapter—Strategies 10 through 18—which primarily relate to retaining employer participation and keeping employers happy with the arrangement. Happy employers contribute to successful work experiences for youth, and the strategies discussed in this chapter will help to make that happen.

**Table 7.1.** Strategies to address employer expectations

| Employer expectation | Strategies |
|---|---|
| Competent and convenient assistance in receiving youth referrals | 1. Conduct informational interviews. |
| | 2. Use business language. |
| | 3. Establish a single point of contact. |
| | 4. Maintain professional and responsive contact. |
| | 5. Underpromise and overdeliver. |
| Matching of youth skills and interests to job tasks and documenting their capacity to perform them | 6. Know both the youth's abilities and interests and the employer's circumstances thoroughly. |
| | 7. Identify tasks that are important to both the youth and the employer. |
| | 8. Customize assignments as necessary. |
| | 9. Propose and negotiate task assignments. |

*(continued)*

**Table 7.1.**  *(continued)*

| Employer expectation | Strategies |
|---|---|
| Support in training and monitoring the youth at the worksite | 10. Clarify employer expectations about job training, coaching, and follow-up. |
| | 11. Follow through on agreed follow-up procedures. |
| | 12. Solicit employers' feedback on service from the transition program. |
| | 13. Adjust support and service to employers based on their feedback. |
| Formal and informal disability awareness (when the youth chooses to disclose a disability) | 14. Deliver information about specific accommodations required by the youth. |
| | 15. Ask what further information and help the employer desires. |
| | 16. Provide disability awareness information based on what the employer requests. |
| | 17. Model interaction and support appropriate for the youth. |
| | 18. Provide periodic guidance and information as necessary. |

## STRATEGIES FOR KEEPING EMPLOYERS HAPPY

Most people have heard advertisements with such tag lines as, "We give service after the sale," or "Backed by the best warranty in the business." Often, our decision to purchase a product or service is influenced by how well we think the company will honor such promises. More important, the likelihood that we will remain a customer of that business—and that we will tell our friends about how good that company is—depends on how we are treated after we buy its product or service. Simply stated, we are loyal to companies that treat us right.

This same concept applies to maintaining good, productive relationships with employers who participate in transition programs and provide work experiences for youth. It is one thing to get an employer to "buy into" the idea of hosting youth in their workplaces but quite another to help the employer do it well and stay committed to doing so. Transition specialists should therefore think of each employer as one of their customers.

Transition specialists can use the strategies in this chapter to generate satisfied and therefore repeat employer partners for transition and youth employment programs. By keeping the employer satisfied, the work experience is more likely to be successful for the youth, the employer is often willing to host additional youth, and the employer is likely to tell other employers about his or her positive experience. After all, many marketing experts will tell you that excellent customer service is the best marketing strategy of all (e.g., AppointmentPlus, 2018; Shuey, 2017). Satisfied employers will tell other employers how good your service is and therefore how beneficial it is to provide work experiences for youth.

The following sections provide some useful and effective strategies to meet—and in most cases exceed—employers' expectations. The strategies have been shown to lead to satisfied and long-term employer partners (Simonsen et al., 2011). These strategies build on those introduced in Chapter 6 and are extrapolated from Table 7.1.

## Support in Training and Monitoring the Youth at the Worksite

Transition specialists can employ the following strategies to support employers in training and monitoring the youth during the work experience, and to keep them as happy and long-term customers of transition programs:

## STRATEGY 10
### Clarify employer expectations about job training, coaching, and follow-up.

Just as each youth requires specific supports and accommodations to learn and perform in the workplace, each employer presents a unique set of circumstances that affect the employer's willingness and ability to host youth. Regardless of the degree of workplace support a youth might require, it is important to involve the employer in deciding how the support will be provided. It should not be left to chance. Make sure employer preferences are considered in deciding when, how often, and under what circumstances transition program support is provided on the jobsite. Decisions about how much training or coaching a youth may require are certainly driven by individual youth circumstances; however, these support activities will take place in the employer's workplace and employer input will be necessary. The rule of thumb is to provide as much follow-up as you can until the employer says otherwise; err on the side of providing too much follow-up. It is better for the employer to ask that you reduce follow-up than for the employer to be frustrated because the transition professional has dropped a youth into a workplace without the necessary support.

Often, it is useful to develop a written plan for follow-up after the youth is placed. Such a plan identifies the agreed-on responsibilities of the employer, the youth, and the transition professional; basic contact information; the nature of the expected follow-up, such as initial training, coaching, and/or decision making; the expected frequency and duration of the follow-up; contingencies for increasing or decreasing follow-up contact; the basic expectation of all parties; and other factors that might be important for clarifying roles. Chapter 8 offers more discussion about this and provides a sample Work Experience Agreement for this purpose.

## STRATEGY 11
### Follow through on agreed follow-up procedures.

Once everyone agrees on how the work experience will be monitored, the transition specialist must execute on what was promised: *service after the sale*. This follow-up includes being on the jobsite as often as the employer expects or requests. It may even be helpful to be there more often than expected, as long as it is not an imposition.

This strategy also presumes that transition specialists will be as responsive as possible to all employer requests, including attending immediately to requests for assistance with a youth. For example, one employer was concerned that a youth was not keeping up with his tasks during his work experience and was disrupting the workplace by constantly talking to himself. After receiving the call from the employer about the situation, the transition professional arranged to be at the jobsite first thing the next day to observe the youth and identify strategies to intervene. Upon observation, it was quickly determined that the youth was simply talking himself through the steps of his tasks because he could not remember them. Consequently, he was slow to complete his work. Both problems were solved when the transition professional developed a picture prompt notebook that the youth followed to move through his tasks. This action not only made the work experience more successful for the youth, but it also showed the employer a high level of responsiveness to his request for help and a high level of competence in resolving the situation. The work experience ultimately led to a full-time job for the youth at that worksite, as well as an employer who was happy with the performance of a productive employee.

Other guidelines for responsive employer relationships include

- Return telephone calls, texts, and e-mail messages within 24 hours—or, better yet, before the end of the business day.

- Confirm appointments 1 day ahead of time. This communicates that you respect the employer's time and also provides an opportunity to quickly prepare for any additional requests the employer might make in advance of a scheduled meeting.

- Drop everything and respond immediately in cases of emergencies or pressing situations. Such responsiveness communicates a concern for the circumstances of the employer and may in fact make the difference between keeping and losing that employer as a long-term partner.

- Underpromise and overdeliver. The most effective transition professionals who have the best relationships with employers work to "dazzle" employers with postplacement service.

In Chapter 6, the customer service concept of underpromising and overdelivering—doing more or giving more service than promised—was introduced as a strategy to deliver competent assistance to employers as they consider receiving youth referrals. The application of this concept is so important to winning employer goodwill and garnering their positive regard that it bears repeating here in the context of ongoing support to employer partners. People always want to work with people they like and trust and who offer to make the situation better than it was before they met. It adds value to the relationship in the eyes of the employer. Underpromising and overdelivering is a proven way to get employers to like you, to trust you, and to think they are better off for having known you. Examples of overdelivering on promises follow.

- After helping a company to hire a student he represents, a transition specialist promises to assist the company's human resource director in advertising additional openings to other schools and employment agencies in the community.

- A transition specialist stops by a company's office just to bring cookies for the coworkers of a student doing an internship there.

- One transition specialist arranged for a youth to participate in an internship at a local printing company. She recommends the printing company whenever she hears that other companies where she has students in work experiences need printing jobs completed.

- An employer requested that a transition specialist contact her by the following week with useful accommodation information about a youth at the workplace. The transition professional provided the information the following day.

- A transition specialist offered three potential times to be available for a meeting after the employer asked for one.

The gesture does not have to be grand or significant. It only matters that the employer gets more than expected because it communicates to the employer that the transition specialist clearly respects and is interested in the betterment of the enterprise. It also demonstrates the thoughtfulness of the transition specialist, something that is likely to be greatly appreciated. It is impossible to overestimate the goodwill that will result from such actions. This strategy is probably one of the most important to maintaining a long-lasting and positive relationship—and it is usually relatively effortless. In each of the previous examples, it is easy to guess who the employer will call for future job openings and who will tell other employers that this transition professional is more than "on the ball."

## Responsiveness to Workplace Problems

What happens when things go wrong? Another aspect of follow-up on agreed-on procedures is being responsive to problems that arise. Invariably, there will be a situation when a youth performs poorly or exhibits challenging behavior in the workplace. Many youth will have had few, if any, previous experiences in the workplace, and they may not—in spite of the best efforts to prepare them—fully understand workplace expectations or know how to handle new situations. There may even be mistakes in matching individual youth with the right workplace environment. When things go wrong, how can the transition specialist ensure that the employer remains a partner?

Think again of the employer as a customer of transition services. Most customers tend to have a higher tolerance for mistakes if there is a timely and genuine response that communicates that the situation will be addressed. Attending to the problem immediately and encouraging feedback from unsatisfied customers are essential customer service activities that the business world has long adopted (Mowatt, 2019; Performance Research Associates, 2012). Often the customer knows exactly what the solution might be to "fix" the problem. Yet even for situations in which this is not the case, identifying how the problem can be addressed, and then coupling that action with a service that adds value to the encounter, breeds strong customer loyalty (Patton & Bluel, 2000; Performance Research Associates, 2012). This added value is often important because simply fixing the immediate problem is not always sufficient to make the customer happy. This strategy was effective when a potentially serious problem arose in a transition program workplace.

For example, a transition specialist helped to secure a work trial for a youth at a local grocery store that is part of a large national chain. The purpose of the trial was to expose the youth to a few stock clerk tasks to see if he could perform them in an authentic environment, to understand if he would like the type of work and the environment, and to determine the best type of job coaching support. This information would help to identify future employment goals and would be a stepping stone for later job development.

The trial did not go well. In fact, on the second day at the store, the youth erupted with loud yelling and threw items from an entire shelf on the floor, breaking most of them. The store manager called the transition specialist, who immediately went to the store. He not only helped to clean up the mess, but he also solicited another colleague to take the youth home because the store manager no longer wanted him there. The transition specialist offered to pay for the damages (an offer that the store manager refused). The manager was impressed with the responsiveness of the transition specialist and the genuine concern he expressed for the problems that the youth created for the store.

The manager was even more impressed when he received a sincere note of apology from the transition specialist, who took responsibility for not being aware that the youth would display such inappropriate behaviors in the workplace. In the note, he also asked what else he could do to remedy the problems that were created by the situation. Although the youth was not permitted to return to the worksite, the manager remained willing to host other youth for work trials because the transition specialist was responsive in addressing the situation, helped to correct the problem the store experienced, apologized for the problem, and offered to make up for whatever the problem caused.

A well-handled problem or complaint has the potential to lead to more customer loyalty than existed before the complaint. The following are suggestions for when things go wrong.

1. *Listen* to the complaint. An attentive ear is always appreciated. Do not become defensive, but instead acknowledge the employer's concerns.

2. *Apologize* sincerely. Saying that you are sorry about the problem, even if it is not your fault, is the first step to diffusing a difficult situation.

3. *Ask what you can do* to make the situation better. Offer to help fix whatever the problem is.

4. *Provide extras.* Offer additional help in rectifying the problem. Consider if there is something you can offer in addition to whatever it took to fix the problem, such as when the transition specialist in the example helped clean up the mess created by the youth.

The store in the example above provided work experience opportunities for many years following this episode as a result of the transition specialist's responsiveness. The store could have discontinued as a partner with the transition program after the episode, but the response to the problem certainly increased the likelihood that it would remain involved. An important note: a failed trial work experience is not really a failure, because youth and transition specialists can learn from it. The most important lesson for the student and the transition specialist in the example above was that a work environment with the constant presence of people moving—like a grocery store—was not a good match for this youth. He subsequently found a job in a home improvement store warehouse, where he could work with few people interrupting him.

 **STRATEGY 12**
**Solicit employers' feedback on service from the transition program.**

It is obviously important to get employers' feedback on how youth are performing. However, it is even more important from a customer service perspective for transition specialists to ask for feedback from employers on what they think about the transition program's service. To elicit useful feedback, transition specialists should ask these basic questions of employer partners:

1. What does the employer like about the transition program's service?

2. What does the employer not like about it?

3. What can be improved?

These questions may be asked informally during a telephone call or a visit or in a more formal way through a brief written survey such as the Employer Satisfaction Questionnaire provided in Appendix 7.1. Regardless of how employers' views are solicited, the key is that this information must be gathered. This communicates concern for the employers' operation, impresses on employers that there is concern, and—most important—gives the transition specialist the chance to act on the feedback so that he or she can improve service to the employer. Many work experiences can be saved by acting on employer feedback.

It is also useful and important to solicit feedback about the youth's performance so that the proper support can be provided to the youth. A useful performance appraisal for soliciting employer feedback on youth performance is included in Appendix 7.2. Ensuring effective support to youth in the workplace goes hand in hand with keeping employers happy with the experience. Chapter 8 explores in detail the subject of youth support in the workplace.

## STRATEGY 13
### Adjust support and service to employers based on their feedback.

Feedback is only useful if it is acted on. If employer feedback indicates that they want more follow up on youth on the job, the transition program should provide it. If employers want less, back off. If employers ask for faster response time to a youth problem, respond quickly. Again, such service improvement efforts impress employers. They also increase the likelihood that the employer will do two things: 1) continue the partnership with the transition program and 2) tell other employers about the program's responsiveness. Remember: Good service is also good marketing!

Implementation of high-quality support to employer partners involves a continuous process of delivering service (i.e., facilitating youth placement in the workplace), soliciting feedback about the service, and responding to the feedback and adjusting the service accordingly. These points form the feedback loop shown in Figure 7.1.

As employers provide feedback, transition specialists need to be ready to address occasionally negative feedback. This is what helps to improve and sustain relationships with employers. To handle employers' complaints, transition specialists should do the following.

- Listen. Do not argue or be defensive. Ask for or offer solutions to fix the problem. Nobody ever wins an argument with customers. Even if you know the customer is wrong, make him or her feel that he or she is right. Sometimes a complaining customer just wants to be heard. The same concept applies to employer partners, whom you should regard as your customers.

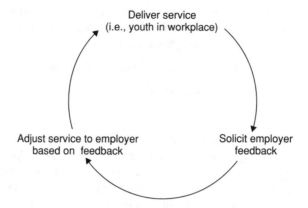

**Figure 7.1.**   Feedback loop of implementing quality service to employers.

- Never ignore or minimize employers' concerns or complaints. Doing so is delivering a message that you do not care about them as partners, in which case you might as well forget them because they will not likely do business with you again. Chances are that they will also tell other employers about their dissatisfaction, spoiling your reputation and your opportunity to develop new employer partners.

- Offer to correct the problem, as in the previous example of the youth in the trial work experience at the grocery store.

- Improve and deliver service to the employer accordingly.

## Formal and Informal Disability Awareness

As discussed in Chapter 4, whether or not to disclose a disability is a personal decision that each youth should make; this is not for transition specialists to decide. The same is true about *how* a disability is disclosed in cases where youth want and need to disclose a disability. The strategies that follow should only be used after youth have given permission to transition specialist to disclose the youth's disability, and related needs for accommodation, to potential and current employer partners. Review Chapter 4, to ensure that you are clear on how to help youth make decisions about whether, how, and to whom to make disclosures about their disability before proceeding with the following strategies.

 **STRATEGY 14**
**Deliver information about specific**
**accommodations required by the youth.**

Any discussion about accommodations required by individual youth should be in the context of the specific work environment and specific work tasks. This is best done during negotiations with employers (see Chapter 6), but it can happen any time after the placement when accommodation needs are recognized. Remember to keep the employer's perspective in mind. Accommodations might look very different through an employer's lens than through a disability advocate's lens.

Therefore, it is most effective to describe accommodations in terms of how they will help the youth perform to the employer's satisfaction, rather than in terms of legal requirements.

As previously noted, the employer is only legally bound to provide accommodations when the youth is hired for a defined company position, not necessarily for other types of work experiences, such as work sampling or unpaid internships, where the youth is not an actual employee of the company. Even then, accommodations are only required if they are necessary for the employee to perform the *essential* functions of the job—that is, those tasks that are required as identified in a formal job description. Some youth will be able to perform jobs with standard job descriptions with or without accommodations. Even if these accommodations might be extensive, such as wheelchair accessibility or modified keyboards, the employer must offer them if they are not an undue hardship on the company.

Many youth with disabilities, however, may only be able to perform some tasks within a standard job description. In these cases and in cases of unpaid work experiences, the employer is under no obligation to provide accommodations or to hire the youth. This is distinctly different from educational settings governed by special education law, under which schools must provide learning and physical accommodations. Thus, it is all the more important to be prepared to negotiate with prospective employers based on a youth's positive traits and potential contributions to the company. Then, whatever accommodations are necessary will be seen as minimally intrusive and ultimately beneficial to the youth's performance at the worksite.

Transition specialists should be direct and open about whatever accommodations might be necessary and should then work with the employer to identify the most effective way to provide the accommodations. Specialists should clarify what their responsibility will be in arranging the accommodations and what the employer's responsibility or preference might be in providing them.

## STRATEGY 15
### Ask what further information and help the employer desires.

Employers who are unfamiliar with or new to youth with disabilities may not always know how to ask, or what to ask, about supporting and accommodating youth. How to properly communicate with youth about their disability and related accommodations is also a common employer question. Therefore, it will often be important and necessary not to wait for the employer to ask but to solicit his or her concerns so that he or she will be comfortable in supporting and accommodating the youth. This is easy when the accommodations are straightforward, such as giving written directions to the youth rather than verbal directions. When the accommodations are extensive or involved, however, much more support by the transition specialist will be required so that the employer is comfortable.

From the very beginning of the placement and periodically thereafter, it may be useful to ask the employer the following questions:

- Do you feel comfortable with the accommodations we have in place?

- Are they helping the youth to complete the assigned tasks?

- Are the youth's coworkers familiar and comfortable with the accommodations?

- Is it easy for you to communicate with the youth? If not, how can I help?

Soliciting this information is similar in concept to Strategy 12 because it is a type of customer service issue. Of course, it is important for the youth to be properly accommodated, but the accommodation must work for the employer (see Mutual Benefit Through Disability Disclosure and Accommodation). Employers' comfort with disability and accommodations is important to their ongoing comfort and satisfaction with partnering with youth transition programs. One employer stated after a transition specialist worked with him to make accommodations for a student worker with complex support needs, "I never encountered an individual like this and I had my doubts. But it worked out well with the help of [transition specialist]. I would not judge a person again based on disability."

---

### Mutual Benefit Through Disability Disclosure and Accommodation

Cynthia's severe dyslexia is not readily apparent upon first meeting her; however, whenever she must read directions, she needs quite a bit of extra time to get through them. Without accommodating for this, Cynthia is prone to making significant mistakes. She was fired from one job due to errors in following directions, but she really wanted to work and was interested in animal care.

Cynthia's transition teacher found a local veterinarian who also operated a boarding facility for dogs and cats and who was looking for animal attendants. The teacher explained Cynthia's love of animals. She also informed the veterinarian, with Cynthia's permission, that Cynthia had a reading disability. During a subsequent job interview, the teacher, the veterinarian, and Cynthia together talked about ways to accommodate her and to provide alternate ways to follow feeding and playtime directions on the boarding orders.

With the veterinarian's input, it was decided that the office assistant would read the orders aloud to Cynthia when an animal was initially brought in for boarding. This proved to be a very effective approach because Cynthia's excellent recall ability enabled her to remember each animal's care needs. She unfailingly carried out her tasks for the entire school year she worked at the boarding facility. This was made possible by disability disclosure to the veterinarian and the other coworkers, joint problem solving to determine an effective accommodation, and the attentive work of the transition teacher to make sure it worked for everyone.

---

### STRATEGY 16
### Provide disability awareness
### information based on what the employer requests.

Transition professionals can and should offer to provide disability awareness information to employers, although that information should not be forced if it is not needed. If it is needed, then it should be based on a particular employer's needs and request. There are many sources of disability awareness materials available through advocacy, business, and government entities, such as the U.S. Department of Labor, Office of Disability Employment Policy (https://www.dol.gov/odep). However, the best source of disability awareness is the youth themselves—who can explain, sometimes with the transition specialist's assistance, what help they need and why.

One employer was particularly concerned about coworkers' responses to having a young man with a significant communication disability in the workplace. She asked the transition specialist to provide a general disability awareness training session to the staff, as well as to offer specific techniques to the coworkers on how to interact effectively with the youth. This employer-initiated awareness training was useful in the youth's eventual acceptance into that workplace. Just as important, it was useful in making the supervisor and the staff in that workplace comfortable with the youth.

Another transition specialist was asked by an employer who hired a youth with autism spectrum disorder to provide some basic information on autism that he could share with staff and coworkers. The employer wanted to help his staff better understand the youth's behaviors, particularly the youth's difficulty following social and verbal cues. The transition specialist provided a basic one-page fact sheet on the nature of autism and the various ways it was manifested. It was particularly helpful in the case of this particular youth, whose social interactions were complicated because the youth often did not respond to nuanced communications or took them literally. The youth was confused and unresponsive if his supervisor said, "Hurry up with those packets or we'll have hell to pay." Once the supervisor learned to say, "Please finish five packets by 12 o'clock," the youth was very compliant. Teaching coworkers to communicate in concrete terms rather than using metaphors was a big help to this employer's ability to support the youth's placement in the workplace.

The format of providing disability awareness information—whether it is delivered informally as needed or formally through written materials or training sessions—is often based on what the employer asks for, on feedback solicited from the employer by transition specialists, and on the workplace environment. Transition specialists should to be ready to respond to what the employer needs to make the situation work for them.

## STRATEGY 17
## Model interaction and support appropriate for the youth.

Every time the transition specialist is at the workplace, he or she has an opportunity to show, by modeling, how best to interact with and support specific youth workers. This is especially true when a youth has unique or involved accommodation needs. Although this helps to ensure that the youth will receive the necessary support in performing assigned tasks and interacting with coworkers, it is also important in helping supervisors and coworkers become comfortable in interacting with the youth (see Modeling Interaction Breaks the Ice).

## STRATEGY 18
## Provide periodic guidance and information as necessary.

Follow up, both self-initiated and based on employer feedback, is again useful and necessary here, just as in Strategies 11 and 12. It is important for the transition specialist not to assume that everything is working fine as long as there is no request from the employer. Checking in periodically to see how accommodations are working gives the employer the impression that the transition specialist wants the partnership to work for the employer as much as for the youth. In addition, there is always the possibility that new wrinkles will occur in the workplace that require adjustment of accommodation or reacquaintance with disability awareness issues after the youth begins the work experience.

---

### Modeling Interaction Breaks the Ice

William started working in a retail clothing chain store as a markdown attendant. His job entailed going from section to section in the store using a handheld scanner to scan items on display. If it was time to lower the price on an item, the scanner printed a sticker with the lower price, which William then put on the scanned item. Normally, this was a fill-in responsibility for other employees whose primary duty was waiting on customers. The job was customized for William through negotiation with the store manager so that more customers could be served in the store while he handled the markdowns.

The transition specialist inquired after a week on the job about William's performance and if there was anything she needed to do to help make the arrangements work. The store's sales associates knew William had a disability and were uncomfortable around him at first. They were not sure how to interact with him. The store manager asked if the transition specialist could come to a staff meeting before the store opened one day and explain William's disability to the sales associates. The transition specialist gladly complied. She also spent part of the day at the store with William modeling to the associates how to interact with William. Within an hour, the ice was broken, and the associates began to comfortably interact with William. It wasn't long before they were inviting him to hang out on breaks with them. This turned into a win-win situation. William succeeded in the workplace and the store (and its employees) benefited from the work he performed.

---

## BE A CUSTOMER SERVICE STAR

Like any customer who is subscribing to a service, employers know good customer service when they see it and when they experience it. From the moment the transition specialist first meets an employer, he or she begins to convey his or her effectiveness—or ineffectiveness—as a service professional. The strategies discussed in this chapter ensure that employers see only competence, responsiveness, and a desire to meet the employer's need—in other words, good customer service.

As transition specialists begin to incorporate these strategies into their repertoire, they are likely to find increasing ease with the whole idea of working with employers as partners and are more likely to become outstanding facilitators of work experience for youth. Transition specialists should ask themselves the following questions as they work to improve their ability to attract and maintain employers as customers of transition programs.

- Do I listen to my employer partners and communicate clearly about what I do and what I can do for them?

- Is it easy for my employer partners to reach me?

- Am I pleasant to work with?

- Do I follow through on commitments I make?

- Do I anticipate problems before they arise and propose solutions?

- Are my proposed solutions easy to implement in the workplace, and are they as unobtrusive as possible?

- Do I respond quickly when my employer partners need me?

- Do I invite employer partners to give me feedback on how I am doing to meet their needs?

- Do I take ownership if something goes wrong?

- If my employer partner is not happy with my service, do I take steps to correct it?

- Do my employer partners see me as a valuable resource?

The aim, of course, is to be able to answer "yes" to all of these questions.

Outstanding performance rarely goes unrecognized by any customer. The same applies to employers who you should now be thinking of as your customers. Outstanding performers are able to develop and sustain partnerships with employers of all kinds. They are the transition "stars." They can readily answer the important question about customer service to employers: How does what I do look in the eyes of the employer? Seeing the situation from the lens of the employer will often clarify the best approaches to keeping employers interested in hosting youth in the workplace.

## SUMMARY

As in Chapter 6, it is useful to emphasize that the success of linking youth with work is as much about meeting employers' needs as it is about serving youth. A corollary to this concept is that the success of youth in the workplace is as much about keeping employers happy with the arrangement as it is about supporting youth. One cannot happen without the other—youth cannot be successful, and employers cannot benefit, unless there is a simultaneous recognition that both have something to gain by good service from transition specialists who are supporting the work experience.

Persuading an employer to commit to bringing a youth into the workplace may seem like the goal, but it is just the beginning. Delivering promised services in a timely, convenient, effective, responsive, and value-added way so that the employer remains satisfied is in fact the larger goal. It is not sufficient to simply convince employers to host youth in their workplaces. Responsive postplacement service to employers will keep them convinced. This chapter provided strategies to significantly increase the likelihood that employers remain willing to stay involved and provide youth with the kind of work experience they need to advance their career progression.

Once employers are recruited to willingly provide their workplaces for youth work experiences, and once there are approaches in place to ensure the employers' ongoing satisfaction with the arrangement, there is still the critical matter of making sure the experience offers the best opportunity for youth to benefit from the work experience. This will require effective accommodation and support strategies so that youth have access to tasks they need to learn. Youth will also need to perform the tasks in a way that not only meets the expectations of the employer but also accommodates their individual learning styles. Finally, youth will frequently need feedback from transition specialists about how they are performing and how the work experience relates to other school and academic goals. Chapter 8 provides considerable detail about making sure youth are supported effectively on the job and are receiving maximum learning benefits.

## LEARNING LAB:
### Keeping Employers Happy

1. Contact an employer with whom you have worked in the past. Or, through a colleague, find an employer who has hosted youth in the workplace. Arrange to interview the employer using the Employer Satisfaction Questionnaire in Appendix 7.1. After completing the survey, answer these questions:

   a. What can you learn from what the employer found most important?

   b. What can you learn from what the employer found least important?

   c. What does the response to the question about recommending services to other employers tell you about how to keep employers happy with participating in transition programs?

2. List five things that you or any transition specialist can do to ensure that employers stay interested in maintaining a partnership.

## REFERENCES

AppointmentPlus. (2018). *Why customer service is really a marketing strategy*. AppointmentPlus Blog. Retrieved from https://www.appointmentplus.com/blog/customer-service-as-a-marketing-strategy/

Luecking, R. (2004). *In their own words: Employer perspectives on youth with disabilities in the workplace*. Minneapolis: University of Minnesota, Institute on Community Integration, National Center on Secondary Education and Transition.

Luecking, R. & Fabian, E. (2015). *Employer preferences in hiring youth with disabilities*. Center on Transition to Employment for Youth with Disabilities, TransCen, Inc, Rockville, MD. *Practice Brief, 1, 16*.

Luecking, R. G., Fabian, E. S., & Tilson, G. P. (2004). *Working relationships: Creating career opportunities for job seekers with disabilities through employer partnerships*. Baltimore, MD: Paul H. Brookes Publishing Co.

Mowatt, J. (2019). *Keeping customers when things go wrong* (Customer Experience Articles). Retrieved from https://jeffmowatt.com/article/keeping-customers-when-things-go-wrong/

Patton, J., & Bluel, W. (2000). *After the sale: How to manage product service for customer satisfaction and profit.* Rego Park, NY: Solomon Press.

Performance Research Associates. (2012). *Delivering knock your socks off service* (5th ed.). New York, NY: American Management Association.

Shuey, G. (2017). *Like PB&J: Customer service as a marketing strategy.* Retrieved from https://www.business.com/articles/customer-service-as-a-marketing-strategy/

Simonsen, M., Fabian, E., & Luecking, R. (2015). Employer preferences in hiring youth with disabilities. *Journal of Rehabilitation, 81,* 9–18.

# Chapter 7 Appendices

- Appendix 7.1: Employer Satisfaction Questionnaire
- Appendix 7.2: Youth Performance Feedback

# Employer Satisfaction Questionnaire

1. How would you rate your overall relationship with our program?

   ☐ Excellent ☐ Good ☐ Not very good ☐ Poor

   Suggestions/comments

2. How would you rate our ability to help make the student's placement work for you?

   ☐ Excellent ☐ Good ☐ Not very good ☐ Poor

   Suggestions/comments

3. How would you rate our program's willingness to listen to and respond to your interests and needs?

   ☐ Excellent ☐ Good ☐ Not very good ☐ Poor

   Suggestions/comments

4. What aspect of our program's services is most important to you?

5. What aspect of our services is least important to you?

6. What changes could we make to enhance our relationship with you or other employers?

7. Would you recommend our services to other employers in our community?

   ☐ Yes ☐ No

   Why or why not?

8. Other comments?

*Thank you for taking the time to share your thoughts with us!*

Adapted from Luecking, R. G., Fabian, E. S., & Tilson, G. P. (2004). *Working relationships: Creating career opportunities for job seekers with disabilities through employer partnerships* (p. 193). Baltimore, MD: Paul H. Brookes Publishing Co.

In *The Way to Work: How to Facilitate Work Experiences for Youth in Transition, Second Edition,* by Richard G. Luecking (2020, Paul H. Brookes Publishing Co., Inc.)

# Youth Performance Feedback

Date: _____

Student: _____     Transition specialist: _____

Job site: _____     Supervisor: _____

Start date: _____     Date of last appraisal: _____

Please rate the student's performance in each of the following areas on a 1–5 scale with 5 being *Outstanding* and 1 being *Unsatisfactory*. Comments by the supervisor, student, and transition specialist are encouraged.

|  | Rating | Comments |
|---|---|---|
| Appearance |  |  |
| Attendance |  |  |
| Punctuality |  |  |
| Interaction with supervisor |  |  |
| Interaction with co-worker(s) |  |  |
| Response to criticism |  |  |
| Initiative |  |  |
| Independent problem-solving |  |  |

*(continued)*

|  | Rating | Comments |
|---|---|---|
| Productivity/timeliness | | |
| Quality of work | | |
| Safety | | |
| Other: | | |
| Other: | | |
| Overall performance | | |

**Recommendations**

**Signatures**

Student: _____ Date: _____

Supervisor: _____ Date: _____

Transition specialist: _____ Date: _____

# Supporting Youth in the Workplace

**By completing this chapter, the reader will**

- Identify considerations for planning to support youth in the workplace
- Learn strategies for identifying and implementing effective supports and accommodations in the workplace
- Learn about accommodations in various workplace contexts
- Complete a Learning Lab on supports and accommodations

*"I don't read too well. My teacher and
my boss worked with me so that my work was set up
so I don't have to read. I listen to instructions on my cell phone."*
Joseph

*"Freddy is nonverbal and can't read. I was amazed when
he was taught by his teacher how to measure and mix ingredients
by simple markings on the measuring cups at the bakery where he works."*
Freddy's Mom

Dillon has delivered mail throughout a large medical facility since high school, with help from a number of supports and accommodations. He uses a motorized wheelchair with a basket mounted on the front to carry the mail. As he has limited reading skills, he has a coworker who organizes the mail according to color codes for each department. He knows where to go throughout the medical campus because a job coach taught him the route when he first started. His speech is difficult to understand, but his receptive language is strong and he is quick with a greeting to the people in each department where he delivers the mail. All potential barriers to workplace success for Dillon have been effectively addressed through customized job tasks, physical accommodations, coworker support, and specific workplace prompts.

For another student, Frances, it was apparent before her first work experience that behavior and impulsiveness would need to be addressed and accommodated. She tended to lose her temper when she became frustrated with tasks. She often made mistakes when she became distracted or rushed through a task. When she began a work experience as a dental office assistant helping with filing and billing the lead receptionist offered to mentor Frances in these tasks. They soon become fast friends. Her mentor modeled communication with customers and coworkers, showed her basic filing and billing procedures, and gave regular feedback on Frances' work and communication. Because of this guidance, Frances exhibited none of the anticipated potentially problematic work behaviors. This work experience as a dental office assistant turned into a paid part-time job before she graduated high school. This became possible because her support needs were successfully addressed.

Helping youth get their feet in the door of employers is not the end of the responsibilities of transition specialists. In many respects, it is just the beginning. Once youth have found a work experience, they need to have the chance to learn in the workplace, perform assigned tasks, and meet employer expectations. To do so, they will need varying degrees of support to be successful. The types of support they need will depend on each youth's characteristics and employer circumstances. Some youth will need only a little help to acclimate to a particular workplace. However, many will require carefully planned processes, supports, equipment, or adaptations to the work environment. Whether these work supports are extensive, as in Dillon's case, or relatively straightforward as with Frances, they must address specific issues related to work behavior and performance.

Regardless of the degree of support required, all youth benefit from oversight and guidance from transition specialists when on a worksite. This is because anyone new to a workplace may need help learning new skills, following directions, taking initiative, making judgments, communicating with coworkers, fitting in socially, or any number of other aspects of functioning successfully in a work setting. For effective learning to occur at the workplace, for the youth to perform to the satisfaction of employers, and for potential problems at the workplace to be addressed, careful and well-planned support from transition specialists will often be necessary. In any case, it is the responsibility of transition specialists to support youth, or arrange supports for youth, once the youth are in the workplace. Crossing fingers and hoping it works out will never get it done. We can't "drop the ball." Neither the youth nor the employer can afford for that to happen.

Helping youth with disabilities succeed in the workplace requires two general areas of attention. The first is oversight and support during the work experience itself, which includes such basic activities as teaching someone how to do various job tasks, giving feedback on performance, and providing regular follow-up. The second area is facilitating accommodations that might be necessary because of barriers related to disability, such as modifications or adjustments to the work environment or the conditions of work. This chapter addresses both issues by discussing and providing strategies for assistance, guidance, advice, modifications, and adjustments that may be necessary or useful for ensuring successful work experiences for youth.

## IMPORTANCE OF WORKPLACE SUPPORTS AND ACCOMMODATIONS

For all youth, with or without disabilities, who are new to or inexperienced in the workplace, there are important considerations. How comfortable will they be in the new environment? How confident will they be in their ability to learn and perform work tasks? How competent will they be in performing the assigned tasks? For youth with disabilities, there may be additional considerations. What barriers might there be to work performance? How well will they be able to address barriers through specific accommodations so they can perform at their best? These youth are likely to need some form of support from transition specialists. They might also benefit from help and guidance from a key coworker who acts as an on-the-job mentor (see Chapter 9 for a detailed discussion of mentors).

In any case, the successes of people with disabilities who are strategically supported in the workplace are well documented. Effective accommodations for youth and adults with disabilities range from supports afforded by rapidly advancing technology aides to straightforward and low-tech workplace adaptations. On the high-tech end of that spectrum, for example, augmentative communication supports—including a range of specific computer-aided devices, as well as carefully crafted methods of e-mail communication—have provided much wider access to workplaces for people with communication disabilities (Armstrong, Gentry, & Wehman, 2013). Balser (2007) reported that, with the design and application of assistive technology in the workplace, individuals with significant mobility disabilities can experience improved employment access and success. Numerous other examples illustrate the application of very complex computer adaptations that have supported workers with a variety of disabilities and accommodation needs, allowing them to accomplish a variety of work tasks (e.g., de Jonge, Scherer, & Rodger, 2007; Jette, 2017; Patterson & Cavanaugh, 2012).

In addition to technology-related supports, there are numerous studies and documentation of employment success when specially trained and assigned job coaches are available for people requiring a high level of support (e.g., Becker, Drake, & Bond, 2011; Wehman, Chan, Ditchman, & Kang, 2014; Wehman, Inge, Revell, & Brooke, 2007). Methodology has also been widely reported that draws on naturally existing and internal workplace supports, such as coworker mentors, that contribute to successful work performance by youth with high support and accommodation needs (see Chapter 9). The real-world anecdotes presented throughout this book illustrate the workplace supports that contribute to successful job performance for workers with disabilities.

Workplace supports are those activities and circumstances that enable the youth to adjust and perform in the workplace. Accommodations are those things that directly address disability-related barriers. Although supports and accommodations can mean different things, combining well-considered workplace support with suitable accommodation for disability-related barriers increases the likelihood that *any youth* can experience success in the workplace. To help them do so, transition specialists need to be familiar with the context of both workplace supports and accommodations so they can be prepared to help implement these supports and accommodations. To begin, the section that follows considers workplace supports.

## CONTEXT FOR WORKPLACE SUPPORTS

During the development of an asset-based inventory (see Chapter 3), potential support needs of the youth should have been identified. Then, as a work experience is being developed and negotiated between the youth and the host employer, the youth's support needs can be part of the discussion, along with matching the youth's goals, strengths, and needs to the employer's goals, expectations, and requirements of the employer. Indeed, from the very first negotiation of a work experience to its completion, there are many facets to the experience for which youth may require supports, including

- Managing schedules and other logistics

- Getting comfortable with the worksite (and vice versa)

- Learning and applying new skills

- Developing social skills and fitting into the culture of the workplace

- Receiving and incorporating regular feedback and evaluation of performance

Clearly the type, level, and amount of support will vary from person to person and across situations. In addition, it is very important to note that the youth is not the only one who will require some level of support. Supervisors, coworkers, or anyone who might be at the worksite may also need support from the transition specialist so that they, in turn, can comfortably and effectively support the youth's work experience and also benefit from the experience. After all, this experience should ideally be beneficial to all involved parties.

It is helpful to think of workplace support on a continuum from minimal to extensive. Only very basic support will be necessary for youth who are very independent and for whom accommodations are relatively easy to implement. Support may consist of a series of check-in calls and visits; supervisors and coworkers typically provide the primary supports under these circumstances. Moderate support may be necessary for youth who require a more structured approach, whereby the transition specialist is at the worksite on a regular basis and may provide hands-on assistance to the youth, especially at the beginning of the work experience. Specialized accommodations may or may not be needed for these youth.

Extensive support is needed for youth whose support needs are significant. Such support may include frequent hands-on involvement of the transition specialist (e.g., full-time job coaching). These youth may also need complex accommodations. Whether the supports are basic, moderate, or extensive, it is always important to involve supervisors and coworkers in the process of deciding how the supports will be arranged. In all cases, it is useful to identify supports within the workplace—notably, coworkers or supervisors who can act as mentors to the youth, as in Frances' case at the beginning of this chapter and as we discuss in detail in Chapter 9.

## SIX STEPS TO PROVIDING EFFECTIVE WORKPLACE SUPPORTS

By following an organized sequence of activities, transition specialists can assist youth to approach the work experience with the highest probability of valuable learning occurring. They can also anticipate and therefore avoid or minimize problems in youth work experiences. By conducting the kinds of advanced planning discussed in Chapter 3, particularly completing an asset-based inventory, indicates what types of support youth might need prior to the work experience. Once the site for the work experience is negotiated, it will be necessary to determine how these anticipated supports will apply given the specific features and circumstances of that worksite. Figure 8.1 provides a schematic representation of six basic steps for identifying and implementing workplace support, which are discussed in detail in the following sections.

### Step 1: Clarify the Employer's Requirements and Expectations of the Work Experience

Finding a suitable workplace experience for youth is only the beginning. Transition specialists must follow up by planning and providing postplacement support. Leaving youth to fend for themselves once the work experience placement is made can have disastrous consequences at worst; at best, the experience will be only marginally useful for the youth's career development. In addition, carefully planned and responsive postplacement support is equally important to the employer. The last thing employers want to experience is what one employer called "the drop-off-and-see-you-later approach."

From the outset, transition specialists should determine employer expectations. It is important that all requirements, policies, and procedures are spelled out clearly. Clarify general issues such as dress code, punctuality expectations, and places in the worksite that pose safety risks or are off limits to the youth. If it is a volunteer experience, the employer's expectations will likely be modest;

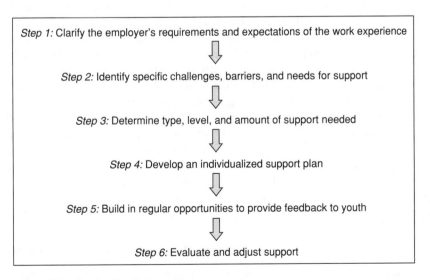

*Step 1:* Clarify the employer's requirements and expectations of the work experience

*Step 2:* Identify specific challenges, barriers, and needs for support

*Step 3:* Determine type, level, and amount of support needed

*Step 4:* Develop an individualized support plan

*Step 5:* Build in regular opportunities to provide feedback to youth

*Step 6:* Evaluate and adjust support

**Figure 8.1.** Six steps for effective workplace supports.

expectations will likely involve when to be there, what to observe, what general task assignments the youth will complete, and how the youth can stay unobtrusive and safe. For paid employment, however, the expectations for youth performance will be understandably elevated to include productivity requirements and higher standards of workplace social behavior. Accordingly, transition specialists must understand these expectations in order to identify what supports will allow the youth to meet these expectations. Without a clear grasp of what the employer expects, it will be difficult to know how to support and accommodate any youth in the work experience.

One way to clarify employer expectations is to provide a format for outlining them. Although most often employer expectations are arrived at informally through verbal discussion and agreement, it can be very helpful to document them for planning and review purposes. A convenient tool for this purpose is a basic written agreement between the employer, the youth, and the supporting school or organization. The Work Experience Agreement included in Appendix 8.1 can be adapted for use in setting up the work experience so that from the beginning, all parties are clear about the expectations and goals of the experience. Once employer expectations are clarified, it is then possible to help the youth identify and implement the supports that will best enable him or her to meet the employer's expectations.

## Step 2: Identify Specific Challenges, Barriers, and Needs for Support

As discussed in Chapter 3, individualized, person-centered, and self-directed planning precedes any activity that puts youth in the workplace. An essential aspect of this process is identifying potential work barriers and ways of compensating for them. Considering supports and accommodations early in the game will be invaluable once youth are in the workplace. From the moment transition specialists begin working with youth—using processes such as the asset-based inventory to ascertain their goals, skills, interests, and other attributes—they can begin to also pinpoint those areas that might pose a challenge to the youth's success in the workplace. This is why it is so important to determine employer expectations before organizing specific supports and accommodations for youth. It is equally important to make adjustments after the placement as some support needs will often become apparent only after the youth begins the work experience.

For example, Marlon's support needs were extensive and required careful planning. In addition to transportation arrangements, it was important to have someone teach him assigned tasks and coach him as he initially learned to perform them. The specific tasks had to be negotiated and customized because he would not be able to do anything that might require reading or calculating. These needs were well known before the work experience search began. It was therefore clear how these needed to be considered both before and during the work experience. That is, the necessary supports were part of the negotiation with the employer and adjustments were made as necessary when he began to perform specific tasks in the workplace.

## Step 3: Determine the Type, Level, and Amount of Support Needed

To determine the type, level, and amount of support needed, transition specialists can begin with the following questions.

- *Has the youth ever had a work experience or worked before?* If the youth has had other work experiences, then the transition specialist should find out as much as possible about the circumstance of that experience: what went well, what did not, what supports worked, and so forth. If not, then the transition specialist will need to ensure a thorough orientation to the new workplace. Additional oversight may be necessary at the beginning of the work experience.

- *What is the youth's preferred learning style?* Auditory learners will need verbal instructions from supervisors and coworkers. Hands-on learners will need to be shown the work tasks and given opportunities to try them, with feedback. Other learning styles will require other approaches. In each case, the transition specialist will need to make sure that the most appropriate presentation of tasks is available at the worksite.

- *Does the youth need a little or a lot of oversight?* This has implications not only for how often the transition specialist visits the site (see Step 4), but also for how much and what kind of orientation the worksite supervisor will need as he or she begins working with the youth.

- *If the youth has had previous work experiences, have there been problems or difficulty?* Inappropriate social behavior, tardiness, or poor task completion in previous work experiences will indicate a need to find ways to minimize their occurrence in the new experience. Such occurrences might also determine how often the transition specialist visits the youth on site or how much assistance the worksite supervisor will need in organizing and overseeing work assignments.

- *How well is the youth able to speak up for him- or herself?* Reinforcing self-determination training and preparing the workplace supervisor for eliciting youth responses may be a necessary support intervention for many youth.

- *How extensive will the support need to be?* Will they be modest, such as minor adjustments to how instructions are provided to accommodate a specific learning challenge? Or will they be extensive, such as customized or individualized task assignments or on-site and continuous job coaching?

The transition specialist needs to involve the youth and the employer in determining the type, level, and amount of support that will be provided. In all cases, however, the transition specialist must be on top of what is needed at the start of the work experience and have a full understanding of how things are progressing for the duration of the experience. There are a host of other possible considerations when identifying potential support needs. Each youth is unique in this respect, and the previous questions are only examples of what might have to be considered. Although it is impossible to anticipate every potential performance hurdle or support requirement, the better acquainted the transition specialist and the employer are with the youth's specific support needs, the more likely it is that the work experience will get off to a good start.

## Step 4: Develop an Individualized Support Plan

To keep the work experience on the right track and to ensure that individual youth receive the support they need for optimal workplace performance, a well-considered plan is helpful. Appendix 8.2 provides an individual support plan template for conceptualizing and planning for work experience supports. The plan does not have to be complex or even in writing. It does help, however, to think about at least these three questions: Who will provide most of the support? What specific supports and accommodations need to be in place? How will they be implemented?

**Who Will Support the Youth?**     An obvious place to start is by identifying the designated supervisor of the youth during the work experience. The person supervising the youth, as well as the intensity of supervision, will vary considerably, depending on the nature of the work experience (e.g., unpaid, paid), who has time to devote to overseeing the youth's performance and communicating with the transition specialist, and the complexity of the work tasks to be assumed by the youth. Most often, identifying the youth's workplace supervisor is easy and self-evident, but it will be necessary to have a person on record who will supervise the youth, who oversees the youth's work, and who will offer feedback about the youth's performance to the transition program.

In addition to the person designated as the youth's supervisor, it is useful to identify coworkers who might be willing to serve as formal or informal mentors to the youth, as discussed in detail in the next chapter. A workplace "champion"—one who supports, encourages, guides, and helps represent the youth—can make all the difference in how well the youth is accepted in the workplace, how well coworkers respond to the youth, and how much the youth is able to learn during the work experience. In addition, a workplace mentor can keep transition specialists apprised of the youth's progress and help identify emerging challenges before they become major problems. In effect, this will be the "go-to person" for the youth when he or she has questions or needs direction at the workplace and the key contact with whom the transition specialist will communicate regularly about the work experience.

**Face in the Place**     Regardless of who is the designated workplace supervisor or if a workplace mentor is identified, the transition specialist will always have a need to have a "face in the place." Often in the crush of supporting multiple youth who are spread among many worksites, transition specialists are challenged to give each youth as much oversight and attention at the workplace as he or she needs. It is critically important, however, that scheduled and unscheduled visits to the youth in the workplace occur. Site visits can be noted in the individual support plan. These visits are important because they provide

- Visual context for evaluating the work experience (i.e., seeing youth perform ensures that feedback is accurate and on target)

- An opportunity to identify the need for adjustments in task assignments or to facilitate specific accommodations

- An opportunity to solicit feedback from employers and coworkers

- An opportunity to troubleshoot and correct problems that arise in the workplace

Areas that might require the intervention of transition specialists include lack of production, mistakes performing tasks, work and social behavior, attendance, and taking direction and feedback, among a host of other possible matters. Being in the workplace to observe these things will enable them to be addressed in a timely fashion.

Two additional things to keep in mind when determining how often to visit youth at the workplace include the status of the work experience and the preferences of the youth and employer. Go more often when youth start at the workplace, go immediately and return as often as necessary when there are problems, and go less often when youth are more experienced and established. Go more when youth seem to be more comfortable in the presence of the transition specialist, less when the youth does not want to stand out or be stigmatized because of the presence of a transition specialist. Go as often as the employer wants—some will be reassured by more visits; others will consider them an imposition. It is always best to err on the side of more visits than less, but ultimately the frequency of visits will be individually determined based on youth characteristics, workplace circumstances, and employer expectations.

**What Supports Need to Be in Place?**    The type and extent of supports that may be necessary are based on both the assessed support needs of the youth and the expectations of the employer. Later in this chapter, possible accommodations for each phase of the work experience will be provided. It is also important that required supports be related to learning expectations—that is, how does the work experience relate to school coursework, and how does it relate, if at all, to specific individualized education program (IEP) goals? Relationship of the work experience to academic coursework or educational objectives might also influence what supports the youth receives.

**How Will Supports Be Implemented?**    Implementation of the individual support plan will be guided in part by the decision of the youth to disclose disability. As discussed in considerable detail in Chapter 4, disclosure is a personal decision that only the youth can make. He or she may decide to disclose a disability to receive specific supports and accommodations. In that case, asking for and negotiating specific supports and accommodations will need to be included in the plan. The absence of disclosure, however, does not mean the absence of support need. If the youth decides not to disclose, then supports will need to be implemented without reference to disability and in the context of what will need to be in place for the youth to perform at his or her best.

It is often helpful to have a checklist to provide direction to the activities of the transition specialists during worksite visits, as well as to create a record of the purpose and results of the visits. A format for this purpose is the Worksite Visit Checklist provided in Appendix 8.3.

Regardless of the nature or duration of the work experience, youth will better internalize learning from the experience if there are goals for the experience that the youth and transition specialist jointly identify. It is often useful for the transition specialists and the youth to work together to incorporate these goals into a learning contract that specifies these goals and expectations for performance (see the Work Experience Agreement in Appendix 8.1). A formal agreement of this nature will not be necessary or appropriate for all youth, but in many situations, it can be a useful tool when organizing the work experience and structuring the oversight provided by the transition specialist.

Finally, to increase the likelihood of work experience success, the company and its operation needs to be considered. The best workplace supports

- Reflect the business environment

- Are as unobtrusive as possible

- Ultimately help the youth contribute to the employers' operations

- Are made with both the youth's and the employer's input

## Step 5: Build in Regular Opportunities to Provide Feedback to Youth

It is natural and appropriate to solicit feedback about the youth's performance from the person designated as the youth's supervisor. In fact, the most organized and best work experiences include a formal process for evaluating the experience, such as weekly feedback, feedback in the midpoint of the work experience, and at the end of the experience. Again, the frequency of the feedback will be determined by individual youth support needs and employer expectations.

Transition specialists can provide employers with the Work Experience Evaluation form included in Appendix 8.4 to facilitate this process. Proactive solicitation of employer feedback is necessary for all kinds of reasons. For example, employers may hesitate to be direct about a youth's performance, or they may not know how to best frame the feedback due to discomfort or inexperience with disability. In any case, organizing structured feedback allows the transition specialist to promptly address any problem at the worksite. Just as important, if the youth's performance is good or exceptional, it allows the transition specialist to provide positive feedback to the youth to both reinforce and celebrate the achievements along the way!

Much can also be gained from soliciting informal feedback about the youth's work experience from mentors and coworkers. This chapter has already discussed the value of having a mentor as a go-to person. Because mentors are likely to be people with a vested interest in helping the youth get the most from the work experience, they tend to be keenly aware of how youth are doing and what issues have arisen at the workplace. Similarly, coworkers see and know how the youth performs and are therefore useful sources of information about the youth's progress in the work experience.

No matter the nature of the feedback—positive or negative—from supervisors, mentors, or coworkers, it is critical for the transition specialist to ask what else he or she can do to help support the youth. Transition specialists who ask whether they can help the youth with learning task performance, help the supervisor explain and reinforce work rules, or discuss a workplace problem leave the impression that they care about how the workplace is benefiting from the experience and that the opinions of the people at the workplace are valued. Most important, this assistance encourages people at the worksite to suggest ways to improve the experience so that when feedback is provided to the youth, it is based on specific reports from those who know firsthand how the youth is doing in the experience.

Ultimately, this information is only valuable if it is passed on to the youth in some fashion to help him or her learn from it. When giving feedback, transition specialists should be direct, provide feedback regularly, look for opportunities to praise, and note exceptional performance. One helpful tool to structure feedback to youth is the Daily Work Report in Appendix 8.5.

## Step 6: Evaluate and Adjust Support

Throughout the work experience, transition specialists should consider: What is working? What is not? Do I need to be at the workplace more or less often? Are there issues with supervision? Do the workplace supervisor and coworkers need help communicating with the youth? Are there issues that arose that I did not expect? Signs of difficulty may include spotty attendance, tardiness, poor task performance, slow production rate, inappropriate social interaction, or any number of things in work and social skill areas. Feedback from the workplace will help enable transition specialists to identify the kinds of supports that work well, work fairly well, or do not work at all for a particular individual. Chances are good that most youth will encounter some situations or problems that call for revising the approach to workplace supports.

Typical areas in which adjustment of the transition specialist's support might be necessary include the following.

- *Frequency of feedback to the employer or youth:* For example, transition specialists should provide more feedback when there is a specific problem, such as attendance, and provide less feedback when the employer or youth complains that the transition specialist is hovering over the youth too much.

- *Nature of feedback to the employer or youth:* For example, the transition specialist can model for the employer how to interact with the youth, rather than telling the employer how to do it. When offering feedback to the youth, the specialist might decide to meet with the youth off site rather than at the workplace to discuss a problem that is sensitive in nature.

- *Frequency of on-site visits:* For example, the transition specialist may opt to visit more when there are performance issues that need specific supports, or visit less once an effective mentoring relationship is established.

- *Refining the instruction given to the youth:* For instance, the transition specialist may replace a verbal prompt with a picture prompt when steps are missed, or break the task down into smaller steps.

- *Adjusting or refining accommodation for accessibility and/or learning:* There are a host of considerations and options for facilitating and adjusting the type of accommodations that youth may require to fully participate in what the work experience has to offer and to fully take advantage of the learning opportunities it presents. The next section covers them in detail.

## CONSIDERATIONS CONCERNING WORKPLACE ACCOMMODATIONS

Accommodations are a part of any support strategy. Legal definitions of *accommodation* will be covered later in this chapter. For now, *accommodation* will be defined simply as any strategy that alleviates or lessens the effects of a specific disability-related barrier. Accommodations are a way to help a youth succeed in a work environment. When organizing a successful work experience, you might ask these types of questions: Do youth have the skill and know-how to accomplish a given task? Will they need an accommodation to make them competent to perform the task? What accommodation would that be? With effective accommodation and resulting effective task performance comes youth confidence in their own ability to do the job as well as increasing comfort in the workplace.

Accommodations can be high tech, low tech—or no tech! They can be categorized in three primary areas.

1. *Physical*—using adaptive equipment, assistive devices, and specific apps, for instance, and making changes to facilities and equipment (e.g., putting in ramps, elevating a desk to accommodate a wheelchair, providing assistive or adaptive equipment, making materials available in large print)

2. *Specialized services*—providing sign language interpreters, readers, job coaches, and personal care attendants, for example

3. *Customized solutions*—changing procedures, restructuring tasks, reassigning tasks, giving instructions in different formats, using flexible schedules, and assigning a workplace mentor, among others

When a youth requires an assistive device, equipment, specialized service, or other substantial accommodation to succeed at a worksite, the transition specialist should help the individual obtain this accommodation. Most employers will welcome the help that the transition specialist can provide in identifying and implementing workplace accommodations. Remember, an accommodation is essentially any strategy that eliminates or lessens the effects of a specific barrier faced by a person with a disability. A barrier is an obstacle that may exist at home, in school, at the workplace, in the community, or in getting to and from places. In the context of youth work experiences, an accommodation is any change in the environment or work process that makes it possible for a youth with a disability to enjoy access to and participation in a workplace opportunity.

Notably, the *obstacle* that the disability creates—not the disability itself—determines the accommodation. For example, stairs are barriers to a youth who uses a wheelchair, a fast-paced work environment is a barrier to a youth who needs to work at a deliberate pace, and reading below grade level may be a barrier for a youth who wants to work in a bookstore. Cerebral palsy is not a barrier for the youth who uses a wheelchair. Emotional disability is not a barrier for the youth who cannot work at a fast pace. A learning disability is not a barrier for the youth who reads below grade level. In other words, the disability itself does not indicate the accommodation but the barrier that is shaped by the specific circumstances of the youth's disability in the context of where he or she will work. Thus, barriers are unique for each youth—even for youth with the same disability. Likewise, barriers are unique to each workplace—even for employers in the same industry.

## Legal Requirements and Workplace Accommodations for Youth

It is worth reiterating that accommodations that employers make on behalf of youth in work experiences are not necessarily those required by law. Title I of the Americans with Disabilities Act (ADA) of 1990 (PL 101-336) requires employers with 15 or more employees to make reasonable accommodations for qualified job applicants and employees with disabilities. Under the law, *reasonable accommodations* are adjustments and modifications that range from making the physical work environment accessible, to providing assistive technology, to offering flexible work scheduling for qualified individuals. They are not required if the applicant or the employee cannot perform the *essential functions* of the job—that is, those tasks ordinarily required of a position or that are outlined in a formal job description. Accommodations are also not required if their costs constitute an undue hardship for the employer.

As noted, the ADA requires reasonable accommodations in the context of youth work experiences only if a youth is being considered for a standard paid job, if the youth can reasonably be expected to perform the essential functions of that job if the accommodations are made, *and* if the costs of providing the accommodations are not considered excessive. For work experiences in which there is no legal employer–employee relationship (e.g., work sampling, unpaid internships, career explorations, job shadowing), employers are not required to provide accommodations, reasonable or not. In addition, even when there is a formal employer–employee relationship, the employer still may not be legally required to provide accommodation under conditions of unusual work circumstances, such as customized jobs for which no previous job description existed.

This is distinctly different from education settings governed by the Individuals with Disabilities Education Improvement Act of 2004 (PL 108-446), under which schools must provide learning and physical accommodations if they are identified as necessary in the IEP. Thus, it is extremely important to be prepared to negotiate with prospective employers based on a youth's positive traits and potential contribution to the company. Necessary accommodations are then seen as minimally intrusive and ultimately beneficial to the youth's performance on the job.

Experience by colleagues around the country with literally thousands of employers confirms that most employers are quite willing to work with youth and transition specialists in implementing necessary accommodations, no matter the circumstance of the youth or the presence or absence of a legal obligation, as long as they receive competent help and service from the specialist (see Chapter 7). This is the case even when accommodations far exceed any pertinent legal requirements or if the accommodations are extensive or complex, as in Dillon's case at the beginning of this chapter. Thus, the main issue of accommodating youth in work experiences is not a legal one but a practical one. Can the accommodations be implemented in such a way that they will provide the youth an opportunity to get the most out of the work experience? Can they be implemented in a way that does not overly tax either the resources or the patience of the employer? Most often the answer is yes, but such implementation requires planning. The individualized support plan should always include planning for accommodations if they are needed.

## Accommodations for Each Component of the Work Experience

When there is a need for physical accommodations, such as wheelchair access, or service accommodations, such as sign language interpretation, the process of identifying these accommodations is relatively straightforward. However, when youth present other needs for accommodations that are less obvious or less common, careful analysis of these needs—and perhaps even some creative approaches—may be required. Furthermore, accommodations may be necessary at any phase of the work experience process. The following sections outline junctures in the work experience when such specific accommodations may be necessary, along with potential approaches to accommodations during these phases of the work experience. In each case, the identification and implementation of effective accommodations will require the transition specialist to establish a good relationship with the employer, characterized by respect for the employer's operation and clear communication about the nature of the accommodation and why it will help the youth succeed.

***Application and Interview Process***    With the exception of career explorations and worksite visits, there almost always is a process for applying and interviewing prior to the start of the experience. Many experiences, such as internships, apprenticeships, or paid employment, will require that the youth participate in a standard interview and selection process. In such circumstances, it may be necessary for youth to ask for (or to receive help asking for) accommodations that will enable them to illustrate their suitability to perform in the prospective job. There are a number of alternative ways to accomplish this by lessening potential barriers in completing applications or participating in interviews. Several ideas for making accommodations that might help youth put their best foot forward to prospective employers are listed next.

- Provide help and clarification in completing applications and arranging interviews

- Allow the youth to take the application home

- Obtain the application information through a verbal interview rather than in writing

- Conduct interviews in an informal environment that is free of distractions

- Minimize the number of introductions made or assure the youth that there will be time later to get to know everyone he or she meets

- Describe the job tasks clearly and concisely, and break down tasks into steps

- Demonstrate job tasks, in addition to or instead of describing them verbally

- Allow the youth to demonstrate a task skill through a "working interview" in place of participating in a verbal interview

- Adjust the interview length according to the youth's ability to concentrate and remain attentive

***Initial Training and Orientation***    Each youth's needs in this area are different, depending on the youth's learning style and the skill requirements of the tasks to which he or she will be assigned. Starting a work experience is a potentially anxious time for youth, especially if experience in the workplace is limited; hence, accommodations might be useful for increasing the youth's comfort and confidence when he or she starts a new work experience. The following list includes several potential accommodations for workplace training and orientation.

- Tailor training to the youth's preferred learning style (e.g., verbal instructions, written instructions, demonstration, tactile prompting, a combination of styles)

- Break down tasks into clearly defined, smaller steps or components

- Provide additional training and additional training time

- Develop a consistent routine or sequence for the job tasks, and train the youth to follow the routine or sequence

- Create pictures or diagrams to train and prompt the youth through a task sequence

- Provide extra time to orient the youth to the employer's rules and performance expectations

- Reinforce verbal training with written or visual material

- Provide additional coaching, on-the-job training, or retraining as necessary

- Supplement standard employer orientation and training procedures with coaching from the transition specialist

- Discuss and role-play appropriate workplace social skills and behavior

**On-the-Job Performance**      It is not uncommon for anyone new to a job or inexperienced in the workplace to occasionally fall short of performance expectations. For youth who have specific barriers to performance due to disability, there may be several areas where work performance may be impeded and therefore require accommodation. These include challenges related to attendance, stamina and stress, concentration, meeting deadlines, memory, vision, writing and spelling, and performing calculations. Several potential approaches to accommodations in each of these areas are outlined next. Remember, the specific accommodation needs of the individual youth and the circumstances of each individual workplace ultimately dictate what kind of accommodation will be helpful or required. In addition, input from employers about performance expectations and input from the youth are important prerequisites to deciding what accommodations will work best and how they will be applied. For any area of accommodation need, transition specialists should monitor the effectiveness of accommodations and supports and be alert to the need to modify if necessary.

   *General potential accommodations may include*

- Restructuring or modifying job tasks to include a few basic and essential tasks for completing basic assignments

- Providing additional coaching

- Arranging the assistance of existing workplace supports such as regular supervisor or coworker feedback

- Assigning a mentor to provide daily guidance and to assist the youth to set workplace goals

- Providing praise, positive reinforcement, and constructive suggestions for improvement

- Clearly defining work performance expectations and responsibilities and the consequences of not fulfilling them

- Providing written work agreements

- Developing and using self-management and compensatory tools, such as check-lists, to-do lists, and picture prompts

- Allowing time for telephone calls to health care professionals, family members, and others needed for support

*For youth with attendance challenges, accommodation strategies may include*

- Flexible scheduling or time off (when needed for medical appointments, counseling appointments, and so forth)

- Flexible leave for health problems

- Changing the work schedule to less or different hours to accommodate personal circumstances, such as transportation or family issues

- Altering arrival or departure times if transportation is problematic

- Looking for alternative means of transportation, such as a family member or coworker

*For youth with stamina and stress challenges, accommodation strategies may include*

- Arranging flexible scheduling

- Organizing longer or more frequent breaks

- Identifying back-up coverage when the youth needs to take a break

- Identifying work assignments that include self-paced work

- Organizing ad hoc breaks to use stress management techniques

*For youth with concentration difficulties, accommodation strategies may include*

- Minimizing noise and visual distractions in the work area

- Providing a separate work area, private office, or room partitions

- Breaking down large assignments into smaller tasks and steps

- Allowing the youth to listen to soothing music on a smartphone or other device

- Setting up an app on a smartphone or other device to remind youth of task steps

- Reducing clutter in the work area

- Planning for uninterrupted work time

*For challenges with meeting deadlines, accommodation strategies may include*

- Making a daily to-do list, and checking off items as they are completed

- Developing a set routine or sequence for tasks

- Arranging material in order of use

- Setting up an app on a smartphone or other device to remind the youth of task steps

- Arranging for a coworker or mentor to remind the youth of deadlines

- Color coding items or resources

*For youth with memory deficits, accommodation strategies may include*

- Developing a set routine or sequence for tasks

- Allowing the youth to make an audio recording of meetings

- Arranging for written minutes of meetings

- Setting up an app on a smartphone or other device to remind the youth of task steps

- Providing written or picture-coded checklists

- Labelling items and places where they are stored when not in use

- Using cues such as color-coded labels, and posting written or pictorial instructions on or nearby the work area or frequently used equipment

*For youth with visual or reading limitations, accommodation strategies may include*

- Providing information in large print

- Using pictures, symbols, or diagrams instead of words

- Arranging for someone to read written information

- Providing an audio recording of the information

- Using the voice input/output options on computers

- Increasing natural lighting or using

- high-intensity lamps

- Providing glare guards for computer monitors

*For youth with writing and spelling difficulties, accommodation strategies may include*

- Using templates or forms to prompt the provision of needed information

- Allowing verbal responses instead of written responses

- Using the voice input option on computers, smartphones, and other devices

- Using spellcheck software tools

- Using a scribe to assist with written communications

*For youth with calculation limitations, accommodation strategies may include*

- Providing a calculator, large-display calculator, or talking calculator

- Using the calculator app on smartphones and other devices

- Providing a counter or ticker

- Making a precounted or premeasured vessel or jig

***Workplace Integration and Interpersonal Relationships***    Social acceptance of youth with disabilities in the workplace is evident when coworkers are willing to work with the youth, eat lunch or take breaks with him or her, attend company-sponsored social functions with the youth (e.g., birthday parties, holiday gatherings), and invite him or her to socialize outside of work. Transition specialists should be alert to these signs. However, inexperience in the workplace, youthfulness, and coworker misunderstanding about disability can all contribute to difficulties for youth as they strive to feel comfortable and accepted by coworkers and others in the workplace. Often, the transition specialist is in a position to provide guidance to youth about workplace socialization, educate workplace supervisors and coworkers about the youth's need for accommodation, and model appropriate interaction. The list that follows offers strategies to improve the ability of youth to become socially integrated in the workplace and to establish appropriate social relationships with others at the workplace.

- Provide disability awareness and sensitivity training to coworkers

- Model positive, nonpatronizing, and respectful social interaction

- Teach the youth to ask a supervisor or coworker for support and assistance

- Identify a coworker to be a workplace mentor

- Ask a coworker to support the youth in participating in and getting to on- and off-site meetings and work-related social activities

- Model and help the youth practice appropriate workplace social skills and behavior (e.g., how to greet coworkers, when and where to eat at the workplace, how to answer the telephone, how to handle frustration, when to leave or not leave the workstation)

## SUMMARY

The topic of supporting youth in the workplace could encompass an entire book. In this chapter, it has been covered in a few key strategies. All of the support strategies in the world would be rendered ineffective if one important element is overlooked: the match itself. No amount of on-site support, accommodations, personal attention, and effort by a transition specialist or host employer will address a situation in which a youth is ill suited to a particular jobsite, where there is a poor match between the employee's skills and the required tasks, when the individual's personality and temperament are not suited to the workplace environment, or when other discrepancies that should have been discovered early on in the process of seeking a work experience or job.

This chapter provided a six-step strategy for ensuring effective supports that are basic for any youth in any workplace. It also introduced considerations for determining and implementing necessary workplace accommodations for youth with disabilities in various stages of the work experience. The transition specialist must be thinking about the kinds of supports that will be needed from the moment he or she meets a job seeker. Identifying and implementing effective workplace supports cannot be an afterthought. The importance of continually soliciting feedback from the youth and his or her workplace colleagues was discussed, as well as the need for evaluating and adjusting supports and accommodations accordingly. In this regard, the most basic formula for facilitating effective workplace supports includes

- Identifying supports and accommodation needs by starting with each individual youth and his or her circumstances, then matching them to an employer's requirements and expectations for the work experience

- Seeking continual feedback from both the youth and the employer

- Making adjustments in support and accommodations as necessary and as feedback indicates

- Renegotiating tasks, supports, production requirements, and other workplace requirements as necessary

This chapter offered a range of considerations when facilitating supports and accommodations during youth work experiences. Using the individual support plan and with a little customization, transition specialists can put every youth in a position to learn from every work experience.

## LEARNING LAB:
### Solving Workplace and Performance Obstacles

1. Appendix 8.6 provides scenarios that illustrate potential workplace support needs. For each scenario, identify supports or accommodations that might be called for. The first two scenarios are completed as examples for responding. You might want to brainstorm with colleagues regarding the potential supports or accommodations for each example.

2. Identify a youth with whom you have worked who struggled in the workplace. Discuss with colleagues potential supports or accommodations that might address the issues this youth faced.

## REFERENCES

Americans with Disabilities Act of 1990, PL 101-336, 42 U.S.C. §§ 12101 *et seq.*

Armstrong, A., Genter, T., & Wehman, P. (2013). Using technology from school to adulthood; Unleashing the power. In P. Wehman (Ed.). *Life beyond the classroom* (pp. 285–308). Baltimore: Paul H. Brookes Publishing Company.

Balser, D. (2007). Predictors of workplace accommodations for employees with mobility-related disabilities. *Administration & Society, 39,* 656–683.

Becker, D., Drake, R., & Bond, G. (2011). Benchmark outcomes in supported employment. *American Journal of Psychiatric Rehabilitation, 14,* 230–236.

de Jonge, D., Scherer, M., & Rodger, S. (2007). *Assistive technology in the workplace.* New York, NY: Elsevier.

Individuals with Disabilities Education Improvement Act of 2004, PL 108-446, 20 U.S.C. §§ 1400 *et seq.*

Jette, A. (2017). The promise of assistive technology to enhance work participation. *Physical Therapy, 97,* 691–692.

Patterson, K., & Cavenaugh, T. (2012), Assistive technology in the transition education process. In M. Wehmeyer & K. Webb (Eds.), *Handbook for transition education for adolescents with disabilities* (pp. 227–246). New York, NY: Routledge.

Wehman, P., Chan, F., Ditchman, N., & Kang, H. (2014). Effect of supported employment on vocational rehabilitation outcomes of transition-age youth with intellectual and developmental disabilities: A case control study. *Intellectual and Developmental Disabilities, 52,* 296–310.

Wehman, P., Inge, K., Revell, G., & Brooke, V. (2007). *Real work for real pay: Inclusive employment for people with disabilities.* Baltimore, MD: Paul H. Brookes Publishing Co.

# Chapter 8 Appendices

- Appendix 8.1: Work Experience Agreement
- Appendix 8.2: Individual Support Plan Template
- Appendix 8.3: Worksite Visit Checklist
- Appendix 8.4: Work Experience Evaluation
- Appendix 8.5: Daily Work Report
- Appendix 8.6: Learning Lab Activity: Scenarios That Illustrate Worksite Support Needs

# Work Experience Agreement

Student name: _____

Company: _____

Work experience location: _____

Company contact person: _____ Title: _____

Transition specialist: _____

*Work schedule*

| | |
|---|---|
| Sunday | |
| Monday | |
| Tuesday | |
| Wednesday | |
| Thursday | |
| Friday | |
| Saturday | |

Work experience goals/objectives

1. _____

2. _____

3. _____

4. _____

Primary duties

1. _____

2. _____

3. _____

4. _____

*(continued)*

Student agrees to

1. Attend according to agreed-on schedule.

2. Conform to the rules and regulations of the workplace.

3. Notify my supervisor when I will be late or absent.

4. Notify my transition specialist if problems arise or if I have a concern.

_____          _____

Student's signature                                                    Date

Employer/supervisor agrees to

1. *Host   Employ*  (circle one) student per the agreed-on schedule.

2. Conform to federal/state regulations regarding employment, safety, and wages (if applicable).

3. Designate a supervisor/mentor responsible for the student and work experience oversight.

4. Consult with the transition specialist about student performance and participate in evaluating the work experience.

_____          _____

Employer/supervisor's signature                                Date

Transition specialist agrees to

1. Provide/help with training and orientation to the student as necessary.

2. Visit the student at the worksite and provide regular feedback and assistance.

3. Assist the student and employer/supervisor to identify and resolve any performance problem that may arise.

4. Maintain contact with the student and employer/supervisor throughout the work experience.

5. Evaluate the work experience and provide appropriate credit as required.

_____          _____

Transition specialist's signature                                  Date

# Individual Support Plan Template

Student name: _____

Company: _____

Company contact person: _____ Title: _____

Transition specialist: _____

**Who?**

Role of workplace supervisor/mentor (e.g., training, supervision, coaching)

Role of transition specialist (e.g., coaching, acquisition of assistive devices)

Other primary contacts at worksite (e.g., coworkers)

**What?** *(check all that apply)*

☐ Mentor identified                  ☐ Tasks clearly outlined

☐ Physical accessibility ensured     ☐ Task modifications identified and in place

☐ Accommodations identified          ☐ Orientation and training arranged

**How?** *(check all that apply)*

☐ Disclosure decision determined with student

☐ Learning goals identified for work experience

☐ Site visit schedule determined

☐ Feedback/evaluation schedule determined

Other comments

# Worksite Visit Checklist

Student name: _____

Company: _____

Date of visit: _____

*During today's visit*

☐ Observed the student perform assigned tasks

☐ Coached the student in completing task

☐ Gave feedback to student on performance

☐ Spoke with supervisor/mentor about student's performance

☐ Helped make adjustment to task or assignment

☐ Checked on effectiveness of accommodations

☐ Spoke with coworkers about student

☐ Scheduled the next visit

Comments

# Work Experience Evaluation

Student name: _____

Company: _____

**Learning objectives** *(check if met)*

☐ 1. _____

☐ 2. _____

☐ 3. _____

☐ 4. _____

☐ 5. _____

Explanation/comments

Rate the student using the scale provided.

| | Work habits and skills | Rating |
|---|---|---|
| | 1. Accepts direction and feedback | |
| 4   *exceptional* | 2. Maintains good appearance | |
| 3   *better than average* | 3. Attendance is on time | |
| 2   *comparable to average* | 4. Shows enthusiasm for assignments and assigned tasks | |
| | 5. Asks for help when needed | |
| 1   *below average* | 6. Follows instruction | |
| n/a   *does not apply* | 7. Follows rules | |
| | 8. Stays on task | |
| | 9. Meets employer's performance expectations | |
| | 10. Interacts well with other coworkers | |
| | ***Overall rating*** | |

*(continued)*

Additional comments

I agree that this evaluation accurately represents _____ 's work experience.

_____
Student's signature

_____
Date

_____
Supervisor's signature

_____
Date

_____
Transition specialist's signature

_____
Date

# Daily Work Report

Student name: _____ Date: _____

Company supervisor: _____

Transition specialist: _____

*Today during a visit to the worksite, the following
was observed and discussed about the student:*

☐ Came to work on time

☐ Was doing assigned tasks

☐ Stayed on task

☐ Performed to supervisor's expectations

☐ Had a good attitude about work

☐ Asked for help when needed

☐ Interacted well with coworker

Comments

# Learning Lab Activity:
## Scenarios That Illustrate Worksite Support Needs

| Scenario | Potential supports/accommodations |
|---|---|
| Marta is very shy, has limited verbal skills, and does not interview well. | *A working interview where Marta can show how she can perform the tasks* |
| Kirsten is blind and needs close supervision to learn new tasks. She wants to work in an office. | *A workplace mentor, customized tasks, jigs to orient papers* |
| Chris wants to work as an electrician. He has an interview for a work experience with a local company that installs electric charging stations. He has limited hearing. | |
| Kayla has a new supervisor who wants her to work faster at her job sorting and hanging clothes at a large department store. | |
| Shawn is in a work experience performing minor computer and cell phone repair. He continually chatters and makes inappropriate comments about celebrities. His coworkers have complained to the supervisor. | |
| Eric is very active and has to move around constantly. He says and does things to irritate people when he has nothing to do at the lumberyard where he works. | |
| Shengli has difficulty remembering the sequence of one particular work task that has several steps. | |
| Lauren has a work experience in a real estate office. She has trouble using the buttons that operate the copy machine because she cannot reach them from her wheelchair. | |
| José works quickly and accurately doing filing at his job at a construction company office, but he is often late for work or calls in sick. | |
| Roberta likes a strict routine and gets upset when her work tasks are changed. | |

# Facilitating Workplace Mentorship for Youth Workers

Richard G. Luecking and Meredith Gramlich

> **By completing this chapter, the reader will**
>
> - Learn from youth mentoring examples
> - Understand the value of workplace mentoring
> - Learn strategies for identifying and recruiting workplace mentors
> - Identify ways to support workplace mentors
> - Complete a Learning Lab on workplace mentoring

*"Sean gave me a chance to try things out. He showed me what he wanted me to do. Then he let me know how I could do better. He also talked to me about how to talk to customers. He really helped me understand how to do a good job."*

Chris, a youth intern, describing support from Sean, his workplace mentor

Christina always wanted to work with kids. She often babysat for her younger siblings and cousins but wanted to get experience learning how to become a teacher. Together with her transition specialist, Christina explored aftercare programs near her home to identify a good match for learning how aftercare and school programs work and what it takes to be successful. As Christina was under 18, she was not able to be hired as a childcare assistant, but was able to jump right into a volunteer work experience helping the teacher set up the classroom, prepare lesson plans, help with story time, and generally help out with the kids. Christina had the opportunity to observe and practice behavior management and lesson implementation. The teacher mentored her by modeling effective classroom management strategies, lesson planning techniques, and workplace expectations and behaviors. As Christina had demonstrated her commitment and her natural easy rapport with the kids during her volunteer work experience, her supervisor officially hired her as a teacher's aide when she turned 18. As a result of the direct mentoring she received from her supervisor, Christina was able to transition her volunteer work experience into a job that is building her career skills.

Jackson always wanted to work at a gaming store. His transition specialist helped him obtain a work experience running the bumper cars at a nearby amusement center where Jackson was a regular customer. A coworker recognized Jackson and occasionally offered support on and off the job with little suggestions for how to interact with customers and how to do the job more efficiently. Jackson's colleague not only became a touch point for Jackson when he needed help navigating work, they also developed a supportive friendship. This informal mentoring relationship helped Jackson build job skills and social interactions necessary for a successful work experience.

Whether mentoring relationships are informal as in Jackson's case, or more formally arranged as in Christina's, mentors can have a significant impact on youth success in the workplace (Bruce & Bridgeland, 2014; Lindsay & Munson, 2018). Companies adopt many approaches with prospective and current employees to promote the development of the skills needed to enhance productivity and the quality of the workplace. Many of the top-performing organizations include mentoring as a specific strategy to nurture employee performance (Emma, 2018; The National Mentoring Partnership, 2015a; Tellmann, 2017). There are important similarities between this concept and what occurred in the examples above. For the most part, mentoring youth workers offers the same benefit to the company and to the youth as mentoring does for all employees, of any age, experience, or need for support. For youth who may have limited experience in the workplace, mentoring has a particularly useful function of acclimating youth to job duties and performance expectations (Lindsay & Munson, 2018; Timmons, Mack, Sims, Hare, & Wills, 2006). Companies benefit in a number of ways, not the least of which is that mentoring youth workers contributes to the development of the future workforce. As discussed later in the chapter, in companies where there is mentoring for youth with disabilities, either formally or informally, there is an extra bonus of authentic, person-specific, disability awareness that is often absent from most company diversity training programs (Morrison, Phillips, & Chan, 2016).

There are many definitions of "mentoring" and of "mentor." For the purpose of youth work experience discussed throughout this book, *mentoring* is defined as a trusting and supportive relationship, formally or informally designated, which pairs youth with well-established persons at the workplace. Similarly, *mentor* is defined as a well-established person at the workplace who is given, volunteers for, or naturally assumes the role of mentoring a youth in the workplace.

An effective workplace mentor models and reinforces behavioral characteristics that will contribute to the youth's successful work experience. An effective mentor relationship benefits not only the youth, but the mentor, the company, and the transition program overseeing the work experience. This chapter discusses how mentoring relationships can provide valuable support to youth in the workplace as they build skills, confidence, initiative, and responsible work behavior. It also discusses how the work experience works for everyone involved.

# WHY MENTORING IS EFFECTIVE

The value of experienced and mature adults mentoring and providing guidance to youth has long been recognized in a host of contexts, including at work where effective mentors are able to model and encourage skills and positive behaviors (National Mentoring Partnership, 2015b; Sipe, 1999). In addition, strong relationships with adults have been shown to be of critical importance to youth, especially those with barriers to social acceptance, such as is the case with many youth with disabilities (Shields, 2016; Spencer & Rhodes, 2014). Furthermore, literature on the value of workplace mentoring generally, and on career development in particular, has consistently shown associations between mentor support and career advancement (Ghosh & Reio, 2013). Thus, it is clear that informal and formal workplace mentors have the potential to be key ingredients in shaping career development of all youth, but especially youth with disabilities (American Association of People with Disabilities [AAPD], 2018).

Among the many advantages of facilitating workplace mentors include the help they provide youth as they develop social and work competencies, make connections with coworkers, and navigate both the physical and social circumstances that are unique to each workplace. In short, having a workplace mentor provides a nonjudgmental, but available, adult helper who can impart crucial job-related and social skills, enrich and expand the youth's social connections, both in and outside of work, and enhance self-concept and optimism for the future. For youth with disabilities, workplace mentors provide two additional benefits. First, they can reinforce self-determination because the youth is able to try more at the workplace experience, which in turn will enable the youth to have a larger repertoire of work experiences from which to draw important self-awareness about workplace likes and dislikes and career knowledge so as to make better-informed future job and career decisions. Second, the help and guidance provided by mentors offer many youth with disabilities the opportunity to take more active roles in the workplace, which in turn encourages youth to take a more active role in their own career planning process. In short, workplace mentors can give meaningful feedback on workplace behaviors, open doors to new opportunities, and help youth establish and make use of connections in and out of the workplace. Specific benefits of workplace mentoring for youth are outlined next.

## Increased Comfort and Acceptance in the Workplace

Everyone needs help orienting to a new job. Anyone of any age at any point in their career who is starting a new job might think: "How will I fit in?" "Can I do the job?" "Will my coworkers accept me?" "What if I make mistakes?" "Who should I ask for help?" "Where do people eat lunch?" "How do I do my timesheet?" "When and where do I take breaks?" Uncertainty regarding these questions is significantly magnified for youth who have had few, if any, experiences in the workplace. The presence of an experienced, mature person who can mentor youth on the job can go a long way in helping youth fit in, know what to do, understand workplace expectations and protocol, and minimize the anxiety that youth may feel in a new workplace and likely their first career experience.

As youth struggle to learn new tasks, meet and interact with coworkers, and acquire effective work behaviors, access to established and trusted coworkers as mentors can significantly affect integration into the workplace and learning on the job. As mentioned earlier, this relationship can be informal, where an interested coworker naturally assumes this role, or it can be a formally designated person who will guide the youth in managing the work tasks and the social relationships in the workplace.

For example, Javon was excited about his opportunity to work in a wet basement recovery business, where his customized work experience responsibilities included categorizing and filing invoices electronically and organizing and maintaining the construction materials in the storage facility during delivery and dispersal. Javon was unfamiliar with both filing work and the tasks related to organizing the materials. So, he was matched with a colleague, Michael, who served as an informal mentor from whom Javon could learn the ropes and to whom he could go with any questions. Whenever Javon was confused or needed extra support, Michael was available as his go-to work buddy. As a result, Michael and Javon developed a great rapport. They discovered a shared passion for baseball and have gone to some baseball games together.

## Skill Acquisition

One of the best ways to learn a new skill or new work task is to learn from someone who has already mastered that skill or task. In almost every job someone is taught and guided by a valued colleague or coworker. These people, whether it is recognized as such or not, are mentors. The same concept applies to youth in work experiences accessing workplace mentors to help them get maximum learning and benefit from the experience. Youth in the workplace will ideally interact with established workers who will in turn play a role in helping the youth learn their job tasks and refine their task performance. Transition specialists and youth advocates who are facilitating youth work experiences will also be better able to manage the work experience when they can identify and encourage the involvement of workplace mentors who are skilled at their jobs, understand the work culture, and can help youth with task proficiency.

For example, Andrea was hired at a farm in a tailored role mucking animal stalls, feeding the animals, monitoring stock supply needs and placing inventory orders, and developing and distributing marketing materials for farm events. Forever passionate about animals, but also interested in art and computers, this was a great combination of her interests where Andrea got to learn about and contribute to the workings of a farm and also help develop marketing materials. A longtime farm employee was matched with her as a mentor to demonstrate each task and provide guidance when needed. Not only did Andrea become self-sufficient and adept at all her roles, she became a mainstay of the farm and continued working at the farm after her work experience ended.

## Enhanced Work Performance

Learning work tasks is usually not the only expectation for workplace performance. Becoming better at them is almost always a desired outcome. Of course, someone at the workplace who is already good at the task can be of great value to help youth gain proficiency at their work tasks. Also, it is very useful for youth to have someone at the workplace who can provide feedback to them on what to do, how to do it, and how to correct errors. Even more important is someone who can praise and encourage youth as they are learning tasks. Effective mentors do all of this.

Effective mentors also guide youth about acceptable work behaviors that contribute to good work performance. These behaviors might include, among a host of others, how to manage criticism, how to interact with coworkers, how to work as part of a work team, how to manage time, and how to correct errors. Even if the employment specialist is available to be on the job to coach youth on many of these work behaviors, it is beneficial that there be an additional experienced in-house guide to support youth as they strive to learn and improve workplace performance. There is nothing more powerful than direct feedback from a colleague or supervisor. These real-time interactions are concrete and timely and offer real learning and growth opportunities.

For example, Ramone's transition specialist helped him get a paid work experience at a dental office, where he filed patient files, sterilized equipment, and kept the waiting room organized. The transition specialist worked closely with the office staff to identify all the steps needed to accurately file and sterilize the instruments and establish a system of quality control to assure accuracy. Ramone was partnered with a colleague, Maria, as a workplace mentor to check on his filing and other tasks. Not only did Maria work closely with Ramone, but also the transition specialist was able to collaborate and troubleshoot with Maria to help Ramone be successful. With Maria's support, Ramone was a hit in the office, and all the staff welcomed him as a member of the team.

## Social Networking

It is common for any youth to have difficulty integrating into the social network of the workplace (The National Mentoring Partnership, 2015c; Timmons et al., 2006). Although the transition specialist can and should play a role in facilitating social connections, this can best be done by people already well established at the workplace. Workplace mentors can introduce youth to other coworkers, help youth interact appropriately with coworkers, and give the youth status by virtue of association with a popular mentor. Mentors can also show youth the ropes around the workplace. For example, a mentor might clue the youth in on when people take breaks, who he or she can joke with, who not to tease, and how to please the boss.

Nothing eases the anxiety and uncertainties of being in a new workplace better than being included in the social network of the workplace. Mentors can help include youth in workplace gatherings and even after work gatherings. For example, Kirsten's transition specialist developed a tailored opportunity for her at an office retrieving and opening all the mail, date stamping and maintaining the chronology of incoming correspondence, and preparing outgoing mailings. Kirsten was matched with a colleague, Darlene, who determined Kirsten's daily tasks and helped get her set up with what she needed to do. Darlene became an informal mentor for Kirsten as Kirsten navigated her work tasks and the social network of her office. Not only did Darlene give gentle, constructive feedback to help Kirsten succeed in her work assignments and adjust tasks and instructions as needed, she also made sure Kirsten participated in all the office celebrations, drove Kirsten to the company picnic, and celebrated Kirsten's birthday with a big cake and group present! Darlene and a few office colleagues attended one of Kirsten's theater performances as well. As a leader in the office—and model for positive, value-based interactions with Kirsten—Darlene was instrumental in helping Kirsten become an integral part of the office community. This work experience did not just include Kirsten in a positive work environment; it also provided added value for both Kirsten and the employer by creating a win-win situation for everyone involved in Kirsten's daily work duties. Kirsten continues to work in this customized paid job, is completely integrated with her colleagues, and is a core team member.

## Enhanced Self-Concept and Self-Confidence

Adolescents often view themselves through "reflected appraisal"—that is, they tend to see themselves through others' judgments of them or others' perceived judgments (Tellman, 2017). In this regard, a positive mentoring experience can make a big difference in a youth's development. If mentors see youth in a positive light and treat them accordingly, youth's view of themselves can shift to a more positive self-regard as well as change the way they regard others' views of them. Hence, a mentor's positive appraisal can gradually become how the youth sees him- or herself. In short, it feels good to be positively regarded, which leads to increased self-regard, which leads to more confidence, which leads to more work and career success.

A good example is Maya, who expressed an interest in a work experience in the medical field but had very poor grades, was getting in trouble at school, was disrespectful, and was not turning in her work. She did not have much support at home, as her mom was stretched thin by three jobs and little time at home with Maya and her siblings. Maya's transition specialist noted the need for Maya to have a strong mentor to help her see the value of doing her best, presenting her best self, and contributing in a meaningful way to her environment. By incorporating her interests and support needs in her work experience development, Maya's transition specialist developed an opportunity for her in a dental office, where the receptionist, Theresa, expressed an interest in acting as a mentor to support Maya. Theresa took Maya under her wing, gave her constructive feedback, and modeled appropriate work behavior and skill development. Theresa supported Maya with demonstration and feedback on appropriate interactions and tasks, and she guided Maya in next steps needed to be successful at work and school. Maya blossomed during her work experience. Her engagement and behavior at work had a positive impact on her school participation and behavior. Theresa helped Maya not only succeed in her work experience, but also provided guidance and feedback to help Maya see how her behavior affected others and could have a positive impact on her environment.

## Additional Mentoring Benefits for Youth

As youth develop more work experience and pursue their career course, they will need both employment and social contacts. Relationships with mentors offer additional benefit beyond the work experience where they were first matched. In fact, there are several ways in which mentors can help youth outside of work. First, the mentor can recommend youth to potential future employers. Everyone a youth meets expands the network of contacts that is so important to adult job searches (The National Mentoring Partnership, 2015c). Thus, mentors can expand the number of people the youth meets who have work connections and who also may constitute a network from which to identify future work and career opportunities.

For many youth, the relationship with a mentor provides a benefit that goes well beyond the work experience. Outside of work, mentors often help youth become part of a more socially desirable or higher-achieving peer group (Bruce & Bridgeland, 2014). As workplace mentors model mature behavior and informally connect and expose youth to others who exhibit mature behavior, they help youth expand their social behavior repertoire and resist negative influence (The National Mentoring Partnership, 2015c). The potential value for youth who establish relationships, either formally or informally, with workplace mentors is substantial. By virtue of being a caring adult who models workplace professionalism coupled with caring feedback and encouragement, workplace mentors can have profound impact on youth and their life trajectory.

Not every mentoring relationship works well for every youth. However, as noted later in the chapter, factors that contribute to successful mentoring relationships include mentor training, clear expectations, and support from a transition specialist. In any case, it is clear that under the right circumstances mentoring relationships can offer plentiful potential benefits for youth. Mentors, employers, and transition programs also benefit for different reasons, as the following section explains.

## How Mentors Benefit

There are many reasons co-workers may choose to act as mentors; for the same reasons, they may gain as much as the youth from the experience. These reasons include, among others, the chance to positively influence youth, a way to improve their own job performance by showing someone else how to do it, recognition from managers and supervisors for taking on extra work, and satisfaction from helping others (Sipe, 1999; Timmons et al., 2006). Transition specialists can keep these multifaceted reasons in mind when recruiting or identifying potential workplace mentors for youth on the worksite. It is also useful to keep in mind that unless there is some direct benefit to the mentor, either tangible or intangible, the mentor relationship either will not take root or will not work. Mentorship relationships evolve in much the same way as negotiations with employers for youth work experiences discussed in Chapter 7. That is, they require making the proposition attractive to all parties involved. This is discussed further later in the chapter.

## What Companies and Schools Gain from Mentor Relationships

As discussed at the beginning of this chapter, many companies have already adopted mentoring programs for existing employees. Hence, it is not a foreign concept in the workplace. Companies can benefit in many ways when experienced workers are paired with youth workers. These include more direct influence over the development of the future workforce, potentially better productivity by both the youth worker and the mentor, improved oversight and supervision of the youth, and useful conduits for communication with transition specialists involved with the youth.

For the transition specialist—and, by extension, schools and transition programs—there are obvious advantages to having someone mentor the youth's experience and performance in work experience situations. After all, transition specialists cannot be everywhere! Someone to oversee the youth's performance

## Mutual Benefits of Workplace Mentoring

For youth

- Increased comfort and acceptance in the workplace

- Enhanced work performance

- Accelerated acquisition of skills

- Improved work and social behavior

- Increased self-esteem and self-confidence on the current work experience and for the subsequent work experiences

For transition programs

- Increased likelihood of successful work experience for youth participants

- More clear connectivity of learning and work

- Improved, constructive workplace oversight for youth

- Eyes and ears of transition specialist—a key go-to person for the work experience

For mentors

- An opportunity to improve the quality of life for young people

- Chance to hone communication and coaching skills

- Helping to improve quality of education in the community

- Satisfaction in helping others

- Recognition and responsibility from supervisor—improved standing at work

- Continual improvement in skills and effectiveness on the job by sharing and reinforcing knowledge

For employers/companies

- More direct and positive influence on youth

- Enhanced productivity by youth and other employees

- Improved workplace supervision and oversight of youth

- Additional avenue for recognizing and promoting workers who act as mentors

- Enhanced avenue for communication with supervising transition specialist

- Expanded avenues for influencing the future workforce

in the transition specialist's absence, someone to directly help youth learn tasks and give constructive feedback, someone to facilitate the youth's connection to coworkers, and someone to report on the work experience are just a few of the advantages. In short, a mentor becomes the eyes and ears of the transition specialist at the workplace and increases the likelihood that the youth will have a successful work experience. Again (and as the Mutual Benefits of Workplace Mentoring textbox summarizes), under the right circumstances, workplace mentor relationships can benefit everyone. The next section provides strategies for organizing and monitoring mentor relationships to facilitate the most favorable outcome.

## THE BASICS OF IDENTIFYING AND ORGANIZING MENTORING RELATIONSHIPS

Workplace mentoring does not require an extensive time commitment. It also does not need to be a formal designation. Mentoring arrangements range from supportive coworkers who naturally guide and encourage youth during their time at the workplace to more formal and intensive interactions between an assigned mentor and a youth. Coworkers frequently guide and assist one another without having the label of mentor. But they are often in positions to do all of the things that a formally designated mentor would do: be a role model, provide guidance as to work performance and work behavior, and facilitate social relationships at the workplace, as well as any number of other useful roles. As a successful adult worker, a mentor is in a position to model and reinforce work skills and behavior for youth in the workplace.

Mentors are a valuable resource for augmenting the work of facilitating work experiences for youth in transition. For the transition specialist, the effort that goes into fostering workplace mentoring may also vary in intensity, depending on the youth and depending on the workplace. It may involve careful recruitment, selection, and matching of a mentor with a youth, which takes time and careful consideration. More often, however, is the scenario when a transition specialist merely offers support and guidance to a relationship that naturally evolves between youth and an interested or involved supervisor or coworker. In any case, a prerequisite to fostering mentoring relationships is to carefully identify potential mentor roles from among many for individual youth. See the textbox for a summary of workplace mentor functions, as originally identified by Gramlich (1999).

### Identifying Mentors

Once familiar with the supports a youth needs and how that fits with any of the various roles mentors can take on, transition specialists are ready to begin identifying potential workplace mentors, encouraging their involvement with the youth, orienting them to the particular needs of the youth, and supporting them in managing the relationship. Ways in which transition specialists can facilitate the matching of a mentor include the following.

- *Find a champion:* Often there is someone in the work environment who is naturally predisposed to help youth adjust to the workplace. This may be a colleague who is a younger worker him- or herself, who is familiar with disability

**Summary of Mentor Functions**

Workplace mentors perform many important support functions and can do the following:

- Provide the youth with an orientation to the workplace including rules, policies and procedures, as well as unwritten rules such as when to take breaks, how to request help, and so forth

- Help the youth understand his or her job or task responsibilities

- Help the youth resolve conflicts, clarify issues, and cope with stressful situations

- Make suggestions about appropriate work assignments and specifications of the work experience

- Model behaviors that lead to workplace success, including respectful communication and cooperation with coworkers and supervisors

- Guide the youth in work-related decision making, scheduling, and so forth

- Provide feedback necessary for the youth to perform effectively, highlighting strengths and opportunities for improvement

- Coach the youth to improve work performance

- Informally evaluate the youth's performance

- Act as a liaison between the youth and school or transition personnel to share information about the youth's progress and performance in the workplace

- When appropriate, contribute to the design, development, and modification of the youth's work experience objectives

- Help the youth's self-esteem and confidence by providing encouragement and positive feedback

*Source:* Gramlich (1999).

through a family member, or who simply expresses an interest in a particular youth worker.

- *Solicit individual recommendations:* Managers or supervisors may be encouraged to recommend or solicit recommendations for potential mentors from people in the company, especially identifying people who have been mentors in the past. In addition, mentoring may be attractive for someone who wants to add the experience of supervising and mentoring fellow employees to his or her work résumé.

- *Observe co-workers:* There may be people in the workplace who seem especially sympathetic to the youth or who exhibit good communication with youth. They might be tapped to be informal mentors. Also, it often happens that certain coworkers naturally gravitate toward a particular youth in the workplace and vice versa. Transition specialists can cultivate this interest so that the coworker agrees to keep an eye out for that youth. Often this happens naturally—the transition specialist can encourage and support the relationship by being available to the coworker to provide information about how the youth learns or how to give feedback to the youth or any number of specifics that apply to individual youth.

A factor in helping identify potential workplace mentors is the set of traits of established employees who could offer youth workplace support. Characteristics of an effective workplace mentor may include any combination of the following (Bruce & Bridgeland, 2014; Emma, 2018):

- Willing and able to commit the necessary time

- Interested in helping and teaching youth

- Able to communicate effectively with youth

- Able to see mentoring as an opportunity rather than an assignment

- Sensitive to cultural backgrounds

- Capable of encouraging, supporting, motivating, and leading others

- Willing to share constructive criticism and feedback in a supportive, sensitive, and patient manner

- Capable of being nonjudgmental

In addition to any of these factors, there may simply be occasions when a straightforward expression of interest in the youth may open the door for a mentor relationship. Transition specialists alert to these situations are in a position to support and encourage a relationship that can significantly contribute to success of any youth's work experience.

For example, Sharon's lively and dynamic personality helped draw Kendrell out of his shell as she greeted him, asked him about his work, and encouraged him to engage with his coworkers. Kendrell's transition specialist targeted Sharon as a natural mentor because of her demonstrated interest in Kendrell, her magnetic personality, and her centrality in the social network of the workplace. At the interactive children's museum where Kendrell organized supplies, set up activity stations, and copied and restocked marketing materials, Sharon acted as a touchstone for Kendrell to check in for next steps and encouragement. As a workplace mentor, Sharon helped Kendrell to be comfortable in his social interactions at work and gain self-confidence.

## Supporting Mentors and the Mentoring Relationship

Mentors are helpful at any stage of the work experience, including initial orientation to the workplace, throughout the learning and performance of work tasks, and in the final evaluation of the work experience. These stages are each discussed next. Transition specialists should be ready to help mentors understand and fulfill their role, no matter if the mentoring relationship is a formal or an informal one. Sometimes it helps to provide a brief guide to mentors, such as the Quick Tips for Mentors Supporting Youth Workers provided in Appendix 9.1. Mentors will appreciate continual communication, encouragement, and advice as they learn to instruct and guide youth. As a consequence, youth will benefit from the mentor's well-supported guidance.

## Workplace Orientation

Mentors can play a key role in the orientation phase, when youth are first beginning the work experience. They are in a position to discuss with youth upfront employer expectations for the work experience, including performance, punctuality and attendance requirements, dress codes, break and lunch times, and so forth. Transition specialists can help mentors structure and/or deliver this information. It is important also to communicate to the mentor the objectives of the youth's work experience so that the mentor's support will augment the most important aspects of the experience.

Transition specialists will need to orient workplace mentors to each youth, addressing specific issues that may affect the success of the relationship, such as best ways to communicate with the youth, individual learning styles of the youth, and best support strategies, including issues of specific disability accommodation if the youth has agreed to disclose personal disability information (see Chapter 4 for discussions about disability disclosure decisions). Ultimately, the key orientation message that mentors can impart to youth in the workplace is fourfold: "We are happy that you are here. This is what we do here. This is what we expect you to do here. Let's work together to make this a success."

## Learning and Performing Tasks

Many youth and their employers will rely on transition specialists to teach work tasks to youth. Many will need only some initial and occasional guidance from a workplace supervisor or coworker. Many will need very little, if any, structured assistance in learning their workplace tasks. In any case, there are several common strategies and activities that mentors can implement in helping youth learn and perform assigned tasks, including

- Giving basic task instruction (here it is often important for the transition specialist and/or the youth to give the mentor information on the youth's learning style)

- Guiding the youth in decision making and prioritizing work tasks

- Helping the youth resolve conflicts, clarify expectations, and cope with stressful situations

- Making suggestions concerning alternative work assignments if the youth is ready to take on new tasks or if he or she is poorly matched to current tasks

- Providing feedback on the youth's work performance, especially highlighting performance strengths and constructively demonstrating specific areas that need improvement

- Modeling performance of the work tasks and of good work behavior

- Implementing supports and accommodations that might be necessary for individual youth

- Acting as a liaison between the workplace staff and transition program staff

- Keeping it positive by giving regular feedback to the youth on good or improved performance

Most important, youth learn in the workplace when mentors stay positive. It therefore helps when transition specialists model positive feedback to mentors.

## Evaluating the Work Experience

As discussed in Chapter 8, a key support role of the transition specialist is to provide feedback to the youth during the experience and to ultimately evaluate the work experience performance of the youth. When there is a mentor involved, this responsibility becomes potentially much easier, not to mention more effective. Who better to provide the youth with feedback and encouragement than people who have had the best opportunity to observe and encourage their performance? It is thus useful to involve the mentor in periodic feedback sessions with the youth as well as in the wrap-up evaluation of the youth's work experience. Getting feedback from the transition specialist is one thing, especially if it highlights the positive aspects of the youth's performance, but it is quite another to receive direct feedback from someone at the workplace with whom the young worker has a good relationship.

## Finding Balance

One final caution: Transition specialists must ensure that they take the ultimate responsibility for overseeing the work experience. Often transition specialists will need to counsel mentors to refrain from getting too involved, overstepping their roles, or doing things that are more appropriately the role of the transition specialist who is responsible for organizing the work experience. For example, mentors should avoid asking personal questions or inquiring about youths' personal lives unless youth bring it up. When youth do bring it up, mentors should not act as a counselor or therapist. If a thorny issue comes up, the mentor should be encouraged to let the transition specialist know. They can then facilitate whatever response or service might be necessary and appropriate.

Similarly, mentors should be cautioned to minimize the giving of personal advice or being judgmental about issues the youth brings up. The possibilities are vast with adolescents who are just learning their way in the world. Youth have revealed issues as serious as criminal behavior, as life-changing as pregnancies, as problematic as financial difficulties, and as innocent as what course to take the next semester. In each case, workplace mentors are advised to seek the help of transition specialists to make sure youth receive appropriate counsel and are referred to suitable services when necessary or fitting. Mentors should always be encouraged to seek out the transition specialist when they are in doubt about handling any situation related to the youth, especially those related to a personal or life crises. Finding the right balance between constructive guidance and excessive personal involvement sometimes requires a little tweaking, but the mentor relationship can be rewarding and effective for all when transition specialists are alert to these issues and ready to step in to help when necessary.

## MENTORING AS A VEHICLE FOR DISABILITY AWARENESS

Some companies have embraced the concept of introducing disability awareness training in the workplace as an element of a diversity initiative. Similarly, many transition and rehabilitation professionals have promoted disability awareness training to companies, to generate employer interest in hiring people with disabilities. These activities can be potentially effective tools to pave the way for people with disabilities in the workplace. However, these trainings are not likely to have much impact without more proactive activity to apply what is learned. The reasons are twofold. First, diversity programs in companies often do not include disability as a diversity feature (AAPD, 2018). Second, whether or not employers include disability in diversity initiatives, general diversity training is minimally effective in changing hiring behaviors of employers (Luecking, 2008).

Employers who have hosted youth with disabilities and adult workers with disabilities, however, generally express a very positive opinion of these individuals (Luecking, 2005; Simonsen, Fabian, & Luecking, 2015). This suggests that planned exposure to and contact with people with disabilities act to dispel myths, stereotypes, and apprehension about disability. Clearly, work experiences that put youth in the workplace contribute to this phenomenon. Even more important, however, are those activities such as mentoring that purposefully put coworkers in close proximate relationships with youth. In this respect mentoring is an actionable way of promoting disability awareness. Sensitivity to disability occurs not by talking about it or by having presentations about it but by actually interacting with a youth with a disability on a regular basis. Consider these quotes from employers that we have worked with.

- "Before I met James, I had never met anyone as disabled before. I would never have considered such people employable. Now that I know James, I know better."

- "I was assigned to help Joey learn his assignments here. I had to be patient, but what a joy to see him become more and more confident as he became more and more proficient with his work."

- "Deborah was the first person I ever talked to with cerebral palsy. I was nervous talking with her at first, but after we go to know each other, I hardly noticed her disability."

We have heard variations of these comments many, many times. Almost every transition specialist can say the same thing. By promoting the development of mentoring relationships, transition specialists are also promoting, however indirectly or unconsciously, disability awareness. This is the type of disability awareness that can directly affect employers' future hiring behavior.

## SUMMARY

This chapter identified why and how workplace mentor relationships benefit not only youth, but also the companies, mentors, and the transition programs that oversee youths' work experience. Youth have the benefit of a supportive workplace relationship that is likely to significantly enhance the work experience. Transition programs have additional eyes and ears to observe youth workplace performance. Companies experience a higher likelihood that youth will contribute to the operations during the work experience and beyond as they shape the future workforce. And mentors have the opportunity to directly influence the career development of youth and to hone their own communication and work skills.

This chapter covered how to organize and facilitate mentor relationships. It illustrated examples of effective mentor relationships and how they benefited all parties involved. Finally, it discussed the value of mentoring as an element of company diversity training. That is, individual and direct contact with people with disabilities enables workers to develop relationships based on something other than disability, and it is a natural and more effective way to promote disability awareness and understanding. This is a potential advantage for companies and—in a larger context—has the potential to cultivate more workplaces that will be more accepting of young people with disabilities.

## LEARNING LAB:
### Examining the Value of Workplace Mentors

Take a few minutes to reflect on your own past work experience. Ask yourself these questions:

1.   Who acted as a mentor in your early career?

2.   How did the relationship affect your experience then? What made it work?

3.   What might have worked better?

4.   How did it influence your later career?

Think of a youth you know well, someone you helped in the past or are helping now in any capacity. List five characteristics you think a mentor of that youth should have.

## REFERENCES

American Association of People with Disabilities (AAPD). (2018). *Mentoring in real life.* Retrieved from https://www.aapd.com/mentoring-in-real-life/

Bruce, M., & Bridgeland, J. (2014). *The mentoring effect: Young people's perspectives on the outcomes and availability of mentoring.* Washington, DC: The National Mentoring Partnership. Retrieved from https://www.mentoring.org/new-site/wp-content/uploads/2015/09/The_Mentoring_Effect_Full_Report.pdf

Emma, L. (2018). *The advantages of mentoring in the workplace.* http://smallbusiness.chron.com/advantages-mentoring-workplace-18437.html

Ghosh, R., & Reio, T. G. (2013). Career benefits associated with mentoring for mentors: A meta-analysis. *Journal of Vocational Behavior, 83,* 106–116.

Gramlich, M. (1999). *How to facilitate workplace mentoring: A guide for teachers to support employers and student workers.* Rockville, MD: TransCen, Inc.

Lindsay, S., & Munson, M. (2018). *Mentoring for youth with disabilities.* Washington, DC: National Mentoring Partnership. Retrieved from http://nationalmentoringresourcecenter.org/images/PDF/Mentoring_for_Youth_with_Disabilities_Population_Review.pdf

Luecking, R. (2005). *In their own words: Employer perspectives on youth with disabilities in the workplace.* Minneapolis: University of Minnesota, National Center on Secondary Education and Transition.

Luecking, R. (2008). Emerging employer views of people with disabilities and the future of job development. *Journal of Vocational Rehabilitation, 29*, 3–13.

Morrison, B., Phillips, B. N., & Chan, F. (2016). *Diversity training in the workplace: Including disability.* Retrieved from http://vcurrtc.org/resources/content.cfm/1157

The National Mentoring Partnership. (2015a). *Mentoring: At the crossroads of education, business and community—the power and promise of private sector engagement in youth mentoring.* Retrieved from https://www.mentoring.org/new-site/wp-content/uploads/2017/12/MENTOR_EY-whitepaper-report_updated-logo.pdf

The National Mentoring Partnership. (2015b). *Mentoring impact.* Retrieved from https://www.mentoring.org/why-mentoring/mentoring-impact/

The National Mentoring Partnership. (2015c). *Mentoring: A critical support strategy for youth career engagement and workforce development.* Retrieved from https://www.mentoring.org/new-site/wp-content/uploads/2015/09/Career.pdf

Shields, D. (2016). *Building the disability inclusion pipeline through mentoring.* In Real Life Blog Series. Retrieved from https://www.mentoring.org/2016/12/real-life-blog-series-building-disability-inclusion-pipeline-mentoring/

Simonsen, M., Fabian, E., & Luecking, R. (2015). Employer preferences in hiring youth with disabilities. *Journal of Rehabilitation, 81*, 9–18.

Sipe, C. L. (1999). Mentoring adolescents: What have we learned? In J. Grossman (Ed.), *Contemporary issues in mentoring* (pp. 10–23). Philadelphia, PA: Public/Private Ventures.

Spencer, R., & Rhodes, J. E. (2014). Growth promoting relationships with children and adolescents. *New Directions for Youth Development, 144*, 59–72.

Tellmann, B. (2017). *Mentoring and diversity.* Retrieved from https://ndmc.pyd.org/guest-blog-mentoring-and-diversity/ [First published in *ACC Docket, 35*(9), 22–23].

Timmons, J., Mack, M., Sims, A., Hare, R., & Wills, J. (2006). *Paving the way to work: A guide to career focused mentoring for youth with disabilities.* Washington, DC: National Collaborative on Workforce and Disability for Youth, Institute for Educational Leadership.

# Chapter 9 Appendix

- Appendix 9.1: Quick Tips for Mentors Supporting Youth Workers

# Quick Tips for Mentors Supporting Youth Workers

- Model what you expect.

- Give clear, detailed, and repeated directions.

- Communicate your expectations for performance, behavior, and social interactions.

- Explain the consequences of inappropriate behavior.

- Discuss progress and improvements in performance—don't stint the praise!

- Be alert to youth learning styles—ask youth how they best learn new tasks, for example, through oral directions, written directions, or just by demonstration.

- Keep an open door and open mind.

- Listen to and respond to concerns and questions.

- Share with youth "tricks of the trade" and what works for you.

- Stay in regular contact with school and youth agency staff for help, support, and information.

# Connecting With Professional and Agency Partners to Foster and Sustain Work Success

Richard G. Luecking and Kelli Thuli Crane

---

**By completing this chapter, the reader will**

- Learn basic information about common professional and agency partners in the work experience and transition process
- Consider the roles of these partners
- Receive tips for effectively collaborating with these partners
- Experience a Learning Lab on partners and their roles

---

*"Ryan had a team of transition professionals working to make sure that he got a job and that he kept it. It worked out great for him."*
Parent of an employed transitioning youth

---

Because of multiple support needs, Keonte's transition specialist arranged for a team of professionals from cooperating agencies to work together to plan for his transition to postschool employment. His transition team included the school transition specialist, a vocational rehabilitation (VR) counselor, a job coach from a local employment service agency, and a counselor from the public mental health agency. Together they set a goal for a paid work experience in his senior year. To participate in the work experience, Keonte and his transition team identified the need for a work schedule that would accommodate his regular counseling appointments, initial workplace support from the job coach to help him learn social communication skills in a retail environment, and the need for a low-stress environment. After considering his interest in science fiction and books, the team helped him find a job at a used bookstore sorting and retrieving books. With the support of the job coach and a customized schedule, Keonte succeeded in the job. Next stop: community college to begin his pursuit of a degree in literature.

Ramon had several work experiences during his last three years in school through a collaboration between his school, the state VR office, and a local adult employment service provider. The school transition specialist worked with Ramon and his family to gather information about his interests, skills, positive traits, and need for support on the job through an asset-based inventory. This inventory was the basis for developing each of Ramon's work experiences. Through its pre-employment transition services (Pre-ETS), the VR office paid the adult employment service provider to develop and monitor the work experiences. Ramon's last work experience was a paid job at a local dentist office, where he not only performed several clerical tasks, but he also was given the responsibility—because of his pleasant personality—to escort patients to their examination rooms. Ramon exited school with this job with ongoing support services paid by the state intellectual/developmental disabilities (I/DD) service agency. He seamlessly entered his postschool life as an employed adult, thanks to the collaboration between the school, the VR office, the adult employment service provider, and the I/DD agency.

During the middle of her work experience as an associate in a retail clothing store, Hailey's stepfather lost his job. Her older brother was incarcerated shortly thereafter. The family was in crisis. Rent needed to be paid. The family dynamics were disrupted. The support for Hailey and her path to adult employment was threatened. Multiple human service agencies were now in Hailey's life trying help the family manage these crises. The transition specialist contacted professionals from each of these agencies so that she could learn how their services could support Hailey with her work experience and how the family situation might affect Hailey's work experience. Through these contacts the transition specialist was able to advise and support Hailey so that she could get ready to go to work, get there on time, and perform her tasks when she got there. Hailey finished the work experience, got a paid job at another clothing store, and now contributes to the family's income.

Youth with disabilities often interact with multiple programs, entities, and professionals at various times during their movement through secondary education and beyond. In addition to the teachers and education professionals who have an obvious and direct role, others among the long list of potentially involved parties in transition are youth service organizations, employment service agencies, government-sponsored disability employment services, and other community organizations and services. Work experiences for transition-age youth do not operate in a vacuum from the rest of their activities and life circumstances. Similarly, a single transition specialist cannot be all things to all youth. Transition specialists will often need partners to collaborate in the effort to develop work experiences, support youth in the workplace, and address life circumstances that might affect the success of the work experience. Moreover, even if transition specialists do a great job in helping youth succeed in the workplace, the success cannot be sustained if there is no support to ensure comparable achievement after school. Thus, additional support and solid partnerships with other professionals and services may be integral to work experience success and a seamless transition to adult employment, as in Keonte's and Ramon's cases. Or, there may be a need to help youth and their families navigate and involve various social services to address family circumstances, as in Hailey's case. For these reasons, transition specialists will often need to identify and collaborate with agencies, professionals, and ancillary services to help youth achieve and maintain work experience and employment success.

Useful support for individual youth work experience and postschool employment success may include VR, community rehabilitation providers, mental health and/or developmental disabilities services, American Job Centers (AJC), Supplemental Security Income (SSI) and Social Security Disability Insurance (SSDI) benefits counselors, social services, and an array of other generic community resources. This chapter identifies and discusses some of these partners, roles they might play, and considerations for organizing their participation in and support of specific work experience circumstances. In fact, the gold standard of youth outcomes is when they are achieving paid employment and pursuing a clear career path. The effects of youth transition initiatives, and the partnerships that support them, are most appropriately judged against this standard.

## COMMON WORK EXPERIENCE AND TRANSITION PARTNERS

The work of transition specialists becomes easier and more effective when targeted professional and agency partners collaborate with them, as well as with youth and their families, to plan for work experiences and sustained employment. Although there are many more possible services and partners than presented here, this section outlines the roles of several of the most common partners in transition work activities.

### Vocational Rehabilitation

A primary resource for transition employment support is the state VR agency. VR services are available in every community in the country through these state agencies. Each state has its own operational structure for VR services and the agency has slightly different names in different states (e.g., Department of Vocational Rehabilitation, Division of Rehabilitation Services, Rehabilitation Commission). Federal government regulations under which state VR agencies operate provide considerable resources and direction to promote consistent service procedures and practices across the country. Literally, students and youth with disabilities in every community in every state have potential access to VR services if they meet designated criteria. It is important to note that the Workforce Innovation and Opportunity Act (WIOA) of 2014 (PL113-128), which authorizes federal funding for VR services, contains specific provisions related to transition services to students and youth with disabilities. The following is a summary of key WIOA provisions.

- Fifteen percent of each state's funding allocation for VR services must be designated for transition services for students and youth between the ages of 14 and 24

- Half of supported employment service funds are designated for youth with significant disabilities

- Pre-ETS is a category of VR funding that can be applied to five service categories before a student exits school:

  1. Job exploration counseling

  2. Work-based learning experience—which may include in-school or after school opportunities or experiences outside the traditional school setting (including internships) provided in an integrated setting in the community to the extent possible

  3. Counseling on opportunities for enrollment in comprehensive transition or postsecondary educations programs at institutions of higher learning

  4. Workplace readiness training to develop social skills and independent living

  5. Instruction in self-advocacy (including instruction in person-centered planning)

- Interagency collaboration between VR and schools is required so that information is shared, joint planning occurs, and services from each system are jointly coordinated

- Services can be provided to youth potentially eligible for VR services but for whom a case has not yet been initiated

In practical terms, this means that VR has a strong focus on transition and can pay for many services *before* students exit high school. Chief among these services are the development and support of work experiences through the Pre-ETS category of "work-based learning experiences." There are also services available through regular VR services that might benefit youth in transition, such as vocational training, assistive technology services, and supported employment. Different eligibility requirements apply to Pre-ETS and to traditional VR services, as summarized in Table 10.1.

**Table 10.1.** Vocational rehabilitation (VR) program eligibility

| Pre-Employment transition services | Regular VR services |
|---|---|
| To be eligible for pre-employment transition services a student or youth must be | To be eligible for VR from the state VR agency an individual must |
| • Age 14–21 | • Have a physical or mental disability, which results in a substantial impediment to employment |
| • Receiving services through an individualized education program (IEP) or a Section 504 Plan | • Be able to benefit in terms of an employment outcome (a person with an impairment and impediment is *presumed* to be able to benefit; in the rare event that there are serious doubts about ability to benefit, the individual will be offered trial work experiences or a period of extended evaluation to further determine the ability to benefit) |
| • Either eligible for VR services (see adjacent column) or "potentially eligible" | |
| "Potentially eligible" means that the individual is thought to meet the criteria in the adjacent column but has not been formally determined to meet them. That is, all students with disabilities, regardless of whether they have applied for or been determined eligible for the VR program, are potentially eligible. | • Require VR services to prepare for, secure, retain or regain employment |
| | Presumed eligibility: Individuals who receive Social Security Income (SSI) or Social Security Disability Insurance (SSDI) are presumed to be eligible for VR services. |
| | Some states also specify that individuals who are eligible for long-term support from the state intellectual/ developmental disabilities (I/DD) service agency or mental health agency and pursuing competitive or supported employment are presumed eligible for VR services. |

Research has shown the effectiveness of VR services, provided early in the secondary school years, in promoting employment and career development for youth with disabilities (Luecking, Fabian, Contreary, Honeycutt, & Luecking, 2018). Early VR services will often result in partnerships between schools, VR agencies, and VR vendors (e.g., community rehabilitation providers) in joint efforts to assist youth in finding and keeping jobs—including those jobs that are targeted for long-term employment after youth leave school. Ramon's example at the beginning of this chapter is an illustration of how that type of collaboration can benefit youth. Of course, referral for VR services also can happen any time after school exit for those eligible youth who were not connected when still in school.

The range of services that VR can provide youth in transition is considerable and includes those listed in the textbox titled Vocational Rehabilitation (VR) Program Services. However, there is an important distinction between Pre-ETS and regular VR services. Pre-ETS are considered preparatory transition activities that start prior to a formal application for VR services. Pre-ETS will usually start prior to a VR application and formal eligibility determination, and it can continue after a VR case is open. Regular VR services (e.g., vocational training, assistive technology, supported employment) can only be provided after eligibility is formally determined.

---

## Vocational Rehabilitation (VR) Program Services

- Pre-employment transition services (Pre-ETS)

  - Job exploration counseling

  - Work-based learning experiences

  - Counseling on opportunities for enrollment in comprehensive transition or postsecondary education programs at institutions of higher learning

  - Workplace readiness training to develop social skills and independent living

  - Instruction in self-advocacy (including instruction in person-centered planning)

- Assessment for determining eligibility and service needs

- Vocational counseling, guidance, and referral services

- Physical or mental restoration services

- Vocational and other training, including on-the-job training

- Maintenance for additional costs incurred while the individual is receiving certain VR services

- Transportation related to other VR services

- Interpreter services for individuals who are deaf

- Reader services for individuals who are blind

*(continued)*

- Services to assist students with disabilities to transition from school to work

- Personal assistance services while an individual is receiving VR services

- Rehabilitation technology services and devices

- Supported employment services

- Customized employment services

- Job placement services

Notably, VR is not an entitlement service in the way that students with a disability are entitled to educational services. This means that not only do youth have to meet the eligibility requirements outlined in Table 10.1, but services are also contingent on available funding resources, which vary from state to state and are usually not sufficient to serve everyone who might be eligible. Due to finite resources, state VR agencies sometimes operate under an order of selection, which mandates that caseloads first include individuals whose disabilities are classified as "significant"—that is, those who require the greatest support to become employed. Nevertheless, because of the array of services that might be available through VR and because of the potentially important role VR can play in augmenting and supporting employment pursuits for people with disabilities, every transition specialist should be aware of this important resource and know how to partner and to link youth with the local VR agency. The textbox titled Way2Work Maryland illustrates how one state is approaching the application of VR services to students in secondary school.

### Way2Work Maryland

Way2Work Maryland is a statewide initiative designed to implement promising school-to-work transition practices in concert with specific provisions of the Workforce Innovation and Opportunity Act (WIOA) of 2014 (PL 113-128). The model incorporates four empirically supported components robustly associated with postschool success for students and youth with disabilities. These components are

1. Early referral to vocational rehabilitation (VR) services, at least 2 years prior to school exit

2. Multiple work-based learning experiences prior to pursuing paid integrated employment

3. Paid integrated employment, including at least one paid job prior to school exit

4.  Strategic and focused service collaboration through a transition team that includes schools, VR, community rehabilitation providers, and American Jobs Centers to maximize partner resources and to ensure that collaborative efforts are directly linked to the pursuit of work experiences, paid integrated employment prior to school exit, and adult employment

Students are connected to Pre-ETS through their local VR office. Once students are approved for Pre-ETS services, they are matched with a community rehabilitation provider (CRP). The CRP, in strong collaboration with the transition team, works closely with the students and their families to identify the youth's interests, preferences, and skills. The CRP then develops a work experience related to the students' identified interests, positive traits, skills, and need for support. Work experiences generally are 6–8 weeks and can be unpaid or paid. The goal of Way2Work Maryland is for students to learn from the work experiences, putting them on the path to integrated community employment.

## State Mental Health/Developmental Disabilities Agencies

In addition to providing services to people with intellectual and developmental disabilities, each state also has a structure for delivering mental health services. These entities may operate from separate state agencies or from the same administrative structure. In some states, they are managed by local community service boards; in others, they are managed through a state administrative structure or through distinct state regions. They also operate under a variety of names and maintain eligibility guidelines that differ from state to state. All of these different entities, processes, and functions may sound confusing. In practice, however, this is less confusing than it sounds, as the applicable state mental health and developmental disability agencies will be well known in school districts and in the local transition service arena. In any case, these services are potentially important to the employment-related activities pursued by youth with disabilities.

For youth with emotional or mental health disabilities, mental health agencies will be potential sources for clinical services, counseling, medication management, and case management. As in Keonte's example at the beginning of this chapter, these services can be critical adjuncts to a youth's work experience. Often, mental health agencies can provide or fund intensive in-the-field case management whereby therapeutic support is made available as an integrated service as youth are pursuing employment. At the same time, such agencies can also manage other concerns, such as relationships with families, judicial systems, substance abuse services, housing, and other life needs that may be affecting their ability to complete school and succeed in work experiences (Wehman, Sutherland, & Achola, 2013). In addition, individual placement and support (IPS) may be available for youth with mental health disabilities. IPS is a model of supported employment for people with serious mental health illness (e.g., schizophrenia spectrum disorder, bipolar disorder, depression). IPS-supported employment helps people living with mental health disabilities work at competitive jobs of their choosing. Although variations of supported employment exist, IPS refers to the evidence-based practice of supported employment that focuses on rapid job-search and placement services. It emphasizes that work is not the result of treatment and recovery but integral to both.

Regarding intellectual and developmental disabilities, I/DD agencies offer case management, housing, and employment services and funding for eligible individuals. Job coaching, supported employment, and customized employment services are the most directly applicable employment-related services for eligible youth provided by I/DD agencies. In most states, funding for these services is not directly available until after the youth exits school, but planning for the receipt of these services before school exit is often a critical feature of transition collaboration. In some communities, the state I/DD agency provides this service; in others, it contracts for this service with community employment service providers, as described in the next section. Ramon benefited from the collaboration with local representatives of the state I/DD agency, who made sure that funding for job coaching was in place immediately upon his exit from public education so that he could keep the job he started while he was a student.

The services available from both mental health and I/DD agencies are eligibility based. Not all youth are eligible for these services. Also, the services provided by mental health and I/DD agencies are dictated by available public funds. Consequently, there are often waiting lists for these services, although some states have made transitioning youth a funding priority (Luecking & D'Agati, 2017). Transition specialists will need to be aware of the circumstances in their local communities so that they can help youth identify and obtain these services accordingly.

## Employment Service Providers

In every community, there are organizations and programs that are contracted by VR or other state agencies to offer job placement, supported employment, customized employment, and other related services. These organizations are often referred to as CRPs or adult employment service agencies. As with VR, when postschool work support will be necessary, it is useful to involve CRPs early in the transition process, such as including them in IEP meetings to involve them in the planning for postschool employment support. For youth work experiences, especially through VR Pre-ETS, CRP services are sometimes used for job development and job coaching for youth while they are still in school. In fact, many transition specialists are employed by CRPs for this purpose when schools need additional help with these activities.

Thus, there are two main roles of CRPs in relation to work experiences for youth. First, they are potential partners in planning for transition and for providing postschool employment services such as supported employment and job placement services. Second, they are potential partners during the development and support of work experiences and jobs while youth are still in school. They may have staff assigned to help youth obtain work and to provide worksite support such as job coaching. Both roles were assumed by a CRP in Ramon's case.

## America's Job/Career Centers

Every state has designated interspersed locations—most often called a One-Stop Career Center, One-Stop Center, or America's Job Center—where anyone, including youth with disabilities, can obtain job search and career information and where multiple services are available in one place. American Job Centers (AJCs) are designed to provide a full range of assistance to job seekers under one roof. Authorized in the WIOA, the centers offer training referrals, career counseling, job listings, and similar employment-related services. Customers can visit a center in person or connect to the center's information online. They also may offer such job search enhancements as résumé writing and interviewing skill classes, as well as job training and youth employment programs for eligible customers. Also among the resources of AJCs are career development information and employer listings that may become contacts for work-based opportunities and jobs. Because state VR agencies and other employment service agencies often are also located there, it is useful for transition specialists to become familiar with how AJCs operate, what services they may offer, and how these services can augment work experience and job development activities.

AJCs and related U.S. Department of Labor–supported programs offer a wide variety of programs to ensure that all youth have the knowledge, skills, and training they need to successfully make the transition to adulthood and careers. These programs do not specifically target, but may include, youth with disabilities. The programs include the following.

- *Youth employment programs* for serving eligible youth, ages 14–24, who face barriers to education, training, and employment. Most of the focus of this program is on out-of-school youth.

- *Job Corps* is the nation's largest and most comprehensive residential education and job training program for at-risk youth, ages 16 through 24. Private companies, state agencies, federal agencies, and unions recruit young people to participate in Job Corps, where they can train for and be placed in jobs.

- *YouthBuild* is a community-based pre-apprenticeship program that provides job training and educational opportunities for at-risk youth ages 16–24 who have previously dropped out of high school. Youth learn vocational skills in construction, as well as in other in-demand industries, including health care, information technology, and hospitality.

- *An apprenticeship program* is a combination of on-the-job training and related classroom instruction in which workers learn the practical and theoretical aspects of a highly skilled occupation. Applicants for apprenticeship programs must be at least 16 years old and meet the program sponsor's qualifications.

For transition specialists and the youth they represent, AJCs can enhance the development of work experiences in the following ways.

- They offer additional sources of career development information. Among the core services available through AJCs are labor market information, information on the area's economy and employers, Internet access to career development information, résumé development, and a host of other services that may provide useful adjuncts to youth, families, transition specialists, and others involved in planning for work experiences.

- They may offer opportunities to gain access to generic (i.e., not disability related) youth employment programs that can provide work experiences and jobs. Through youth programs such as those already mentioned, youth have the option of participating in a host of activities that are designed to give them exposure to work experiences, although there may be a need to assist these youth employment programs in making accommodations for youth with disabilities.

- They may offer access to generic career development and employment training services that are available to adults. Many AJCs have "disability program navigators" who support customers with disabilities in identifying and receiving accommodations during their access to generically available AJC services.

- They provide indefinite, lifelong access to career development assistance. Services of the AJCs are available to any individual older than 18 years at any time in his or her career. This opportunity allows youth to return for career and job search assistance without waiting for eligibility determination or designated program referrals.

## Ancillary Social and Community Services Linkages

Nonwork life circumstances will often significantly influence how successful youth are in work experiences and jobs. Throughout the transition process, youth with disabilities will often require support to obtain and use resources essential to addressing life circumstances that may affect employment success. There are many such situations that occur in anyone's life. However, youth with disabilities are especially vulnerable and often need targeted services that are unrelated to the work experience to properly address them, such as in Hailey's case described in the beginning of this chapter. These situations may include access to or support in maintaining housing; dealing with financial challenges; securing mental health services; coping with health issues; and managing relationship, family, or marital issues—to name only a few.

For these reasons, transition specialists need to be aware of and help link students to supportive services that will help them to address these issues outside of school and work. In many cases, these services will be important partners in helping students and their families plan for the transition to adult life because these supports may be needed at the point of transition and intermittently throughout the students' adult lives. These services include but are not limited to agencies that link people with housing services, income support programs (e.g., Temporary Assistance to Needy Families, food stamps), counseling and mental health services and programs, and various social services agencies (e.g., disability advocacy organizations, family crisis centers, substance abuse intervention services, reproductive counseling services). Just as the employment and career paths of all students are unique, so too are their life circumstances. Thus, is necessary to individualize these services based on a youth's needs. Table 10.2 lists common transition partners and their roles.

## Public Income Benefits Supports

Many youth will be eligible for, or will already be receiving, services from a variety of government-sponsored programs designed to provide youth and their families

**Table 10.2.**   Common transition partners and their roles

| Transition partner | Function | Potential activities to support to work experience and employment |
|---|---|---|
| State vocational rehabilitation agencies | Federally funded program to provide rehabilitation services to individuals with disabilities, including assessment, planning, training, job placement, and other services leading to employment. | Make pre-employment transition services (Pre-ETS) available to youth still in secondary school<br><br>Open cases on referred students well before school exit<br><br>Participate in planning meetings for referred youth (e.g., individualized education programs)<br><br>Facilitate and fund services that contribute to employment goals, such as assistive technology devices, job development, and job coaching |
| Community rehabilitation providers/ Employment service agencies | Private or nonprofit agencies contracted by VR, MH agencies, I/DD agencies and/or school districts to provide job placement, supported employment, and related services. | Cooperatively develop work experiences and jobs with secondary school students<br><br>Contract to provide Pre-ETS<br><br>Cooperate with other partners in work experience service delivery<br><br>Support youth in jobs and community life upon school exit as needed |
| American Job Centers | Centralized location for career and job information, career assessment, career counseling, job training, and job placement services. | Provide career development information and services<br><br>Provide information on job listings<br><br>Offer access to youth employment programs<br><br>Facilitate access to services provided by co-located partners |
| State MH and I/DD agencies | Provides and/or funds case management services, clinical services, vocational services, and supported employment for eligible people with disabilities. | Participate in planning for postsecondary support services<br><br>Provide or fund supported employment and job coaching services<br><br>Provide access to ancillary services such as clinical mental health services, housing, and case management |
| Ancillary health and social service programs | An array of community services to address various social and medical needs of its citizens. | Provide augmentative services for nonwork life needs such as medical services, income support, financial education, child care, and transportation |
| Public income benefits supports | Cash support and medical insurance for financially needy or otherwise eligible individuals. | Provide cash benefits and medical insurance for eligible youth<br><br>Provide information about applicable work incentives<br><br>Services to counsel recipients on effects of earnings on benefits |

*Key:* I/DD, intellectual and developmental disabilities; MH, mental health; VR, vocational rehabilitation.

with income support for their financial needs. These include Temporary Assistance for Needy Families, which provides cash assistance to low-income families, food stamps, medical assistance, and other services. Of particular relevance to transitioning youth with disabilities are two federal income support programs operated by the Social Security Administration (SSA): SSDI and SSI.

SSDI provides benefits, cash payments, and medical insurance called Medicare to individuals with disabilities or blind individuals who are insured by workers' contributions to the Social Security trust fund. To be eligible, a person with a disability must have worked and paid Social Security taxes for a specified amount of time or must be the child of such a worker. SSI makes cash assistance payments to individuals who are older, blind, or have disabilities (including children younger than the age of 18) who have limited income or resources. Beneficiaries also receive medical insurance called Medicaid.

Youth on SSDI or SSI and their families are often concerned about the potential effect of work earnings on their cash benefit and on the associated medical insurance. Because of work incentives offered by SSA, it is most often the case that youth will have more money if they work than if they do not. However, because concerns are common and because there are often complicated procedures for determining how and under what conditions benefits are affected by work, it is useful for youth and their families to contact local SSA resources for advice and help. Benefits counseling is often available from a work incentives expert who can

- Help beneficiaries to navigate the often-complicated public and private benefits programs

- Allow beneficiaries to take full advantage of the array of special work incentives available to them

- Provide counseling that helps beneficiaries plan their employment search so that they ultimately work and earn more

- Place participants in a better position to manage the requirements to report their earnings to SSA so that they do not inadvertently cause a reduction in benefits

Transition specialists should become familiar with benefits counseling resources in their community in order to connect youth and their families to appropriate guidance on managing their benefits when they earn wages (see the textbox Benefits Counseling and Work Experience). Introductory resources on SSI and relevant work incentives can be obtained from several sources, including the local SSA office. SSA also offers comprehensive information about benefits and work incentive rules in what it calls *The Red Book* (see https://www.ssa.gov/redbook/).

---

### Benefits Counseling and Work Experience

Four weeks after Ben started a work experience at an auto body shop, the manager reported that Ben was doing such an outstanding job that he wanted to give him more responsibility and hours. Ben was excited and shared the news with his mother, who instantly became concerned about the cash payments he received under Supplemental Security Income (SSI). The family relied on this cash assistance to help pay bills. The transition specialist working with Ben emphasized to his mother the importance of benefits counseling. She connected Ben's mom with a certified work incentive counselor, who shared information on the various work incentives Ben could take advantage of as a student. Connecting Ben and his mom to a benefits counselor made them more informed about how his earnings could minimally affect his SSI income while he was a student. Ben used this information to start a PASS Plan (Plan to Achieve Self-Support) and started saving for a car. Once Ben buys his own car, he will get himself to and from his job at the auto body shop, where they hired him as a part-time paid employee.

## CONSIDERATIONS FOR EFFECTIVELY IDENTIFYING AND COLLABORATING WITH AGENCY PARTNERS AND ANCILLARY SERVICES

It can be tempting to make a referral to the most convenient, most available, or most familiar service when linking youth to agencies or professionals that are potentially supportive to their efforts to succeed in work experiences and jobs. However, in keeping with what is known to be important and effective for youth in transition—especially the concepts of individual self-determination and informed choice—transition specialists should consider the following items to help them accomplish these linkages.

### Consideration 1

*Make service connections based on the individual youth's needs, not on what happens to be available.* The takeaway here is to avoid the one-size-fits-all approach. It is common, but not always the best option, to steer youth to particular services or agencies based on a disability label. Instead, transition specialists should consider the youth's strengths, needs, existing support system, and the current services they receive to build a profile and determine what new connections will be the best fit.

For instance, Alvin, a youth with intellectual disabilities, was initially referred to a CRP specializing in serving people with intellectual disabilities to help him find a job during his last year in school. Although he wanted to work in an office, the CRP helped him to get a job at a cafeteria cleaning tables with several other individuals with intellectual disabilities. He hated it, and he failed to keep the job. Later, Alvin became involved in a transition program that used an asset-based inventory as a guide to help him obtain a volunteer work experience as an office assistant in an investment firm. This eventually turned into a full-time paid job, which Alvin held when he left school and where he has worked for several years. By individualizing the approach, Alvin's transition specialist was able to steer him to a job and a career path better suited to his interests and capabilities.

## Consideration 2

*Support youth in making their own decisions about services and programs.*
As discussed in Chapter 3, individual choice and self-determination should guide
planning for work experience. Similarly, it should guide linkages to agencies and
services. Transition specialists should provide as much information as possible to
students and families about potential services and potential service agencies so
that they can make informed choices about them.

For one student, Kim, her transition specialist's support of her decisions led
her to pick the service best suited to support her in her postschool career. Kim
was successful in her job as a part-time stock clerk at a large department store.
However, she still needed occasional help from a job coach to make sure she
could learn new tasks when they were assigned to her. As she prepared to leave
the school system, there were four different CRPs funded by the state developmental disability agency that offered to provide job coaching to Kim after
she was no longer a student. Her transition specialist arranged interviews with
representatives from each of the CRPs and helped her to develop questions she
could ask each provider. Kim chose a CRP that answered her question about
what they would do if she lost her job by saying, "We will help you find a new one
that you like."

## Consideration 3

*Help youth navigate supportive services.* Youth often are not aware of what services are available or where to get them. In addition, they often will be understandably confused by the complexities of accessing many of them. Thus, transition
specialists can be important facilitators in this regard.

As one example, due to a family emergency, Sheryl needed help to find a place
to live as well as to contact her mental health counselor about the situation. Her
transition specialist referred her to services that could help her address these circumstances. Without help from a transition specialist, Sheryl may have foundered
for a long time while trying to manage these situations on her own. Not only would
she have been unable to eventually finish her work experience, but also many more
life problems may have resulted.

## Consideration 4

*Help families to support their child to navigate supportive services.* As discussed
in Chapter 5, many families need help to assist their youth to obtain and manage
the myriad resources and services that may support the pursuit of work experiences. This may sometimes mean assisting families with the paperwork associated
with some of these services.

When Joe was about to start a paid job at a local hospital helping in the cardiol-
ogy department, his mother was quite worried about how that might affect his SSI
benefit. She was also not sure how to report his earnings to the local SSA office.
Joe's transition specialist met with Joe's mother and explained that work incentives were available so that Joe could still keep some of his SSI benefits. The transition specialist also provided all of the contact information as well as accompanied
her to the first appointment with the SSA representative. From that point on, Joe's

mother was very supportive of his job and was conscientious about reporting the required earnings information to the SSA office. The transition specialist's support built his mother's confidence and ensured that Joe had a stronger support system for his work experience.

## Consideration 5

*Convene partners around a common goal.* Different purposes or sources of funding of the various programs and services often make it difficult for them to automatically collaborate with one another. As a result they often work in their "silos" operating in isolation from one another. A transition specialist will often need to act as an intermediary or a facilitator to get multiple partners to work together to support a youth's work experience. Pulling them together for meetings is often useful or necessary. At the very least, the transition specialist will need to maintain communication with these partners as well as help them communicate with each other. In the context of work experiences, the collaboration of the partners should always be on the youth's goal to succeed in finding work experiences and performing successfully in the workplace.

For instance, Josie was nearing the end of her internship, in which she was helping to code security badges for a government security agency. With Josie's permission, her transition specialist called a meeting with her VR counselor, her mental health counselor, and her CRP employment specialist to talk about a plan to use her internship as a basis for looking for a permanent job. The plan would have to include VR funding for job coaching, incorporating regularly scheduled mental health counseling with her work schedule, and job development and coaching from the CRP based on her preferences and need for accommodation. The plan led to a successful job experience at a private security company.

## SUMMARY

This chapter explored a selected list of supportive and ancillary services and programs that are often necessary and important to youths' success in work experiences, jobs, and later adult employment. Information was provided on state VR agencies, state mental health and intellectual/developmental disabilities agencies, community rehabilitation providers, American Job Centers, ancillary social service programs, and services that address public income benefits. Any or all of these services may come into play for transition-age youth as they gain work experiences and employment.

For many youth, the end of the secondary education—or postsecondary education, for that matter—does not mean they no longer need support in the workplace. In fact, youth often will need periodic coaching to improve performance, maintain good work behavior, or learn new job tasks. The youth also may encounter nonwork life challenges that may periodically affect work attendance and performance if they are not attended to, such as housing needs, family crises, or personal finance management. Help managing public benefits, such as SSDI and SSI, is a typical ongoing need for many youth with disabilities. For these reasons, it is important for transition specialists to be aware of the purpose and roles of supportive employment and social service partners and be prepared to help students link to those services and programs.

## LEARNING LAB:
## Scoping Out Potential Partners

1. Make an appointment to meet with a VR counselor to learn about the types of local activities and programs for youth in transition in which the VR office is a partner. Ask what services the local VR office typically makes available for youth in transition.

2. Make an appointment to visit the local American Jobs Center in your area to tour the facility.

   • During the visit, interview the staff about services that youth may obtain for employment preparation and development.

   • Find out what other agencies are located there, and determine which of them may offer services that potentially will benefit young job seekers.

   • Find out where and in what format job listings are maintained. Look up several listings to find one that might be appropriate for a youth you know.

## REFERENCES

Luecking, R., & D'Agati, A. D. (2017). Work and employment for people with intellectual and developmental disabilities. In M. Wehmeyer & I. Brown (Eds.), *A comprehensive guide to intellectual and developmental disabilities* (2nd ed., pp. 557–568). Baltimore, MD: Paul H. Brookes Publishing Co.

Luecking, R., Fabian, E., Contreary, K., Honeycutt, T., & Luecking, D. (2018). Vocational rehabilitation outcomes for students participating in a model transition program. *Rehabilitation Counseling Bulletin, 61,* 154–163.

Wehman, P., Sutherland, K., & Achola, E. (2013). Applications for youth with emotional and behavior disorders. In P. Wehman (Ed.), *Life beyond the classroom: Transition strategies for young people with disabilities* (5th ed., pp. 419–446). Baltimore, MD: Paul H. Brookes Publishing Co.

Workforce Innovation and Opportunity Act (WIOA) of 2014, PL 113-128, 29 U.S.C. §§ *et seq.*

# Pursuing Quality Work-Based Learning for All

**By completing this chapter, the reader will**

- Become acquainted with policy and practice issues that may challenge the pursuit of quality work experiences for all youth

- Learn of promising developments that will help address challenges to the pursuit of quality work experiences for all youth

- Identify pragmatic considerations for the ongoing pursuit of quality work experiences

*"Having high aspirations for success can influence the actual outcomes of people with disabilities."*
Wehman (2013, p. xxiv)

The value of work experience has been illustrated throughout this book. Along with an array of strategies to plan, negotiate, and support youth work experiences, there have been numerous case examples illustrating youth in the workplace—what it took to help them get there, what it took to help them get the most out of the experience, and what they may have learned from it. In other words, this book has explained that work experiences are important educational adjuncts and how to make them happen. The challenge now is to make it happen for more youth—regardless of whether youth have so-called low-incidence disabilities or high-incidence disabilities, whether they have one disability label or another, whether they have access to general education or not, or whether they will get a diploma or an alternate certificate of school completion. In other words, should these important features of transition be structured so that they can become readily available for all youth with disabilities? Where do we go from here to make this happen? This final chapter presents considerations and issues that have potential impact on the more widespread adoption of work experiences and work as critical features of the career preparation for youth in transition.

## MEETING THE CHALLENGES TO WORK EXPERIENCE FOR ALL YOUTH

There are four consistent challenges to increasing the opportunity for youth with disabilities to experience more frequent and higher quality work experiences. Among the most significant is the professional development of transition specialists. Currently, preservice and in-service training on how to facilitate work experiences is scarce or sporadically available. The question is, how can transition professionals learn to do this well, and how can they be best supported in helping youth succeed in the workplace?

Another longstanding challenge has been employer engagement, that is, convincing employers to provide work experiences, helping them do it well, and keeping them involved. Yet another challenge is finding the time for youth to fit work experiences into their days given academic requirements, schedules, and other demands for their attention. Finally, the legislated mandates for schools are different than those of their many potential partners, which often leads to disjointed and uncoordinated service delivery to youth in transition. Any of these circumstances can impede the ability of transition professionals to help youth gain access to quality work experiences. These challenges are created by both policy and practice issues. They must be addressed if more youth will benefit from the essential transition service component that work experience is known to be. But they are not insurmountable, owing to evolving policy and practice improvements. Discussions on each of these are presented in the following sections.

### Challenge 1: Scarce or Sporadic Preservice and In-Service Training on How to Facilitate Work Experiences

The frontline practitioners who work directly with youth in facilitating work experiences are, for the most part, the largest intended audience for this book. The quest to do the best job in preparing transition specialists raises these questions:

1.  Are future transition professionals taught how to help youth plan for work experiences and jobs, negotiate with employers, and support youth in the workplace?

2.  Once on the job, do transition professionals receive targeted, ongoing training and support to help youth succeed in the workplace?

Teacher training programs have only recently begun to provide the types of courses or learning opportunities that promote the skills and activities described in this book, which help youth to identify and gain access to workplaces (Morningstar & Clavenna-Deane, 2014). As it stands, teacher certification does not necessarily reflect the need for practical skill in facilitating work experience and jobs for youth. In addition, across the various professional disciplines that interact with transitioning youth, there is not enough practical training content available for transition professionals (Wehmeyer & Webb, 2012). Much of the existing training is sporadically available, overly academically oriented, not specifically focused on work experiences, or all three (Morningstar & Mazzotti, 2014). In addition, many secondary special education curricula no longer include career development courses in favor of more generic preparation to teach academic subjects (Holzberg, Clark, & Morningstar, 2018). The fact is that few preservice and in-service training options provide practical training on how to help youth become employed. This means that transition specialists frequently are "baptized by fire," tasked with helping youth gain access to workplaces and work with little preparation to do so.

For those veteran practitioners already on the job, considerable demands on their time often make it difficult for them to break away for training. A number of factors contribute to this circumstance, including few convenient preservice and in-service learning offerings, difficulty in gaining release time for in-service training, inadequate in-service budgets, and other factors out of the control of personnel who are directly responsible for helping youth participate in these critical contextual educational activities (Butterworth, Migliore, Nord, & Gelb, 2012; Morningstar & Clavenna-Deane, 2014). These circumstances challenge transition specialists to implement strategies that sometimes are characterized more by trial and error than by proven techniques for promoting and supporting youth work experience.

***Meeting the Challenge of Elevating Professional Competence in Delivering Work Experience Services***     There have been major developments in the field of transition that hold significant promise for addressing the challenge of helping transition specialists become proficient in facilitating work experiences. One is federal policy itself. With the passage of the Workforce Innovation and Opportunity Act (WIOA) of 2014 (PL 113-128), there is renewed emphasis on work experiences, specifically how the state vocational rehabilitation (VR) agencies collaborate with schools to provide them. This has resulted in wide attention in the field of school-to-work transition on work experiences and the concomitant need to train professionals how to facilitate them. Consequently, there are more available training opportunities on the topic.

It has become less difficult now to find outlets for in-person and online training of transition specialists that feature work experience strategies. In particular, the proliferation of online learning options has improved access to training when transition specialists are challenged by geography, time constraints, professional responsibilities, and other obstacles. The key is to find those outlets that provide the best learning opportunities. Many colleagues have found that the most effective of such offerings have two things in common:

1.  They feature in-the-field assignments, where trainees are expected to try out specific strategies in the real world. For example, when learning about informational interviews, a strategy discussed in Chapter 6, trainees are assigned the task of conducting one with actual employers.

2.  They provide opportunities for feedback and coaching about how to use and improve upon specific strategies. An experienced professional is available to mentor, coach, and provide feedback to transition specialists learning new skills for facilitating work experiences.

Stand-up training by itself or an online-only experience will likely offer only an abstract glimpse of effective work experience strategies. These types of trainings typically only serve to expose trainees to the content, but do not reinforce the actual acquisition of effective skills. Training needs a learn-by-doing component to ensure that learning about how to facilitate work experiences generalizes to actual practice. In other words, transition specialists should look for opportunities to learn the technique, practice the technique, and get feedback on the technique.

Another facet of elevating professional competence is how well transition specialists are supported by program administrators or managers to learn about and implement effective strategies. The quality and effectiveness of transition programs can improve when they are managed by people who

1. Make sure transition specialists receive training about how to facilitate work experiences before they are assigned the responsibilities to do so

2. Ensure that regular in-service training is available so that transition specialists can improve old skills and learn new ones

3. Set expectations about outcomes, such as how many or what percent of assigned youth are accessing work experiences and how many finish work experiences

4. Provide regular feedback on performance, especially reinforcing and rewarding effective work experience outcomes

5. Keep track of how transition specialists are achieving outcomes, and use this information to gauge the success of the transition program and the youth served by the program

The professional development of transition specialists will be well served when they are given opportunities to receive good training and when they are supported and rewarded for making quality work experiences happen. With the increased expectations that work experiences are more widely available comes the need to train transition specialist how to do it.

## Challenge 2: Employer Engagement

Finding and keeping good workers will always be a goal of businesses and employers. Today more than ever, businesses need access to a skilled and diverse workforce (Society for Human Resource Management, 2019). They cannot stay competitive and increase profitability without qualified personnel. These circumstances seem to offer great promise for both work experience during the formative years of career development, as well as for future employment opportunities for youth in transition. However, convincing employers to take a more active role in youth work experience programs in particular and transition programs in general has been a longstanding problem (Luecking, 2008).

Regardless of job seeker category, studies consistently show that although employers' motivations for participating in transition work experience programs are fairly straightforward, employers' willingness to hire individuals represented by these programs is ultimately influenced by two factors: convenience of access to these job seekers and competent service from employment service programs and transition professionals (Simonsen, Fabian, & Luecking, 2015). Still, transition professionals and youth disability advocates occasionally suggest that employers are the ones who need to do more. It is not unusual to hear them say something to the effect that employers need to "step up to the plate and do their part." It is also common to observe transition specialists trying to "sell" employers on the benefits of hiring people with disabilities such as characterizing people with disabilities as an "untapped resource" (Luecking, 2010). These approaches imply that if only employers were more aware, they would readily consider hiring people with disabilities.

There are two main problems with these messages. First, they do not necessarily put people with disabilities in a favorable light. "Untapped" suggests unwanted, or at best, difficult to find. And promoting "hiring people with disabilities" can be inadvertent stereotyping. Second, these messages do not take employer perspectives into consideration. After all, successful employment initiatives do not occur without knowledge and appreciation of what employers need and how they operate. Similarly, efforts to generate employer engagement in transition programs cannot be successful without regard for or understanding of the real operational demands of employers. In the absence of the strategies discussed in Chapters 6 and 7 of this book, effectively engaging employers so that they are willing and available partners in transition programs will continue to be a challenge.

***Meeting the Challenge of Improving Employer Engagement***    As discussed throughout this book, the competence of both the youth and the transition specialists assisting the youth, to meet employer needs is a better "sell" to employers than any charitable motivation. Therefore, more focused messages to employers include reference to the individual youth's competence, the quality of the assistance the employer might receive from transition specialists, and the service-oriented attention to employer needs that transition specialists can offer. When this is the case, the presence of a disability neither deters nor promotes employer decisions about bringing youth with disabilities into the workplace (Luecking, 2004, 2008). Rather, it is assistance with the operational or bottom line needs of the employer that drives these decisions.

More and more transition programs are starting to understand how this perspective will lead to better employer engagement. They are learning both from business-led programs like Cincinnati Children's Hospital's Project SEARCH, and from those programs that have adopted a business-oriented approach, such as the Marriott Foundation Bridges program. Chapter 1 provided an overview of both of these initiatives. The future of youth transition preparation and the future of work experience in particular may well prosper thanks to the example of these forward-thinking programs. However, these are but two of many examples of business interest and perspective propelling the preparation of youth for jobs and careers. They all serve to teach those in the field better ways to engage businesses in the all-important effort to facilitate the connection of youth to workplaces. Much can be learned by watching these types of business-oriented initiatives and by adopting the approaches that make them successful.

## Challenge 3: Opportunities for Youth to Be Available for Work Experiences

Opportunities to experience work-based learning are restricted for many youth because of academic schedules, course loads, and their desire to pursue extra-curricular and after-school activities, such as sports and clubs. This means that summer and after-school jobs may be among the only available options for many youth to experience work. There are creative efforts to build work experiences into rigorous academic curricula, but it is far less than common. Thus, despite all the evidence that suggests that real work experiences are essential to building careers, there may be few opportunities to build these into secondary and post-secondary educational experiences without a concerted effort to do so. This will challenge educators and means that they will have to create alternative opportunities through project-based learning, youth employment programs, summer jobs programs, and other resources.

Even when class schedules and educational curricula allow for the type of flexibility that enables time for work experiences, there is the issue of making sure that students can maximize the experience by connecting it with curriculum requirements. Pairing work experience with academic content offers a potentially powerful means of preparing youth for successful careers, whether or not youth are receiving special education services (Showalter & Spiker, 2016). In fact, many educators have long advocated for making functional life skills—including those related to career development—a prominent component of the educational curriculum for all youth with disabilities (Clark, Field, Patton, Brolin, & Sitlington, 1994; Wehman, 2013). The call for a functional life skills curriculum is based on the demands of adult life in all domains, including employment.

Several issues challenge this approach, however. First, the realities of standards-driven education often allow little available time for work-based learning activities. Second, educators often receive little guidance on how to best pair knowledge acquisition and skill performance—that is, how to infuse classroom learning with work-based learning and vice versa (Thomas, 2000). Third, school districts and their personnel have long struggled to integrate transition goals, especially career goals, with individualized education programs (IEPs) (Powers et al., 2005). Finally, even for those students whose educational services allow flexible scheduling for work experiences, such as those in nondiploma programs for students with significant disabilities, the programs are not always oriented toward real work learning (Brown & Kessler, 2014).

Given these various challenges, several questions arise:

1.  Will standards-driven academic instruction impede work experiences?

2.  Are there creative ways to integrate work experiences into teaching strategies?

3.  Can youth employment programs facilitate work experiences in lieu of or in conjunction with schools?

***Meeting the Challenge of Youth Availability for Work Experiences***      We can answer the last of these questions first and the answer is a resounding "yes!" As discussed at various junctures in this book, the WIOA is a potential boon to work experience availability. Among other things, it presents a way for VR agencies to provide or pay for services that enable youth to experience work through resources other than schools and outside of school schedules. After-school, weekend, and summer work experiences can be arranged when the local VR agency's pre-employment transition services are applied, as described in the last chapter. These experiences can be facilitated in direct partnership with schools or as totally separate adjuncts to schools' educational services. As also described in the previous chapter, there are a number of other programs that may offer avenues through which work experiences that would not conflict with school schedules are available for youth.

As for integrating work experiences into teaching strategies, one common strategy is called project-based learning. Work experiences in isolation from academic instruction are still useful and important to youth career development, but in tandem with specific courses of instruction, they can be powerful. Work-based learning is one way of learning by doing that reinforces course content. Work co-ops and work internships that are specific to a course of instruction are long-standing examples of this concept. In the absence of ready availability of these types of programs, alternative models of teaching and education exist, which offer enhanced connections between the classroom and the workplace.

Another avenue for pairing work experience with academic content is through contextual teaching and learning. This has the potential to augment standards-driven education with real-world applications. In fact, what is called contextual learning has long been recognized as an effective educational strategy with plenty of research to support its value (Thomas, 2000). Real-world connections are made via the application and integration of content from different subject areas during a project assignment. For example, a teacher can assign students to visit businesses for informational interviews to learn about a company's processes as a project related to any number of academic courses. In this way, concerns about finding time for work experiences in the era of high-stakes testing are minimized, while the learning is augmented by real-world applications. Existing content courses can be augmented with complementary work-based assignments.

## Challenge 4: Disjointed and Uncoordinated Service Delivery

Youth often are eligible for or involved in a host of extra-school services, including mental health services, social and health services, youth employment programs, juvenile corrections services, and many other possible services that typically operate as disparate service systems. The task of linking these services for a singular, coordinated purpose is often difficult, resulting in disjointed or duplicated efforts on behalf of the same youth (GAO, 2014). When these services are unknown to one another, there is often an adverse impact on the ability of youth to pursue work experiences and work, as discussed in the last chapter. The challenge is to integrate service provision in such a way as to support, rather than hinder, successful work experience.

For youth who will need ongoing postschool support, there is an additional challenge: how to seamlessly ensure the provision of support as youth move from the entitlement of special education services to the uncertain availability of adult disability employment and support services. For these youth, one of three scenarios typically occur.

In the first scenario, youth may receive excellent preparation for postschool employment through rigorous curricula and work experience. In the best of circumstances, this preparation is also likely to include individualized and student-driven transition planning and services with strong family involvement, as described in previous chapters. However, these students still may exit school on a waiting list for adult employment services, may experience a delay in receiving necessary postschool support, or may never be helped to make a connection to these

postschool services. This is especially the case for youth with significant disabilities (Callahan, Butterworth, Boone, Condon, & Luecking, 2014; Certo et al., 2009).
For those youth bound for postsecondary education, a related common scenario
includes no connection to the support they may need to complete their coursework or to obtain campus disability services and career services. They are left to
fend for themselves to make the necessary connections. Consequently, these youth
flounder in their postsecondary education or employment life, unlikely to experience any sort of regular employment.

In another scenario, the school system provides a curriculum that is not
bolstered by work experience. In such a case, even if youth eventually become
connected to postschool services or adult services when they leave school, adult
employment services essentially begin from scratch to help these youth and their
families identify job and career goals and to connect them to supportive services
that may help them achieve these goals. For these youth, regular employment
remains an unlikely result.

In either of these two scenarios, the situation is particularly challenging for
youth with behavioral and mental health disabilities. They are more likely to either
drop out of school early (Stark & Noel, 2015) or never opt for adult vocational and
mental health services (Lipscomb, Lacoe, & Haimson, 2018). They are consequently
at higher risk for hospitalization, unemployment, incarceration, and substance
abuse. For this group, early connections to mental health services and opportunities to experience purposeful paid work have been shown to contribute to school
completion and successful adult employment (Clark & Unruh, 2009). Without purposeful attention to transition services, these youth face dismal postschool outcomes. These two scenarios challenge the educational and employment service
systems to find efficient ways to seamlessly build a sequence of work experiences
and work so that youth exit publicly supported education with employment or the
means to continue pursuing employment.

### Meeting the Challenge of Disjointed and Uncoordinated Service Delivery

Fortunately, there is a third scenario, in which school systems work with partners
to facilitate seamless transition to careers and adult life. That is, where students
exit school with a job already in place or with a direct connection to postsecondary
education and training that will lead to employment and a career. In this scenario,
the school and various service partners (e.g., VR agencies, mental health services,
services for people with intellectual and developmental disabilities, employment
service providers, American Job Centers) work together so that transition services
are student driven and involve their families, work-based experiences and employment supplement the academic curricula, and connections with postsecondary
support services such as developmental disabilities, and mental health services,
and/or postsecondary education are made well in advance of projected school
exit. In fact, there have been many demonstrations of school systems and postschool programs collaborating in an effort to create seamless transition into adult
employment.

One of the earliest demonstrations of this type of collaboration was tested
by Certo et al. (2003) and features the seamless transition of youth from school
to adult employment. This approach ensures that—before school exit—youth
with intellectual/developmental disabilities have jobs in place and have identified

agencies to continue to support them in those jobs (Certo & Luecking, 2006). As a result, the first day after school exit looks the same as the day before: same job, same supports. This transition occurs as the result of the collaboration of multiple service partners, including schools, vocational rehabilitation, and developmental disabilities agencies.

Similarly, postsecondary education dual-enrollment models offer additional examples of transition collaboration. The collaboration is mainly between school systems and postsecondary education programs, but the partnerships often include vocational rehabilitation and developmental disabilities agencies as additional collaborators. Grigal and Hart (2009) have developed and evaluated a range of models in which youth with intellectual disabilities are receiving public school special education services that are primarily based on the campuses of two- and four-year colleges. Although there is wide variation in how these models are configured, for the most part they feature a combination of classroom and community-based instruction on functional and life skills, paid and unpaid employment experiences, use of campus facilities (e.g., library, career center, fitness center), and participation in college courses as determined by individual interests, needs, and IEP goals. A critical benefit of this approach is the opportunity for students to interact and spend time with students without disabilities on the campus, thus learning social behaviors and establishing typical friendships. Just as critical is the time spent in community work environments, where youth learn job behaviors and skills that will benefit their career development. The primary objective of these programs is for students to exit mandated publicly supported education with a range of inclusive experiences, work experiences, and employment.

The learning from these programs and models, as well as applicable research, has been translated into models that have been designed to apply to any student with any disability receiving special education services (Luecking, Fabian, Contreary, Honeycutt, & Luecking, 2018; Luecking & Luecking, 2015). The bottom line here is that where the will exists, and when it benefits all parties, effective collaborations can happen. They not only make work experience the center piece of solid transition planning and services, they also result in adult employment outcomes. In other words, work is both a transition intervention and the desired transition outcome.

## WHERE DO WE GO FROM HERE?

The field of school-to-work transition for youth with disabilities has come a long way since it first became a federal policy focus in 1984 (Will, 1984). However, there is still a very long way to go before *all* youth making the transition from publicly supported education can reasonably expect that employment will be a central feature of their adult lives. The good news is that there is much promise in the renewed policy and practice focus on work experience as a vital transition component. There is no reason now not to charge ahead and create as many quality work experiences for as many youth as possible. Many contemporary initiatives illustrate what is possible through a new wave of creative improvements in both the availability of work experiences for youth and the effectiveness of these experiences in promoting meaningful career growth. So much more is now known about how, when, and under what circumstances work experiences will lead to meaningful postschool employment. So, reiterating the concepts and strategies presented throughout this book, here are some final thoughts about elevating the prominence and effectiveness of work experiences and work for youth in transition.

## Early and Often

Exposure to the idea of work and careers should begin as early as students begin school. At minimum, opportunities for career exploration activities, such as job shadowing, should be introduced in middle school. Project-based learning assignments are frequent additional opportunities to introduce aspects of work into the curriculum, which can be done throughout the secondary school years. Of course, work sampling, internships, and all other types of work experiences should be introduced whenever possible. Every opportunity to expose youth to the workplace and to working is valuable for their career development—the more the better! The stage is then set for multiple work experiences throughout high school and beyond, culminating in adult paid employment.

## Paid Work Before School Exit

No matter the academic pressures, no matter if it is during school or a separate experience outside of school, every youth should have the opportunity to have at least one paid job prior to finishing secondary school. If youth go on to postsecondary education, they should also have a paid job experience during that experience as well. Ideally, the job should be related to the course of instruction, but any experience—connected or not—is valuable. One or more paid work experiences on a youth's résumé will significantly bolster later employment success.

## Connections

Work experiences do not happen in a vacuum, nor do they happen without affecting or being affected by other aspects of youths' lives. When necessary, transition specialists should be aware of connecting youth to ancillary social and health services and be ready to collaborate with service partners. Transition specialists will want to maintain and expand the network of employer partners to whose workplaces youth need connections. Most important, these connections should include collaborations that focus on making work experience happen for youth commonly served by schools and multiple other entities.

## Employers as Transition Program Customers

To connect youth with workplaces, it is essential to become more and more skilled at partnering with employers. One way to promote such partnership development is to regard employers as customers whose needs you strive to meet. After all, the success of linking youth to the workplace is as much about meeting employer needs as it is serving youth, as Chapters 6 and 7 illustrated.

## Youth and Family Empowerment

Remember that nothing about youth should happen without their input. Not only does this create more youth buy-in to work experience planning, but it also is likely to contribute to a more successful work experience. As the youth empowerment movement gathers momentum, stakeholders in transition will be more and more reluctant to accept less than self-determined employment. Families are primary among the stakeholders. They can and should be engaged to the extent they are able and to the extent they choose. They know the youth best and can have important influence on the success of any work experience.

## Assess for Success

Any information gathered for planning work experiences should be with an eye to positive youth attributes. Regardless of the accommodations or supports youth may require to plan for and obtain work experience, their skills, interests, and positive traits should guide the match to a workplace. The asset-based inventory introduced in Chapter 3 is a useful way to organize information gathered about youth in preparation for work experience. Transition specialists who can identify and promote the best features of youth will always be successful in helping youth succeed in the workplace.

## Heightened Expectations

The premise of this book is that all youth who want to work can work. My experience implementing transition programs and models, as well as the experiences of numerous skilled colleagues throughout the country, shows that even those youth who do not know if they can or want to work will opt for it under circumstances that expose them to it. Remember that experience precedes interest! Being exposed to work experiences and being shown how to use their best traits and interests as the basis for pursuing work will help all youth find the way to work. The presumption of employability should guide our work as transition specialists. Recent policy initiatives and practice improvements make this more of a reality than ever before. They provide a welcomed push for higher expectations for youth employment.

## CONCLUSION

It is my sincere hope that the strategies provided in this book make at least a modest contribution to expanding both the number and quality of available work experiences for youth. Work is a good thing! Let's all continue to do our very best to help youth experience it.

## REFERENCES

Brown, L., & Kessler, K. (2014). Generating integrated work sites for individuals with significant intellectual disabilities. *Journal of Vocational Rehabilitation, 40*, 85–97.

Butterworth, J., Migliore, A., Nord, D., & Gelb, A. (2012). Improving the employment outcomes of job seekers with intellectual and developmental disabilities: Training and mentoring intervention for employment consultants. *Journal of Rehabilitation, 78*, 20–29.

Certo, N., & Luecking, R. (2006). Service integration and school to work transition: Customized employment as an outcome for youth with significant disabilities. *Journal of Applied Rehabilitation Counseling, 37*, 29–35.

Certo, N., Luecking, R., Murphy, S., Brown, L., Courey, S., & Belanger, D. (2009). Seamless transition and long term support for individuals with severe intellectual disabilities. *Research and Practice for Persons with Severe Disabilities, 33*, 85–95.

Certo, N. J., Mautz, D., Pumpian, I., Sax, C., Smalley, K., Wade, H., . . . Batterman, N. (2003). A review and discussion of a model for seamless transition to adulthood. *Education and Training in Mental Retardation and Developmental Disabilities, 21*, 33–42.

Callahan, M., Butterworth, J., Boone, J., Condon, E., & Luecking, R. (2014). Ensuring employment outcomes: Preparing students for a working life. In M. Agran, F. Brown, C. Hughes, C. Quirk, & D. Ryndak (Eds.), *Equity and full participation for individuals with severe disabilities: A vision for the future* (pp. 253–274). Baltimore, MD: Paul H. Brookes Publishing Co.

Clark, G., Field, S., Patton, J., Brolin, D., & Sitlington, P. (1994). Life skills instruction: A necessary component of all students with disabilities. A position statement of the Division of Career Development and Transition. *Career Development for Exceptional Individuals, 17*, 125–134.

Clark, H., & Unruh, D. (Eds.). (2009). *Transition of youth and young adults with emotional or behavioral difficulties: An evidence-supported handbook.* Baltimore, MD: Paul H. Brookes Publishing Co.

Government Accountability Office (GAO). (2014). *Managing for results: Implementation approaches used to enhance collaboration in interagency groups* (GAO 14-220). Washington, DC: Author.

Grigal, M. E., & Hart, D. (2009). *Think college! Postsecondary education options for students with intellectual disabilities.* Baltimore, MD: Paul H. Brookes Publishing Co.

Holzberg, D. G., Clark, K. A., & Morningstar, M. E. (2018). Transition-focused professional development: An annotated bibliography of essential elements and features of professional development. *Career Development and Transition for Exceptional Individuals, 41*, 50–55.

Lipscomb, S., Lacoe, J., Liu, A., & Haimson, J. (2018). *Preparing for life after high school: The characteristics and experiences of youth in special education: A summary of key findings from the National Longitudinal Transition Study 2012* (NCEE Evaluation Brief). Washington, DC: Institute of Educational Sciences.

Luecking, R. (Ed.). (2004). *In their own words: Employer perspectives on youth with disabilities in the workplace.* Minneapolis: University of Minnesota, Institute on Community Integration, National Center on Secondary Education and Transition.

Luecking, R. (2008). Emerging employer views of people with disabilities and the future of job development. *Journal of Vocational Rehabilitation, 29*, 3–13.

Luecking, R. (2010, November). Enough with the employer awareness already! What else has to happen for access to employment? *APSE Connections.* Rockville, MD: Association of People Supporting Employment First.

Luecking, R., Fabian, E., Contreary, K., Honeycutt, T., & Luecking, D. (2018). Vocational rehabilitation outcomes for students participating in a model transition program. *Rehabilitation Counseling Bulletin, 61*, 154–163.

Luecking, D., & Luecking, R. (2015). Translating research into a seamless transition model. *Career Development and Transition for Exceptional Individuals, 38*, 4–13.

Morningstar, M., & Clavenna-Deane, E. (2014). Preparing secondary special educators and transition specialists. In P. T. Sindelar, E. D. McCray, M. T. Brownell, & B. Lignugaris (Eds.), *Handbook of research on special education teacher preparation.* Florence, KY: Routledge.

Morningstar, M. E., & Mazzotti, V. L. (2014). *Teacher preparation to deliver evidence-based transition planning and services to youth with disabilities* (Document No. IC-1). Retrieved from http://ceedar.education.ufl.edu/wp-content/uploads/2014/08/transition-planning.pdf

Powers, K., Gil-Kashiwabara, E., Geenen, S., Powers, L., Balandran, J., & Palmer, C. (2005). Mandates and effective transition planning practices reflected in IEPs. *Career Development and Transition for Exceptional Individuals, 28*, 47–59.

Showalter, T., & Spiker, K. (2016). *Promising practices in work-based learning for youth.* Washington, DC: National Skills Coalition. https://www.nationalskillscoalition.org/resources/publications/file/10-4-NSC-YouthWorkBasedLearning_v4.pdf

Simonsen, M., Fabian, E., & Luecking, R. (2015). Employer preferences in hiring youth with disabilities. *Journal of Rehabilitation, 81*, 9–18.

Society for Human Resource Management (SHRM). (2019). *The SHRM Skills Gap Survey*. Washington, DC: Author.

Stark, P., & Noel, A. (2015). *Trends in high school dropout and completion rates in the United States: 1972–2012*. Washington, DC: U.S. Department of Education. Retrieved from http://nces.ed.gov/pubsearch/pubsinfo.asp?pubid=2015015

Thomas, J. (2000). *A review of the research on project-based learning*. San Rafael, CA: The Autodesk Foundation.

Wehman, P. (2013). *Life beyond the classroom: Transition strategies for young people with disabilities* (5th ed.). Baltimore, MD: Paul H. Brookes Publishing Co.

Wehmeyer, M., & Webb, K. (2012). *Handbook of transition education for youth with disabilities*. New York, NY: Routledge, Taylor and Francis.

Will, M. (1984). *OSERS programming for the transition of youth with disabilities: Bridges from school to working life*. Washington, DC: Office of Special Education and Rehabilitative Services, U.S. Department of Education.

Workforce Innovation and Opportunity Act (WIOA) of 2014, PL 113-128, 29 U.S.C. §§ *et seq.*

# Index

Page numbers followed by *f*, *b*, and *t* indicate figures, boxes, and tables, respectively.

Accommodations, *see* Supports and accommodations; Workplace accommodations

ADA, *see* Americans with Disabilities Act of 1990

American Job Centers (AJCs), 207, 213–214, 215*t*

Americans with Disabilities Act (ADA) of 1990 (PL 101-336), 30, 35–36
  on reasonable accommodations, 82
  on workplace accommodations, 168–169

Ancillary social and community services linkages, 214, 215*t*, 230
  effectively identifying and collaborating with, 217–219

Application process, workplace accommodations for, 170

Apprenticeships, 7*t*, 10, 25*t*, 213

Assessments, 41–42, 231
  formal and informal, 41
  portfolio, 42*t*
  sibling support in, 106
  situational, 42*t*
  *see also* Planning, work experience

Asset-based and person-centered discovery process, 16

Asset-based approach to work experience development, 52, 53–54*b*

Asset-based inventory, 47–52, 121
  example of completed inventory, 68–76
  template for, 57–65
  Work Experience Plan in, 52–54
  workplace supports and, 160

Asset-based youth profiles, 29, 42*t*
  development of, 46–54
  using asset-based inventory for, 47–52

Assignments
  customization of, 123
  mentoring for learning and performing, 198–199
  proposing and negotiating task, 124

Attendance challenges, workplace accommodations for, 172

Availability of youth for work experiences, 225–227

Bridges From School to Work, 10, 14–15, 225

Business language, 119

Calculation limitations, workplace accommodations for, 173–174

Career awareness, 22

Career decision making, 23

Career exploration, 7*t*, 8, 22, 25*t*, 230

Career placement, 23

Career preparation, 23

Career progression, 22–30
  functions of work experience and, 24–26, 25*t*
  identifying and implementing work experiences and, 27–29, 28*f*
  legal aspects of work experience and, 30–36
  National Standards and Quality Indicators for Secondary Education and Transition (NASET) on, 23–24, 23–24*t*
  promoting work experience success and, 29–30, 30*t*
  timing of work experiences and, 26–27, 26*t*

Challenges of providing quality work experiences
  disjointed and uncoordinated service delivery, 227–229
  employer engagement, 224–225
  opportunities for youth to be available, 225–227
  scarce or sporadic preservice and in-service training, 222–224

Clarification of employer expectations, 139, 161–162

Collaboration, transition, 228–229

Comfort and acceptance in the workplace, mentoring and, 189–190

Community rehabilitation provider, 212

Competent and convenient assistance in receiving youth referrals, 117

Complementary strategies for finding and recruiting employers, 125–127

Concentration difficulties, workplace accommodations for, 172

Conditions of work, 28
Covert awareness, 107
Cultural awareness, 107
Cultural reciprocity, 107–108
Culture, family, 106–108
Customer service stars, transition
    specialists being, 148–149, 230
Customization of assignments, 123

Daily Work Report, 184
Deadlines, workplace accommodations
    for challenges with meeting,
    172–173
Disability awareness, 116, 146–147
    mentoring and, 200
Disclosure, disability
    advantages of, 82–83
    counseling youth about their rights and
        responsibilities with, 91, 91–92t
    deciding on whether to provide, 29,
        81–84, 84t
    disadvantages to, 83–84
    do's and don'ts of, 90–91
    how and what to include in, 85–88
    learning lab on, 92–93
    mutual benefit through, 146b
    representing a youth's disability to
        employers and, 89–91
    scripts for, 87–88b
    timing of, 84–85, 86t
    to whom, 89
Discovery process, 46
    sibling support in, 106
Disjointed and uncoordinated service
    delivery, 227–229
Dislikes and preferences in asset-based
    inventory, 50
Diversity, 99
    cultural reciprocity and, 107–108
    respecting family culture and, 106–108
Division on Career Development and
    Transition (DCDT) of the Council on
    Exceptional Children, 44

Elevator speeches, 125–127
Employers
    asking what further information and help
        is desired by, 145–146
    benefits of mentoring for, 193–195
    benefits of work experience programs
        for, 114–116
    building relationships with
        participating, 18
    challenges with engagement of, 224–225
    complementary strategies for finding and
        recruiting, 125–127

customizing assignments as necessary
    with, 123
disability awareness information for, 116,
    146–147
employer engagement challenges,
    224–225
employer outreach, 29
Employer Satisfaction Questionnaire, 153
establishing a single point of contact
    with, 120
expectations of, 117, 117t, 136–141,
    137–138t
feedback from, 30, 143, 154
finding, strategies for, 125–127
follow-up procedures and, 139–141
formal and informal disability awareness
    and training by, 116
identifying tasks important to, 122
information interviews of, 118–119
liability of, 36
maintaining professional and responsive
    contact with, 120
matching what your offer to needs and
    wants of, 116–124
networking with, 113–114
proposing and negotiating task
    assignments with, 124
reasons for bringing youth with
    disabilities into their workplace,
    115–116
representing a youth's disability to,
    89–91
responsibility in work experiences, 13b
soliciting feedback from, 30,
    142–144, 144f
strategies for successfully working with,
    138–141
as transition program customers, 230
transition specialists thoroughly knowing
    the circumstances of, 121
underpromising and overdelivering to,
    120–121
using business language with, 119
see also Mentoring; Retaining workplace
    partners
Employment service providers, 212
Evaluating and adjusting workplace
    supports, 167
Evaluation, Work Experience, 182–183
Evaluation process, 29
    mentors in, 199
Expectations
    employer, 117, 117t
        clarifying, 139, 161–162
        revisiting, 136–137, 137–138t
        strategies for meeting, 138–141
    heightened, 231
Exposure preceding interest, 45–46b

"Face in the place," 164–165
Fair Labor Standards Act (FLSA) of 1938
    (PL 75-718), 9, 30
    paid work experiences and, 33–34
    provisions for unpaid work experience,
        30–32
Family culture, 106–108
Family support
    example of, 95–97
    implementing work experience, 102–103
    importance of, 97–98
    learning lab on, 110
    in negotiating and organizing work
        experiences, 101–102
    parent-to-parent suggestions for,
        103–105
    in preparation and planning, 99–101
    recognizing successful family–
        professional partnerships and,
        108–109
    respecting family culture and, 106–108
    setting the stage for, 105b
    siblings in, 105–106
    for youth work experiences, 98–99,
        230–231
Family–professional partnerships,
    recognizing, 108–109
Feedback
    adjusting support and service based on,
        143–144, 144f
    building in regular opportunities to
        provide feedback to, 166
    from employers, 30, 142–144, 144f
    evaluating and adjusting workplace
        supports based on, 167
    provided by mentors, 198
    from youth, 30
FLSA, see Fair Labor Standards Act of 1938
Follow-up procedures, 139–141
Formal assessments, 41, 42t
Functions of work experiences, 24–26, 25t

IDEA, see Individuals with Disabilities Act
    of 1990
IDEIA, see Individuals with Disabilities
    Education Improvement Act
    of 2004
IEPs, see Individualized education programs
Individual placement and support (IPS)
    services, 211–212
Individual Support Plan Template, 180
Individualized education programs (IEPs),
    4, 5, 226
    parental approval for, 98
    unpaid work experience and, 31, 32
Individualized work experiences, 16
Individualized workplace supports, 163–166

Individuals with Disabilities Act (IDEA) of
    1990 (PL 101-496), 2
Individuals with Disabilities Education
    Improvement Act (IDEIA) of 2004
    (PL 108-446), 4–5, 35, 40
    on parent involvement, 97–98
    on workplace accommodations, 169
Information gathering for work experience
    planning, 40–43, 42t
Informational interviews, 118–119
Initial training and orientation, workplace
    accommodations for, 170–171
Integration, workplace, 174
Interagency collaboration, 17
Interests and preferences in asset-based
    inventory, 47–48
Internships, 7t, 10, 25t
Interpersonal relationships, 174
Interviews
    informational, 118–119
    workplace accommodations for, 170
    by youth, 42t
Inventory, asset-based, see Asset-based
    inventory
IPS, see Individual placement and support
    services

Job corps, 213
Job shadowing, 7t, 8–9, 25t

Language, business, 119
Legal issues
    disclosure rights and responsibilities, 91,
        91–92t
    liability, 36
    nondiscrimination and reasonable
        accommodations, 35–36
    special education requirements, 4–5
    subminimum wage restrictions, 34–35
    work experience, 30–36
    workplace accommodations and,
        168–169
Liability, employer, 36
Library of Congress, 9
Life and work experiences in asset-based
    inventory, 48–49
Listening to complaints, 142, 143

Marriott Foundation for People with
    Disabilities, 10, 14, 225
Matching of youth skills and interests to job
    tasks, 121
Meals on Wheels, 9
Memory deficits, workplace
    accommodations for, 173

Mentoring
    additional benefits for youth from,
        192–193
    basics of identifying and organizing,
        195–200
    benefits for companies and schools from,
        193–195
    defined, 188
    enhanced self-concept and self-
        confidence and, 192
    enhanced work performance and,
        190–191
    example of, 187–188
    increased comfort and acceptance in the
        workplace due to, 189–190
    for learning and performing tasks,
        198–199
    learning lab on, 201
    skill acquisition through, 190
    social networking and, 191–192
    support for, 197–198
    value of effective, 189–195
    as vehicle for disability awareness, 200
Mentors
    benefits of mentoring for, 193
    in the evaluation process, 199
    finding balance, 199–200
    functions of, 196b
    identifying, 195–197
    quick tips for, 204
    support for, 197–198
    in workplace orientation process, 198
Modeling
    by mentors, 199
    by transition specialists, 147, 148b
Models, work experience, 13–17, 17f

NASET, see National Standards and Quality
        Indicators for Secondary Education
        and Transition
National Center on Secondary Education
        and Transition, 33
National Collaborative on Workforce and
        Disability for Youth (NCWD/Youth),
        84, 91
National Standards and Quality
        Indicators for Secondary Education
        and Transition (NASET), 23–24,
        23–24t
National Technical Assistance Center on
        Transition, 41
NCWD, see National Collaborative on
        Workforce and Disability for Youth
Networking, 113–114, 125, 126b
    social, 191–192
Nondiscrimination and reasonable
        accommodations, 35–36

Observations, 42t
    in identifying mentors, 197
Offering to fix problems, 142, 144
Office of Disability Employment Policy
        (ODEP), 10
On-the-job performance, workplace
        accommodations for, 171–174
Orientation, see Workplace orientation
Outcomes, expected, 27
Overdelivering and underpromising with
        employers, 120–121, 140–141
Overt level of cultural awareness, 107

Paid employment, 7t, 11, 25t, 230
    FLSA provisions for, 33–34
Paid integrated employment experience, 17
Parents, see Family support
Parent-to-parent suggestions for success,
        103–105
Periodic guidance and information provided
        by transition specialists, 147–148
PL 75-718, see Fair Labor Standards Act
        (FLSA) of 1938
PL 101-336, see Americans with Disabilities
        Act (ADA) of 1990
PL 101-476, see Individuals with Disabilities
        Act (IDEA) of 1990
PL 108-446, see Individuals with Disabilities
        Education Improvement Act (IDEIA)
        of 2004
PL 113-128, see Workforce Innovation and
        Opportunities Act (WIOA) of 2014
Planning, work experience, 27
    exposure preceding interest in, 45–46b
    gathering information for, 40–43, 42t
    guiding principles for, 43–46
    strategies for involving families in,
        99–101
    Work Experience Plan in, 52–54, 66–67,
        77–78
    see also Asset-based inventory; Asset-
        based and person-centered discovery
        process
Portfolio assessments, 42t
Positive Personal Profile, 46–47
Possibilities and ideas in asset-based
        inventory, 52
Pre-employment transition services (Pre-
        ETS), 11, 208, 209
Preparation, strategies for involving families
        in, 99–101
Problems, handling, 141–144, 144f
Professional and agency partners
    America's Job/Career Centers, 207,
        213–214, 215t
    ancillary social and community services
        linkages, 214, 215t

common, 207–217
effectively identifying and collaborating with, 217–219
employment service providers, 212
example of, 205–206
learning lab on, 220
public income benefits supports, 214–217, 215*t*
state mental health/developmental disabilities agencies, 211–212, 215*t*
value of, 206–207
*see also* Vocational rehabilitation (VR) agencies
Professional and responsive contact with employers, maintaining, 120
Project SEARCH, 15–16, 225
Project-based learning, 227
Proposing and negotiating task assignments, 124
Public income benefits supports, 214–217, 215*t*
Purpose of work experience, 27

*Quality Work Experience Characteristics*, 12
Quality work experiences, 11–13
challenges of providing, 222–229
improvement in, 18–19
value of, 221–222

Reasonable accommodations, 168–169
Reciprocity, cultural, 107–108
Recruiting of employers, strategies for, 125–127
Reflected appraisal, 192
Retaining workplace partners, 135–136
responsiveness to workplace problems and, 141–144, 144*f*
revisiting employer expectations in, 136–137, 137–138*t*
strategies for keeping employers happy and, 138–141
support in training and monitoring youth at the worksite and, 139–141
Revisiting employer expectations, 136–137, 137–138*t*

Scarce or sporadic preservice and in-service training, 222–224
School or program records, 42*t*
Seamless transition models, 16–17, 17*f*
Searching for work experience, 51–52
Self-concept and mentoring, 192
Self-confidence and mentoring, 192
Self-determination, 44

Service after the sale, 116, 139
Service learning, 7*t*, 9, 25*t*
Siblings, 105–106
Single point of contact with employers, 120
Site supervision, 28
Situational assessments, 42*t*
Skill acquisition through mentoring, 190
Skills, knowledge, and abilities in asset-based inventory, 49–50
Social networking, 191–192
Social Security Disability Insurance (SSDI), 207, 215–216
Special education law, work experience requirements under, 4–5
SSDI, *see* Social Security Disability Insurance
SSI, *see* Supplemental Security Income
Stamina and stress challenges, workplace accommodations for, 172
State mental health/developmental disabilities agencies, 211–212, 215*t*
Stipend jobs, 7*t*, 10
Subminimum wage restrictions, 34–35
Subtle awareness, 107
Success, promoting work experience, 29–30, 30*t*
Supplemental Security Income (SSI), 207, 215–216
Supports and accommodations, 29
in asset-based inventory, 50, 51
delivering information about specific requirements for, 144–145
importance of, 159–160
on the job site, 29
for mentoring, 197–198
mutual benefit through disclosure and, 146*b*
respecting family culture and, 106–108
in training and monitoring youth at the worksite, 139–141
*see also* Family support; Workplace supports
Systematic and program benefits of work experience, 5–6, 6*t*

Task assignments, *see* Assignments
Terminology, business, 119
Timing
of disability disclosure, 84–85, 86*t*
of work experiences, 26–27, 26*t*
Training
disability awareness, 116, 146–147
scarce or sporadic preservice and in-service, 222–224
workplace accommodations for initial, 170–171
Transition models, seamless, 16–17, 17*f*

Transition planning, 4–5
  assessment in, 40–41
  collaboration in, 228–229
  *see also* Planning, work experience
Transition Service Integration Model
    (TSIM), 16–17, 17*f*
  identifying specific challenges, barriers,
    and needs for support, 162
Transition specialists, 18
  asking what further information and help
    the employer desires, 145–146
  being customer service stars, 148–149
  building in regular opportunities to
    provide feedback to youth, 166
  complementary strategies for finding and
    recruiting employers, 125–127
  cultural reciprocity and, 107–108
  customizing assignments as
    necessary, 123
  delivering information about specific
    accommodations required by youth,
    144–145
  determining type, level, and amount of
    support needed, 162–163
  developing individualized support plans,
    163–166
  establishing a single point of contact with
    employers, 120
  giving employers what they want,
    116–124
  identifying tasks that are important
    to both the youth and the
    employer, 122
  informational interviews by, 118–119
  knowing the youth's capabilities/interests
    and employer's circumstances
    thoroughly, 121
  learning lab on, 127–128
  maintaining professional and responsive
    contact with employers, 120
  modeling interaction and support
    appropriate for youth, 147, 148*b*
  networking by, 113–114
  proposing and negotiating task
    assignments, 124
  providing disability awareness
    information, 116, 146–147
  providing periodic guidance and
    information as necessary, 147–148
  recognizing successful family–
    professional partnerships, 108–109
  respecting family culture, 106–108
  responsiveness to workplace problems,
    141–144, 144*f*
  revisiting employer expectations,
    136–137, 137–138*t*
  scarce or sporadic preservice and in-
    service training for, 222–224

  soliciting feedback from employers,
    142–144, 144*f*
  and support in training and monitoring
    youth at the worksite, 139–141
  underpromising and overdelivering to
    employers, 120–121, 140–141
  using business language, 119
  working with parents, 97–98, 99, 104
Transportation resources in asset-based
    inventory, 51
Turning "negatives" into "positives," 43
Types of work experiences, 6–11, 7*t*

Underpromising and overdelivering to
    employers, 120–121, 140–141
Unpaid work experience, FLSA provisions
    for, 30–32
U.S. Department of Labor, 33–34

Visual or reading limitations, workplace
    accommodations for, 173
Vocational rehabilitation (VR) agencies, 2,
    5–6, 207, 215*t*
  early case initiation, 17
  effectiveness of, 209
  key Workforce Innovation and
    Opportunities Act (WIOA) provisions
    for, 207–208
  pre-employment transition services
    (Pre-ETS), 11
  program eligibility for, 208*t*
  services provided by, 209–210*b*
  Way2Work Maryland, 210–211*b*
Voice recognition software, 1
VR, *see* Vocational rehabilitation agencies

Way2Work Maryland, 210–211*b*
WIOA, *see* Workforce Innovation and
    Opportunities Act of 2014 (PL
    113-128)
Words to avoid with employers, 119
Work experience
  accommodations for each component of,
    169–174
  apprenticeships, 7*t*, 10, 25*t*, 213
  benefits to students and youth, 3–4
  career exploration, 7*t*, 8, 25*t*
  career progression and, 22–30
  challenges of providing, 222–229
  defining, 3
  disjointed and uncoordinated service
    delivery of, 227–229
  examples of, 1–3, 21–22, 39–40, 79–81,
    96–97
  functions of, 24–26, 25*t*

importance of, 3–6
improving the quality and availability of, 18–19, 229–231
internships, 7*t*, *10*, 25*t*
job shadowing, 7*t*, 8–9, 25*t*
legal aspects of, 30–36
legal special education requirements and, 4–5
models for, 13–17, 17*f*
organization of, 7–8
paid employment, 7*t*, 11, 25*t*
process for identifying and implementing, 27–29, 28*f*
promoting success in, 29–30, 30*t*
quality, 11–13
service learning, 7*t*, *9*, 25*t*
stipend jobs, 7*t*, 10
systematic and program benefits of, 5–6, 6*t*
timing of, 26–27, 26*t*
types and uses of, 6–11, 7*t*
work sampling, 7*t*, 9, 25*t*
*see also* Family support; Planning, work experience
Work Experience Agreement, 178
Work Experience Evaluation, 182–183
Work Experience Plan, 52–54
example of completed plan, 77–78
template for, 66–67
Work sampling, 7*t*, 9, 25*t*
Workforce Innovation and Opportunities Act (WIOA) of 2014 (PL 113-128), 2, 17, 30, 207–208, 223
subminimum wage restrictions, 34–35
Workplace accommodations, 167–168
in application and interview process, 170
for each component of the work experience, 169–174
general, 171–172
for initial training and orientation, 170–171
legal requirements and, 168–169
for on-the-job performance, 171–174
types of, 168
Workplace integration and interpersonal relationships, 174
Workplace orientation
accommodations for, 170–171
mentors involved in, 198
Workplace partners, *see* Employers; Retaining workplace partners
Workplace performance and mentoring, 190–191
Workplace policies and procedures, 29

Workplace problems, responsiveness to, 141–144, 144*f*
Workplace supports, 157–159
building in regular opportunities to provide feedback to youth in, 166
clarifying the employer's requirements and expectations and, 161–162
considerations concerning accommodations in, 167–174
context for, 160
determining type, level, and amount of needed, 162–163
developing individualized plan for, 163–166
evaluating and adjusting, 167
identifying specific challenges, barriers, and needs for, 162, 175, 185
importance of, 159–160
learning lab on, 175, 185
steps to providing effective, 161–167, 161*f*
workplace integration and interpersonal relationships and, 174
*see also* Mentoring
Worksite Visit Checklist, 181
Writing and spelling difficulties, workplace accommodations for, 173

Youth with disabilities
benefits of work experience for, 3–4
challenges with finding opportunities for, 225–227
customizing assignments as necessary for, 123
delivering information about specific accommodations required by, 144–145
developing individualized support plan for, 163–166
feedback from, 30
follow-up procedures for, 139–141
heightened expectations for, 231
identifying tasks important to, 122
laws limiting work hours of, 33
proposing and negotiating task assignments for, 124
responsibility in work experiences, 12*b*
siblings of, 105–106
support in training and monitoring, 139–141
*see also* Asset-based inventory; Disclosure, disability; Family Support; Workplace supports
YouthBuild, 213